Identities in Flux

SUNY series, Afro-Latinx Futures

Vanessa K. Valdés, editor

Identities in Flux

Race, Migration, and Citizenship in Brazil

NIYI AFOLABI

SUNY
PRESS

For information, contact State University of New York Press, Albany, NY
www.sunypress.edu

Library of Congress Cataloging-in-Publication Data

Name: Afolabi, Niyi, author.
Title: Identities in flux : race, migration, and citizenship in Brazil /
  Niyi Afolabi.
Description: Albany : State University of New York Press, [2021] | Series:
  SUNY series, Afro-Latinx futures | Includes bibliographical references
  and index.
Identifiers: LCCN 2020024651 | ISBN 9781438482491 (hardcover : alk. paper) |
  ISBN 9781438482507 (pbk. : alk. paper) | ISBN 9781438482514 (ebook)
Subjects: LCSH: Brazilian literature—History and criticism. | Blacks in
  literature. | Race in literature. | Blacks—Race identity—Brazil. |
  Brazil—Civilization—African influences.
Classification: LCC PQ9523.B57 A46 2021 | DDC 869.09/981—dc23
LC record available at https://lccn.loc.gov/2020024651

10 9 8 7 6 5 4 3 2 1

To my beloved father, J.O. Afolabi
On my silver jubilee, you departed.
Gratitude for the vision,
Three decades after,
In peace, you rest.

Contents

Preface

After close to forty years of interacting with Brazil, intellectually, socially, culturally, and spiritually, in part due to my own African connections with this Southern American country, I was compelled to ask myself a few cogent questions, only a decade ago: (1) Why is Brazil so intrinsically connected to Africa, especially given its more visible Yoruba spiritual rootedness? (2) What could be teased out, among its historical, literary, and cultural manifestations as defining "archetypal" icons or subjects that constitute foundational essences for Afro-Brazilian identities? (3) How exhaustive are these predominant elements, and why are what is left out not a deliberate omission but a consequence of limited space and time for inclusion? (4) Why are other vital forces of the culinary, the architectural, the carnivalesque, the sacred, even the popular and the profane all conflated within cultural and historical production? And (5), why are other intellectual and archival agencies so extensive that one book cannot possibly exhaust all the daunting possibilities? Since answers are often embedded within questions, let me suggest that my effort here, which one of the anonymous readers delightfully qualified as "ambitious," has barely scratched the surface of an expansive treasure grove for future research. I am quite pleased with what I consider a major milestone in my navigation of Afro-Brazilian Studies. Afro-Brazilian identities are indeed constantly in flux due to their shifting historical and contemporary realities as they struggle to make sense of the self that is consistently oppressed by the pyramid of power and racial relations.

Acknowledgments

Many individuals and institutions have contributed to the emergence of this book. First, I thank the anonymous publisher that inadvertently spent three long years on the editorial processing of my most recent book. As fate would have it, during that long moment of suspense, I summoned the energy to focus on another book while waiting for Godot. To my surprise, and against the grain of all absurdist reality, Godot actually showed up. Unfortunately, the long wait had taken its toll and I had moved on in my placement decision. This book thus comes as a fortu- itous consolation to that nagging editorial experience. Second, I thank the Warfield Center for African and African American Studies and the Department of African and African Diaspora Studies at the University of Texas at Austin for sponsoring my field research in Brazil for the last ten years. Third, I thank the Office of the Vice President for Research for the generous publication subvention grant as well as the College of Liberal Arts for the Humanities Research Award's consolation prize, which metaphorically "crowned" my efforts by speaking with me in double sense.

I must not forget to thank the many centers, institutes, and libraries in Brazil that opened their gates to my enquiries every time I came knocking on their doors by providing me access to invaluable information through granted interviews, archival research, material culture, as well as many memorable moments of human interactions and spirited discussions. Though all of those who helped me are too numerous to mention, I particularly thank João Reis, Florentina Souza, Jeferson Bacelar, Lande Onawale, Katuka, Lisa Castillo, Felipe Rodrigues, Maria Antonieta Antonacci, Vagner Gonçalves da Silva, João Dias, Paulo Lins, Zézé Motta, and Júnia Ferreira Furtado. Equally deserving of my gratitude is the editorial and production team at SUNY Press. As a dynamic collective, they form a meticulous force that painstakingly made the book the best it could be. I thank, among others, Vanessa K. Valdés, Rebecca Colesworthy, James Peltz, Eileen Nizer, Fran Keneston, and Matthew Phillips.

Finally, but definitely not the least, I thank the ever-present spirit of my mother, Ogboja Jengbetiele, who keeps me forging ahead in the midst of many mysterious eyes that often propel me to higher grounds in my quests for meaning.

Introduction

In Defense of Identity

Identities in Flux seeks to understand how the concepts of race, migration, and citizenship in Brazil interact in literary and cultural terrains. At the core of race relations in Brazilian culture lies the question of miscegenation or race-mixture, which has been compellingly advanced by Gilberto Freyre and powerfully critiqued by scholars (Isfahani-Hammond, 2005) as they grapple with the theoretical and social implications of violent plantation sexual relations that have challenged the seeming positive cultural hybridizations in the Americas. While slavery remains at the center of these complex relations, it also undermines the contradictions of assimilationism at the expense of racism. Though hybridity was politicized as a desirable system of racial reconciliation in which the plantation culture privileges African, indigenous, and European contact without any sense of hierarchy, the reality of colonial power relations proves otherwise. The quest for resolution of identity crisis calls for the questioning of citizenship when identities are constantly in motion and in the process inhibits collective social mobilization against racial oppressions.

When located in the context of decolonial frameworks (Maldonado-Torres, 2018), this project redeems Brazilian cultural icons who were once considered dislocated subjects of colonial power relations during enslavement and after. Similarly, these potential agents of reconstruction redefine themselves against the grain of past dehumanization and along the lines of theories articulated by Frantz Fanon (2004, 2008), Aimé Césaire (2000), Sylvia Wynter (2003), and Walter Mignolo (2000). As identities migrating from colonized spaces of damnation, inferiority, and oppression to insurgent positionalities that restore their humanity and

1

dignity, these archetypal subjects offer new ways of envisioning regeneration of the human spirit. Migrating identities in the transnational frame are thus not fixed but shifting and political. Race relations in the specific case of Brazil are borne out of historical racial inequalities that morph from their original dislocation to a new location where a series of negotiation processes shift from assimilation and integration toward potential upward mobility. Even when communities and social movements contest the state by challenging the official representation of citizenship through a demand for equality despite difference, the ultimate sense of resolution lies in the flux of identities that is amenable to social change.

"Racial democracy," as interrogated by scholars, has been subjected to a rigorous analysis that has further complicated our understanding of racism or its assumed lack thereof in the mythical racial paradise that Brazil is projected to be. Recent scholarship (Caldwell, 2007; Pinho, 2010; Sterling, 2012; Smith, 2016; Aidoo, 2018; Mitchell-Walthour, 2018) differs in their positionings on Brazilian racial identity yet agree on the crisis of black citizenship given the persistence of inequalities and ambiguous ethnoracial citizenship (Mitchell, 2017) that make a definitive identification impossible given the possibilities of claiming fluid identities. By virtue of a luso-tropical miscegenation thesis, racial hybridity offers a terrain of struggle in which Brazilians could claim whiteness, blackness, or race mixture depending on their politics of identity. Embedded in this fluid terrain is what I propose as "migrating identity."

In overlapping issues of race and gender with the problematic of "mestiço essentialism" (28), which comes against the grain of "racial anti-essentialism" (179) or the Brazilian hegemonic framework of racial democracy, Caldwell deploys the black women's movement in Brazil as a case study in how black women's identity challenges the political discussion of race as a fluid or hybrid phenomenon in her text *Negras in Brazil: Re-envisioning Black Women, Citizenship, and the Politics of Identity* (2007). The quest for racial equality by black women thus plays out in symbologies such as hairstyles, carnival costumes, and musical lyrics, among others. Caldwell burdens herself in critiquing Gilberto Freyre's advancement of Brazil as a "Luso-tropical Racial Democracy" (31) by suggesting that "proponents of miscegenation and racial democracy have tended to conflate biological mixture between racial groups with social integration" (35). In other words, interracial sexual interaction and miscegenation do not translate into equal racial treatments. Unlike Caldwell's direct assault on race relations, in her study *Mama Africa: Reinventing Blackness in Bahia* (2010), Pinho evokes

Africa as a signifying trope in Afro-Bahian construction of black identity by drawing on the strength of the *blocos afros* (Afro-Carnival cultural movements and organizations) that not only draw pan African connections with New World spaces of Jamaica, Cuba, and the United States, but also market this new black consciousness or re-Africanization through music, hairstyles, clothes, and religious practices, by expecting their adherents to model their Afrocentric black body against the readily Europeanized model of beauty enshrined in racial democracy. Pinho however takes issues with this simplistic marketing of *baianidade* (Bahian identity) by questioning its commercial partnership with the tourism industry. In other words, Pinho highlights the contraditions of these otherwise well-intentioned cultural movements by suggesting that they succeed in establishing a forceful political black identity while failing to bring about a more inclusive discussion on racial equality and pragmatic humanity.

In her comparative and seminal work on Afro-Brazilian roots and rites, *African Roots, Brazilian Rites: Cultural and National Identity in Brazil* (2012), Sterling seems to pick up from Pinho with a more forceful focus on the convergence of the sacred and the popular when it comes to how to politicize public rituals and festivals in order to effect social change through political agency. Drawing specifically on Candomblé religious rituals, street performances, poetry, and hip-hop cultural manifestations, Sterling methodically rejects hybrid national identity by challenging Edouard Glissant's notion of "rhizome" identity that privileges European roots. Rather, she insists on the celebration of African roots through which Afro-Brazilians are able to dialogue with their ancestry as well as reject state-sponsored "Afro-Brazilian identity" that is conflated within racial democracy. While Sterling's arguments are culturally anchored, those of Smith are more transnationally and anthropologically encompassing. In *Afro-Paradise: Blackness, Violence, and Performance in Brazil* (2016), Smith unveils the many complex levels of anti-black violence and racism in Brazil. Structuring her book performatively, she highlights critical moments in which racialized bodies experience violent encounters with the police and during which the myth of racial democracy is more visibly contested by the sheer power of police violence against mostly black bodies. The author dramatizes how a theatrical group in Bahia, "Culture Shock," relives the relics of modern slavery through the denigration of black citizenship by the "terrorist" hand of the white State and the surveillance implicit in grotesque police raids. Drawing on the analogy of the black body as a "wandering ghost" susceptible to torture, pain, and war, she shifts the social analytic framing of race from language and discourse to "ways that gestures, looks, feeling, seeing, and hearing define material realities of the nation, and particularly the lived realities of blackness" (161). While framing her thesis in dialogue with more contemporary Black Lives Matter movement in the United States, she turns the metonymic drama of Afro-Brazilians into a commendable transnational paradigm of contestation against normalized violence against black bodies.

Along similar lines of unveiling the violence of the state against black bodies as examined by Smith in the context of the instrumentality of the police, Aidoo offers in *Slavery Unseen: Sex, Power, and Violence in Brazilian History* (2018) a largely understudied aspect in Brazilian Studies, especially as it relates to sexual violence. Drawing on several narratives of interracial sexual violence that included European travel records and Inquisition trials as well as literature, the author argues that racial democracy was forged within concealed acts of colonial sexual violence that included rape, sodomy of male slaves, and prostitution. While the scope and depth of Aidoo's examination of Brazil's anti-black racial violence is extensive, its main thrust lies in the revelation that Brazil masks racial violence, sexual exploitation, and white patriarchy. But the issue of black identity in contrast with the mixed-race identity continues to be problematic as the racial democracy myth compelled many to auto-identify as white or brown even when they are obviously black by phenotype. And this is where Mitchell-Walthour's *The Politics of Blackness: Racial Identity and Political Behavior in Contemporary Brazil* (2017) is timely. Against the prevalent studies that focus on the privilege accorded by race-mixture, Mitchell-Walthour investigates black identity from the perspectives of ethnoracial identification, political inequality, and the intersections of race, class, and gender. The investment in knowing how black identity impacts political underrepresentation is rewarding in order to determine political participation and the benefits of affirmative action policies. Regardless of the limitations of the methodology, the study improves our appreciation of ethnoracial politics and the implications of black political identity and behavior.

The challenge to ethnoracial citizenship that the foregoing review presents offers the opportunity to engage the case studies presented in this book. From the problematic of mestiço essentialism (Caldwell), Afro-Bahian identity (Pinho), convergence between the sacred and the popular (Sterling), state violence against black bodies (Smith), sexual violence (Aidoo), to the quest for black political participation (Mitchell-

Walthour), the diverse perspectives contest Brazilian racial democracy while complicating the crisis of identity for Afro-Brazilians. The five iconic historical figures that form the corpus of this study have been carefully selected to make a statement on how race mixture or racial hybridity has not really eliminated racial discrimination in Brazil. Rather, it has allowed for a further complication of the racial problem by promoting racial ambiguity that further fragments the citizenry into shades of color that make national identity impossible despite the claim of multiculturalism. The life and trials of Manuel Querino as masterly fictionalized by Jorge Amado as Pedro Archanjo in *Tent of Miracles* offers a compelling treatise on Afro-Brazilian stereotypes and racial hybridity. In order to understand the contending racial opposites within Archanjo, one must make sense of the protagonist's initial desire to become a medical doctor (a position considered in the nineteenth century as exclusively reserved for the white elite) without success and his neglect as an ethnographer of Afro-Brazilian studies and African influences on Brazil. Zumbi dos Palmares, the leader of the most populous runaway slave communities in the seventeenth century, was initially perceived as an anti-Brazilian rebel until the Unified Black Movement transformed him into the hero of the Black Consciousness Day since the late 1970s. Beyond Querino and Zumbi, three other icons, Xica da Silva, Black Orpheus, and the City of God perform shifting identitarian roles as they challenge the myth of racial democracy. In the case of Xica da Silva, an eighteenth-century hypersexualized mixed-race woman shifted from being the mistress of a Portuguese elite to being accorded freedom from slavery, only to be abandoned and humiliated by being denied the benefits of full citizenship. As a national stereotype of a "miscegenated" woman, her identity is questionable within the context of racial democracy. Black identity is also problematized in the carnivalesque character of Black Orpheus and the ghetto-stuck characters in City of God where the violence around them becomes a self-fulfilling prophecy and identity. These identities are migrating and shifting. They are not fixed as they undergo the perpetual fragmentation that the myth of racial democracy engenders.

Defining Concepts

This study argues that the quest for identity has been laden with various racialized challenges and coping strategies through the course of the tortuous journey of negotiating identities in the Brazilian miscegenated world. Despite the convenient claim about the "racial paradise" that the Portuguese colonial slave-labor project bequeathed to its ex-colonies such as Brazil, Goa, Macau, and the five Lusophone African countries (Angola, Mozambique, Cape Verde, Guinea-Bissau, and São Tomé and Príncipe), the persistence of social exclusion and economic inequalities proves otherwise. While the miscegenated identity of those of "mixed race" is praised as a social ideal, the realities of this dualized personality are anything but celebratory in the midst of oppressive conditions of survival and negotiations. This study serves as a multilayered and nuanced interrogation of economic disempowerment as the critical weapon that negated the possibility of any equality since the holders of this economic power were not ready to negotiate such a determinant power in the functioning of the Portuguese colonial empire. Countering the fallacious arguments of Gilberto Freyre in his numerous works, this study challenges such claims of racial erasure and the existence of a "colonial family" in a context where the "Casa Grande" and the "Senzala" remain literally separated and unequal.

In the specific case of Brazilian fraudulent "racial democracy," and looking deeper into the problematic "cosmic race" produced through sexual violence and economic exploitation, this study argues that, as a matter of fact, the identity produced through this interlocking relationship was more of a shifting one, a "migrating identity" that constantly and strategically negotiated its being and relevance according to contexts and convenience as a matter of survival. In addition to reviewing historical and critical literature, the study deploys a number of case studies to unveil the contradictions of the claim of a uniform Lusophone Atlantic, and demonstrates that Lusotropicalism was more of a burden than an asset. In so doing, such iconic symbols of national identity as Zumbi, Xica da Silva, Pedro Archanjo, Orpheus, and the favelado are interrogated by juxtaposition with works by various cultural producers to arrive at a sustainable theoretical proposition on shifting Brazilianness and Afro-Atlanticity. In addition, the implied dislocations of these characters are juxtaposed with their real relocations through highlighted social inequalities and problematized "racial harmony."

While the case studies primarily focus on Brazil, this book's conceptualization extends well beyond Brazil as it interrogates the Afro-Atlantic Lusophonia in terms of historical and cultural intersections between Portugal, Africa, and Brazil during slavery and colonialism, in order to better understand the transnational movements of ideas, people, and cultures over many centuries. These intersections, these movements, ultimately constitute how we engage this unique diaspora of Lusotropicalism and the cultural political challenges it poses for the miscegenated and migrating identities thereby produced. Some of the questions to be interrogated include: To what extent does the Afro-Atlantic Lusophonia replicate or problematize the "Black Atlantic" as theorized by Paul Gilroy? How does Gilberto Freyre's "Lusotropicalism" complicate or expantiate such a paradigm? Beyond these two formulations, is there a differentiating or inclusive paradigm that better captures the Lusophone Atlantic while taking into consideration the uniqueness of the individual historical units of Africa, Europe, the Americas, Asia, and the Caribbean, in order not to limit analysis of case studies to external influences and impositions without regard for indigenous articulations of identity, resistance, and sociohistorical formations?

To better appreciate the interlocking dynamics of the concepts and terminologies deployed in this book, namely, "migrating identities," "dislocation," "relocation," and "Afro-Brazilian Diaspora," it is necessary to have working definitions of such ideas from the outset. Based on the central thesis that the Atlantic is a space of migration, whether voluntary or involuntary, the negotiation of place, space, and identity as the migrant moves from one location to the other, deals with the implied dislocation from the old setting, and the inevitable relocation in the new setting, and the adaptation of such a decisive experience into a survivalist trigger; it is indeed a perpetual process of naming and renaming the shifting identities that occur in the individual or group. This negotiation is performed primarily by those in migration, and secondarily by scholars of the phenomenon.

By "migrating identities," I refer to those collectives and individuals subjected to forced and voluntary migrations whether as enslaved, colonized, labor-driven, or politically displaced subjects through natural disasters or economic exigencies. This broad definition allows for nuanced understanding of case studies, as the characters, cultural productions, and settings analyzed vary from case to case, especially since the timeframe of the nineteenth and twentieth centuries is quite broad. I am not suggesting that the "identity" that is migrating is in any way fixed, even before migration; but in the very least, the migrant has a sense of place and origin before the migration took place. Unlike voluntary migration, which can be planned by the migrant in a three-part sequence ("pre-migration," "physical migration," and "post-migration"), involuntary migration, such as transatlantic slavery, is never planned by the migrant, but rather is imposed as a brutal consequence of imperial economic greed. In both instances of voluntary and involuntary migrating identities, however, a lasting trauma is implied as the migrant adjusts through a series of coping mechanisms that may not be limited to assimilation, invocation of memory, nostalgia, and even real and symbolic rebellion, resistance, or creative cultural and spiritual adaptations. Of particular relevance is the view of Vijay Agnew in *Diaspora, Memory, and Identity* (2005) when the critic articulates a "dynamic tension every day between living 'here' and remembering 'there,' between memories of places of origins and entanglements with places of residence, and between the metaphorical and the physical home" (4). Yet, beyond the physical and metaphorical place or space, Stuart Hall in "Cultural Identity and Diaspora" (1993) cogently problematizes identity as a dynamic process when he theorizes: "Perhaps instead of thinking of identity as an already accomplished fact, which the new cultural practices then represent, we should think, instead, of identity as a production, which is never complete, always in process, and always constituted within, not outside, representation" (18). Migrating identities are thus subjected to the persistent dynamics of change as they navigate the transformative energies of dislocation and relocation regardless of the historical or contextual frame of reference.

The discussion of "dislocation and relocation" raises a number of questions and issues that relate to the migrating subject's state of being and frame of mind. Through ruptures, disjunctures, and reconfigurations, this perpetually dislocated and relocated subject is a product of two or more worlds who shifts amidst a territoriality well beyond its control, especially between the old "homeland" and the newly adopted "hostland." Even the notion of the center in relation to the margin is constantly shifting to the extent that the newly reconfigured Afro-Atlantic subject may well be at the mercy of constant conflicts, internal divisions, movements, fractures, and an elusive cohesion that is complicated by multiple identities as the subject tends to break away from colonizing hegemony and is yet implicated in it as a hybrid personality that cannot be restored to the original state of purity. Can this subject be exclusively dislocated or reciprocally dislocated and relocated over time, depending on contexts and specific moments of identitarian consciousness? For Homi Bhabha in *The Location of Culture* (1994), the dislocated subject occupies, indeed, a "third space," an "in-between space" that carries the ultimate meaning of culture since this same character is able to disrupt colonial hegemony from within, not so much as a split subject, but by playing on the power of marginality imposed on it, and through this power, recast social and cultural meaning through subversion by creatively playing in the margins and on the interstices of cultural identity. Yet the dislocated subject may well be coping with a larger sense of belonging neither to a homeland nor to a hostland, in which case the sense of place is problematized, as there is really no fixed center or "home" since this subject often feels torn between the two or more spaces through the crisis of consciousness and of identity. Even when "relocation" seems to conjure up positive vibrations for the dislocated subject, the sentiments of memory or nostalgia complicate this positive feeling as it endeavors to recuperate what appears "lost" and necessary to regain through the symbolic recourse to remembrance. In the process, a fluidity of the subject emerges, as when confronting the often romantic memories of the old home with the harsh realities of the new residence. In sum, while not interchangeable, dislocation and relocation are two sides of the same coin for the migrating subject and must be considered hand-in-hand to get the full import of the dialectical intersectionality of norm and deviation in the process of becoming or of problematic transatlantic identity formation.

The "Afro-Brazilian world" refers to the Africa-influenced expansive space that suffered under Portuguese colonial oppression was later reconfigured into shifting identities due to the problematic myth of racial democracy. In order to understand the paradoxes of reversal deployed to counter dislocating structures through cultural production, this book serves as an urgent call for intervention. While studies have been conducted about dislocations of Afro-Brazilians from political power through the myth of racial democracy that disenfranchises through economic disparities, these works do not provide answers beyond the more obvious (slavery, miscegenation, and the fallacy of assimilation thesis), thus avoiding the real issue: the direct impact of racial and economic disempowerment. In recasting dislocation as an economic and racial consequence of a deliberately structured reality, this book sets out to present strategic modes of dislocations and concrete counter-dislocation measures that challenge abusive processes that deprive marginalized populations of human and civil rights. Ultimately, beyond being an academic exercise and labor of love, this study seeks to demand social justice for dislocated populations in Brazil—mostly black and brown.

Socioeconomics of Post-Abolition Migrating Identities

This book argues that slavery was only partially responsible for the contemporary marginalization of the Afro-Brazilian population, which has been "migrating" between slavery, urban poverty, marginalization, social exclusion, economic deprivation, educational inadequacy, and political powerlessness, among other agencies of social death. Beyond slavery, the draconian structural policies adopted by the violent instrumentalities of the State in the post-abolition era have maintained socioeconomic and political disparities for more than a century. It is against this background that this book raises a number of research questions that further elucidate the intricacies of migrating identities in the Afro-Brazilian world. What, for example, were the significant consequences of slavery in Brazil in concrete terms? What specifically has changed for Afro-Brazilians since the abolition of slavery in 1888? Which texts (canonical or otherwise) have manifested and/or contributed to highlight dislocations in socioeconomic, cultural, and political terms? What strategies have been adopted "against" the state by cultural producers representing "counter-dislocation" voices from the urban periphery? What is the place of postmodern cultural production in relation to traditional expression, and how is this new wave challenging old ways of cultural dissemination in relation to shifting power dynamics?

Other questions seek to understand the aftermath of such exclusionary politics in terms of counter-strategies designed to advance social equality. One wonders, for example, why a radical social upheaval has been avoided in Brazil to date despite signs and signatures of tensions and agitations among social movements clamoring for change and social justice? Is there any place for negotiations in a dire state of affairs that could easily deteriorate into systematic "social death"? What is the role of culture in these wishful "negotiations" and what are its limits? What are the possibilities and potentialities of social regeneration without uprooting hegemonic and dislocating forces which seem to remain intact in the post-abolition era? Of what ideological or pragmatic significance is negotiation in the midst of a stifling economic condition that ultimately requires structural overhaul and redistribution of state resources in order to redress conscious and unconscious dislocations? At what point in the cultural-political negotiation process will sociopolitical actors realize the limits and cooptation alternatives available to them, and how do these alternatives negate their original resistant ideological goals? In answering these questions, the book argues that shifting identities will be inevitable if lasting structural changes are not effected by the state.

Though many studies on Brazilian slavery have glossed over the subject of the economic impact of this heinous crime against humanity, a few have focused on slave resistance as well as on the import of miscegenation as a strategic measure to "harmonize" the differences between the races that contributed to the making of contemporary Brazil. Yet even though miscegenation is sometimes taken as a potential "solution" to social inequalities, this paradigm is yet to be interrogated beyond the facile cultural harmony it brings about. In fact, the violence it conjures up in the colonial setting fails to rationalize such problematic harmonious relations. The reality is that miscegenation was not just a cultural or social arrangement, it was (and is) also an economic one. The convenience of having intercourse with both the Amerindian and African women in colonial Brazil yielded many unspoken benefits to the colonizer. Economically speaking, these women would bring to the world biracial children, who, in addition to "belonging" to the colonizer, were also born into slavery despite the privileges attached to them as biological children. Despite such "privileges," they were still considered slaves who could be sold out to other plantations as well as forced to work just like any of the Africans turned into slaves in the Americas. Socially speaking, these biracial subjects often served as "foremen" and thus had control over African slaves in the colony—forgetting that they themselves were the offspring of slaves. The hierarchy thus created exacerbated tensions as the miscegenated children came next in terms of power dynamics right after the colonizer, while the Amerindians and the Africans remained at the bottom.

That colonial set-up has not changed to date in the polarized Brazilian political structure. The complex Brazilian race relations are arguably the aftermath of that colonial engineering that lasted for more than three centuries. With a recent Brazilian census indicating that over fifty percent of the population as biracial, the inevitable rungs on the economic ladder are, in descending order, the rich white elites, the mixed-raced middle class, and the black poor. According to Robert Brent Toplin, this economic division or social stratification is not in any way troubling to the Brazilian white elites because it is in their best interest to continue to dominate other races.[1] Octávio Ianni goes even further by suggesting that capital accumulation in Latin America came about through slavery while capitalist expansion equally led to the slave crisis, considering that the European Industrial Revolution necessitated the abolition of slavery.[2] This dialectical relationship between slavery and capitalism leads today to the same gap between the haves and the have-nots as well as to the attendant racial antagonisms that pervade the Brazilian society in the twenty-first century.

Racialized policies of Brazil in the colonial era have remained unchanged except for some structural changes geared toward improved racial relations. The same way slaves were kept in a lamentable socio-economic situation as objects and chattel, likewise, most black Brazilian poor wander aimlessly through the favelas of life in contemporary Brazil when it comes to economic empowerment. Though no official discrimination laws were enacted in Brazil as in apartheid South Africa, racist policies were practiced in order to keep blacks disempowered, uneducated, subservient, and disenfranchised. Brazilian elites continue to need cheap labor in order to maintain profits in their privileged "national" and "transnational" businesses, the same way that they needed African slaves in the colonial plantations and mines. The white minority in Brazil will not voluntarily share economic power with disenfranchised blacks because it is not in their short-term interest to do so. Political efforts to "unify" white and black Brazilians have not worked despite various affirmative action policies introduced by the Workers' Party (*Partido dos Trabalhadores* [PT]), especially in the era of the Lula presidency. This is so because class discrimination has always been in place to ensure that white elites assume their privileged space in the natural order of things in the Brazilian economic apartheid. The European foray into Brazil, while often treated as a coincidence, was a well-planned voyage of exploitation and not simply of discovery. European monarchs had traded with their royal counterparts in Africa before the advent of slavery and colonialism. They even went to the extent of trading ambassadors or emissaries and exchanged gifts. Thus the claim that they did not know Africa or Latin America had mineral wealth, spices, and natives whose labor could be easily exploited was sheer nonsense. Amerindians and Africans were imposed the burden of mining precious stones and gold, and also cultivating the land for both food and cash crops while the colonizer became the controller of virgin lands "in the middle of nowhere" in Africa as well as in the New World.

Slavery was thus a vital economic activity for the survival of even European economies. This explains why emancipation did not come very easily. Even in the case of Brazil, where independence was declared by the heir to the Portuguese throne, the race-mixture experimentation was not as easy as it has been represented. Despite the efforts to integrate slaves after abolition in Brazil, the process was slow and painstaking. Political and economic factors had to be considered. Now that slaves were not needed for the industrializing post-abolition economy, they could not all be repatriated back to Africa, not even all those who committed "treason" by attempting to overthrow the colonial government in Bahia before abolition, such as the Malês in the nineteenth century.[3] There is no question that economic and political factors contributed to the "race-mixture" experiment. It was born less of the benevolent desire to attain racial equality than of the need to create a semblance of racial tolerance and co-existence. In the colonial capital of Bahia alone in the early eighteenth century, it was reported that African descendants constituted 96% of the population.[4] Yet Brazilian slave owners were also noted to have been very harsh with their slaves.[5] Gilberto Freyre's claim that Brazilian slavery was more compassionate than other slaveries is untenable. Often framed as the Tannenebaum thesis, the Freyrean argument appears to have assumed the humane treatment of the African slaves by the colonial slave owners. If indeed the circumstances of the slaves were humane, what explains the many slave revolts of the nineteenth century? Even after abolition of slavery and independence from Portugal, the slave owners were still hoping to keep their slaves. Brazil's close ties with Europe at a time when slavery was being perceived as an impediment to development contributed to its decision to also abolish slavery, even though it was a gradual process. The Brazilian economy was not in any way threatened by the emancipation of slaves. Rather, the Brazilian government felt that free labor would ultimately be more lucrative than slave labor due to technological advances, modernization, and industrialization. Besides, the emancipated slaves constituted the lowest economic class, and, lacking technological know-how, would have no choice but to return to the petty occupations they were used to before abolition. The lack of upward mobility for blacks was thus blamed not on racial discrimination, but on class: their place in the social hierarchy brought with it immense odds, which alone would prevent them from prospering.

Summary of Chapters

In seven chapters, the conceptual framework of *Identities in Flux* interrogates and exemplifies the viability of a paradigmatic shift in explicating marginalized and dislocated populations, especially in Brazil. Interdisciplinary in focus and context, the book has necessitated fieldwork, theoretical thrust, and applications that vary from chapter to chapter. Through archival materials, scholarly dialogues with prominent and emergent cultural and institutional "memories," as well as local social interpreters of Afro-Brazilian cultural production, especially in Bahia, the entire book maps the cause-effect analysis of slavery and its aftermath in social policy and execution. Chapter 1, "The Afro-Brazilian Diaspora: From Slavery to Migrating Identities," traces the history of Portuguese colonialism in the lusophone world with specific emphasis on the impacts of slavery and colonialism in Brazil. In addition, African resistance, adaptations, and relics of renaissance are analyzed to highlight survivalist tendencies that attempted to create counter-dislocation paradigmatic shifts even at the stage of the conquering mission of the Portuguese. While chapter 1 provides the historical context, chapter 2, "Zumbi dos Palmares: Relocating History, Film, and Print," compares and contrasts dramatic and cinematic renditions of a social icon while highlighting some historical and biographical elements deployed to fashion a persona and a legend that document one of the lasting icons of Brazilian social history. While this chapter focuses principally on the dramatic text *Arena Conta Zumbi*, the cinematic interpretation of the life of Zumbi dos Palmares in *Quilombo*, as directed by Carlos Diegues, is also revisited. Chapter 3, "Xica da Silva: Sexualized and Miscegenated Body Politics," explores the shifting versions of the legacy of Xica da Silva as portrayed in film and fiction, while focusing on the significance of her sacrificial strategies to "free" herself from slavery and enjoin others to do the same. Chapter 4, "Manuel Querino: African Contributions to Brazil," provides a case study that examines the contributions of the works of Manuel Querino (1890–1920) to the discourses on African retentions in Brazil.

The remaining chapters provide archetypal exemplification of iconic essences that have become part of Brazilian cultural and national consciousness. Chapter 5, "Jorge Amado's Poetic License: Fictionalizing History," delves into a comparison of history, biography, and authorial license in the invention of Pedro Archanjo in his famed *Tenda dos Milagres*. Chapter 6, "Black Orpheus: Regeneration of Greco-Yoruba Mythologies," investigates the emergence of Black Orpheus as an Afro-Brazilian character by studying fictional (*Invenção de Orfeu* by Jorge de Lima; *Orfeu da Conceição* by Vinícius de Moraes) and cinematic adaptations over the years—from Greek dramatic versions, to Brazilian dramatic pieces that led to two cinematic adaptations: *Orfeu Negro* (1959) and *Orfeu* (2000).

Finally, chapter 7, "City of God: The Ghettoization of Violence," high-lights "gangsta" violence that is overlapped with drug trafficking in the "Hollywoodified" favela community of Cidade de Deus (City of God) in the urban peripheries of Rio de Janeiro.

Chapter 1

The Afro-Brazilian Diaspora

From Slavery to Migrating Identities

Lusotropicalism as a Defining (Post)Colonial Concept

When in the 1930s, Gilberto Freyre wrote *Casa Grande e Senzala* (The Masters and the Slaves), little did he know that his book would one day be considered a classic, and that his "Lusotropicalist Idea" would revolutionize the entire lusophone world and become one of the foundational and most interrogated paradigms among scholars in the field. Though he did not use the term himself (it was later coined by critics), his idea was that the Portuguese had a special disposition to adapt and mix with other cultures, thus resulting in a desirable race mixture devoid of racism. He later popularized the idea in the 1950s, traveling throughout the Portuguese empire and producing a sizeable body of work,[1] of which *O Luso e o Trópico* (1961) may be considered a synthesis. Gilberto Freyre had set out to explain the formation of Brazilian society and the place of the Portuguese, the Amerindian, and the African in that historical formation. Yet this concept would later be used by the Portuguese in the 1970s to justify its mission to colonize Africa as well as Asia. Despite the decolonization wars of 1960–1974 in Portuguese-speaking Africa, miscegenation had taken root and continued to generate debates on both sides of the Atlantic—not only among the Portuguese, Brazilians, and Africans, but also among historians, sociologists, and anthropologists, who are still trying to make sense of the liabilities and assets of such a complex social theory.[2]

In Brazil, the intellectual debate on race mixture was primarily ideologically inclined, between those from the southern part of Brazil, mostly European and Japanese immigrants who felt Brazil should become another American melting pot where African descendants and Amerindians are treated equally, and those from the Northeast, mostly in favor of the plantation economy, who defended more traditional positions. The definition of what constituted and should constitute Brazilian social formation was at the crux of the controversy—since Gilberto Freyre in *Casa Grande e Senzala* set out to define Brazilian society in the 1930s. Implicitly, the two sides of the debate could not avoid the issue of race since, on the one hand, Brazilian identity was predicated on a colonial formation based on slavery, hence the origin of racial inequalities; and on the other hand, Portugal was deemed a weak colonial power that lacked the complex state structure of other colonial powers. Brazil was, after all, a modern and modernizing nation influenced by European immigration and industrialization, and thus a newly formed nation that was quite different demographically from the Portuguese roots that Lusotropicalism tended to associate with the unique ability for racial harmony.

While Freyre's theory proposed a counter-narrative to the negativity and brutality of Portuguese colonization, it could not undo the racist doctrines of the nineteenth and twentieth centuries. And neither could the concrete reality of that which Freyre described—the race mixture between the Amerindian, the African, and the Portuguese—undo the violence suffered by the African slaves under the colonial power of the Portuguese.

Freyre's main argument was that under the Estado Novo in Brazil, a system of governance that claimed Brazil as a "racial democracy," Brazilian national identity was at the heart of the official government's political discourse that argued that the plantation economy during the colonial era brought about a kind of contradictory but cordial, racial, and cultural intimacy among European masters and African slaves. This dynamic relationship, he argued, led to a unique Brazilian society different from those influenced by the Anglo-Saxon experience, in the United States, for example. Freyre further reasoned that before the arrival of the Portuguese in Brazil, they had undergone similar cultural and racial miscegenation with the Moors, Jews, and Arabs, among other races; and in so doing Portugal was better prepared for what would then happen in colonial Brazil in terms of race-mixture. While Luso-Brazilianists differ about the legacy of Gilberto Freyre, his contribution to the development of a colonial concept later used to justify colonization and racism is unquestionable—though the concept is still contested by black social movements who insist that he contributed to the racial democracy mythology in Brazil, as well as by some apologists of Lusotropicalism in Africa.

While Brazil could pride itself in its natural resources, Portugal could not lay a similar claim to such natural wealth and blessings. When Gilberto Freyre published *Casa Grande e Senzala* in 1933, Portugal was under Salazarian dictatorship (1926–1974) as prompted by a military coup of 1926 that ended the First Republic. Despite the progressive nature of the Republic that had overthrown the Portuguese monarchy in 1910, Salazar felt the need to structure a colonial enterprise in Africa since the previous Portuguese "empires" in India of the sixteenth and seventeenth and in Brazil in the seventeenth and eighteenth centuries had not amounted to much economic prestige for Portugal, ultimately. During the dictatorship of Salazar, African colonies were seen as an economic boost for Portuguese national reputation and identity. By combining the glorious age of discovery with the colonial conquest of Africa,[3] Portugal was able to re-invent its national narrative as a major empire of discovery and colonial expansion. With the emergence of Freyre's ideas about harmonious Portuguese relations in the tropics, Portugal was able to deploy this theory to its own advantage by replacing the more racist image of its colonial policies with one supposedly more humane, less violent, and more cordial in terms of racial relations. Despite these problematic claims of harmony, colonized African countries were administered through an assimilationist policy that divided the populations into three racial categories: Portuguese colonials were citizens, mixed-raced individuals or assimilated Africans were considered as next in rank, and the indigenous people who refused or resisted assimilation fell at the very bottom of the racial hierarchy. At the same time that poor Portuguese immigrants were looking to France, Germany, and England as illegal workers or refugees in the late 1950s, anticolonial sentiments were being expressed by colonized African countries, and this decolonization wave finally took off in 1960—lasting until young Portuguese military officers overthrew the Salazar regime in 1974. Freyre's Lusotropical theory was helpful to Portuguese colonialism in Africa because the Portuguese had successfully implemented this alternative paradigm in Brazil much against the ideals of Soviet communism and American capitalism.

With Portugal's integration into the European Union, the former imperial nation sought to re-invent its image in the committee of nations—from a primarily nation of maritime discoveries and colonial expansion to a tolerant nation of immigrants from the ex-colonies, which further legitimized its claim as a "Lusofonia" or Portuguese commonwealth (CPLP) or even a Portuguese diaspora. As a metropolitan bridge between Europe and the Afro-Brazilian diaspora, Portugal sought to represent itself as a transnational Portuguese community that had transcended its brutal colonial and exploitative past. Despite these claims, examples abound of the different experiences of the immigrants from Portuguese-speaking Africa, Eastern European countries, and Brazil, and how, beyond differential treatment and racism, these immigrants were confined to the worst living conditions and communities, systematically exploited, and ultimately found it more difficult to attain Portuguese citizenship than Portuguese descendants. It is in this context that the Lusotropical idea of colonial miscegenation, harmony, and tolerance falls apart. Rather than subscribe to the enduring claim of Portuguese exceptionalism in the world, the reality speaks to the continuity of racial discrimination as even today Portugal continues to deny African influences or cultural presence in Portugal. The result is a systematic social exclusion of Portuguese-speaking Africans who at best become clandestine, marginalized, and invisible. In the final analysis, Lusotropicalism as propounded by Gilberto Freyre ceases from being just a colonial theory and becomes also a postcolonial one.

Of Social Exclusion, Racism, and Identity Formations

The Portuguese initiated the New World slave trade[4] in the sixteenth century, followed by the British, French, Spanish, and Dutch. Portuguese discoveries, despite the claim of maritime adventure, soon turned into a legacy of domination and racism as the ship owners repurposed their vessels and inaugurated the Atlantic slave trade. Slave traders needed to minimize transportation costs to the Americas. Their cargoes were destined to labor on plantations of sugar, coffee, tobacco, and cotton, in rice fields, and in gold and silver mines, among others. For the convenience of domination and acculturation, the Portuguese failed to recognize ethnic diversities among the indigenous populations and referred to native populations as "Indians," while slaves forcibly removed from Africa were called "negroes." Conflating social rank and skin color, they saw blackness and slavery as synonymous. The majority of enslaved

Africans transported to the New World from the sixteenth through the nineteenth centuries were taken from West Africa to the Americas. In the competition among the West European nations to create overseas empires, the Atlantic economic system was focused on producing commercial crops for European industries. In *Paths of the Atlantic Slave Trade* (2011), Ana Lucia Araujo suggests that the form of enslavement was determined by such factors as the disembarking region, the kind of work performed, gender, age, religion, and language, among others. As a consequence of slavery, racism—still today—permeates every facet of modern human life, especially for those who experience it on a daily basis; hence Walter Rodney notes in *How Europe Underdeveloped Africa* (1981) that "no people can enslave another for four centuries without coming out with a notion of superiority, and when the color and other physical traits of those peoples were quite different it was inevitable that the prejudice should take a racist form" (112). For, ultimately, racial attitudes are conditioned by the slave experience and the relationship between the slave and the enslaver.

Despite the semblance of homogeneity in the phrase "lusophone identity," perhaps suggested by linguistic commonalities, the term "lusophone" itself dates back to the ancient Roman province of Lusitania, which reached beyond the Iberian Peninsula to include parts of today's Spain. Today's Portuguese-speaking countries include Portugal, Brazil, Angola, Cape Verde, East Timor, Guinea-Bissau, Mozambique, São Tomé and Príncipe, and Equatorial Guinea. In addition, 1996 saw the creation of the international Community of Portuguese Language Countries (CPLP), which consists of the nine independent countries where the Portuguese language is spoken. Yet, despite linguistic commonalities, the CPLP, and the efforts of Portuguese-diaspora communities to expand and promote the legacy of the Portuguese empire in language and culture, identity formation and ethnicities are complex. Often omitted from the discussion of the Portuguese legacy is the impact of slavery and the resultant racism and miscegenated identities.[5] Portuguese expansionism and exceptionalism would also become its undoing. Having dominated the colonial empire across Africa, Asia, and South America in the sixteenth through eighteenth centuries, it would become subordinate to England in the nineteenth century given the transfer of the Portuguese Crown to Rio de Janeiro in 1808 as well as the discontinuation of the transatlantic slave trade in 1845. As a second-tier colonial power during the scramble for and partitioning of Africa, Portugal deployed violence to maintain its hold on its African ex-colonies. In the case of Brazil, the Portuguese transfer of its capital from Lisbon to Rio de Janeiro between 1808 and 1821 shifted the economic power between Portugal and Brazil, with Brazil as the new economic power in relation to Portugal, even though Brazil would remain a Portuguese colony until its independence in 1822. The Brazilian colonial experience was also marred by economic exploitation and violence against native Amerindian populations as well as Africans taken as slaves. Not even the fallacious Lusotropicalist formulation of Gilberto Freyre about racial harmony can minimize such violence.

The close affiliation among the Portuguese ex-colonies well after independence from Portugal was further accentuated in the era of transnationalism and global diasporas, in which migrations followed paths from Portugal to Brazil, from Brazil to Europe, from Africa to the Americas—to the degree that the Portuguese find themselves settling in Rio de Janeiro, Brazilians in Lisbon, Africans in São Paulo and Salvador and elsewhere in Brazil, with Portuguese migrant populations as well in Massachusetts and Rhode Island. Even in literature, many Afro-Luso-Brazilian works by the likes of Machado de Assis, Adolfo Caminha, Aluísio Azevedo, Pepetela, Manuel Rui, Mia Couto, José Eduardo Agualusa, António Lobo Antunes, and Germano Almeida, to name a few, engage the subjects of dislocation, settlement, crosscultural affinities, and transatlantic journeys; all of which, directly or indirectly, revolve around issues of identity formations and revisionist versions of Portuguese colonial adventures. No other (post)colonial concept does as much justice to these problematic and shifting identities as Gilberto Freyre's *Casa Grande e Senzala*. As controversial as the theory of Lusotropicalism is, it remains the most enduring legacy of the Portuguese multicontinental colonial enterprise. In theorizing on hybridism and miscegenation in the lusophone world, he synthesizes rather seminally that:

> The Portuguese case is one of the most complex and intriguing. If Brazil has been systematically praised as the example of the humanistic and miscegenating characteristic of Portuguese expansion, it has also been used as an argument for the legitimization of later colonialism in Africa, as well as for the construction of a self-representation of Portuguese as non-racists. The Portuguese nation, however, has seldom been described as a miscegenated nation and *mestiça* itself.[6]

Despite the cultural affinities and political tensions between Portugal and its ex-colonies, the relationship remains one of seductive ambivalence and permanent ambiguity. And it is in this respect that identity formations in the lusophone world as well as racial relations will continue to be marred by the legacy of the Lusotropicalist ideology and the attendant processes of inclusive exclusion.[7]

Gilberto Freyre and Anti-Freyrean Echoes

Any discussion of Gilberto Freyre regarding the history, sociology, and cultural interpretation of Brazil is always subject to controversy, because the man and his works emerged at a critical juncture—or disjuncture—of Brazilian history. To fully understand Gilberto Freyre as a social theorist, one must also juxtapose his background and influences with the paradigmatic contributions of his works to a better understanding of Brazilian life. The controversies notwithstanding, there is no gainsaying that Gilberto Freyre has given us cogent insights into understanding the Brazilian identity—whether of the Ameridian, European, African, or mixed-race individual. In the context of understanding colonialism in Africa as well as in other lusophone countries, Freyre's theoretical and identitarian formations reach beyond the confines of Brazil. From a comparative perspective, the resonances propounded in his majestic work, especially in *Casa Grande e Senzala*, are equally found in the United States, Europe, Asia, and Africa. Studies are now emerging about the implicit existence of racism in the purported theory of Brazilian "racial democracy." Though Brazilians themselves are still struggling with that criticism (as a large society often tends to dismiss the racism staring it in the face), a cursory look at the trajectory of Brazil since the abolition of slavery in 1888 confirms that very few changes have occurred to improve racial relations between whites and blacks. In the course of its tortuous history, and specifically during one 400-year span, Brazil claims to have avoided racial tensions and maintained racial harmony. Nothing could be further from the truth. Gilberto Freyre's problematic racial ideology of the 1930s argues that Brazil is made up of a singular harmonious race as represented by the indigenous, African, and European identities.

In suggesting that everyone is Brazilian, discouraging specific ethnic identities, Brazil places in the forefront of its racial ideology a differentiation between its own racial ideology and that of the North American or even South African segregational tendencies. As a result, in Brazil, privileges increase in proportion as darkness of skin decreases. Such a blurred or "collective" identitarian vision makes for a confused racial identity that promotes the denial of blackness or African heritage as an unnecessary form of ancestral connection and pride. Despite this illusion, outside of Nigeria, Brazil has the second-largest African ancestry, with about 80 million of its 180 million population claiming African ancestry. Brazil has thus gotten away with a false posture of being a "multicultural" country while at the same time promoting racist and genocidal policies against the marginalized Afro-Brazilian populations. Yet the Brazilian elite look the other way by maintaining that class rather than race is the cause of the poverty of Afro-Brazilian communities. From inequalities in educational access to inequalities in the labor market, millions of Afro-Brazilians are thus trapped in a vicious cycle of poverty, violence, and social death, as they disproportionately sacrifice their humanity and well-being for the advancement of the white race through the systemic perpetration of veiled racism. Class analysis, while important, cannot dismiss the history of racism and its connectivity with transatlantic slavery. Ultimately, the reality is that the political participation of Afro-Brazilians will be minimized if not prevented entirely by virtue of that disenfranchising history. As Rebecca Reichmann notes, "Overall, Afro-Brazilian candidates were drafted from the working class, whereas whites came from upper-middle and middle-class,"[8] thus giving the white candidates with better educational backgrounds a disproportionate advantage over less-educated Afro-Brazilians.

During the "World Conference Against Racism,"[9] in 2001, Brazil officially acknowledged that racism is prevalent in Brazil, and has since instituted some measures to rectify this crime against humanity. After the conference, a "Durban Declaration" document was drawn up by the participants and representatives. The document sought to formulate a cohesive identity for all African descendants deemed to have been victims of slavery, including those who may have more than one ancestral heritage. The Lula government (January 2002–January 2011) is credited with the largest social programs ever, such as *Bolsa Escola*, *Bolsa Família*, *Fome Zero*, and *Sistema de Quotas* (Affirmative Action). Lula is also considered as the strongest crusader in government for racial equality for Afro-Brazilians in recent years. Some social movements were also able to benefit from these social services, especially the Secretariat for the

Promotion of Racial Equality (SEPPIR). This ministry-level organization was responsible for the coordination of opportunities for Afro-Brazilians and other racial minority groups, as well as for efforts to strengthen Brazilian-African relations. As was the case in the United States, some of these Affirmative Action programs came under attack by the elite, who argued they constituted a violation of the Brazilian constitution as well as a form of reverse racism against whites. Such government efforts could not be initiated before Lula due to the official position on racial democracy: the establishment had embraced Gilberto Freyre's arguments on racial harmony, and their implication that Afro-Brazilians were compelled to subject themselves to "whitening" their dark skin as a social control measure. They were also compelled to use sex (miscegenation) to improve their status and in so doing minimize the effects of racism on their immediate and future generations. This measure is what Carl Degler in *Neither Black Nor White* (1986) refers to as the "mulatto escape hatch," or, frankly, sex as a safety valve. Freyre's miscegenation thesis[10] also plays into the national euphoria during the annual Carnival—a time when not only the racially mixed but blacks and whites alike can enjoy sexual freedom, and in a symbolic way, class freedom as well, at least for some dreamy Carnival days.

Despite the constitutional ban on racism, the fact of the matter remains that racism is alive but veiled in Brazil. Quite often, in the interest of maintaining harmonious relations, Brazilians pretend that racism does not bother them, and this very same inferiority complex can be traced back to the era of slavery when blacks or African descendants were subjugated and expected to know their place over many centuries of enslavement. The consequent silence and lack of open discussions about race, racism, and the consequences of social inequalities result in an odd feeling and acceptance of inferiority on the part of some disadvantaged Afro-Brazilians. In addition to the governmental hypocrisy and denial of racism, darker-skinned Brazilians tend to be so ashamed of their skin color that they would not even openly identify as Afro-Brazilians during national census or while job-hunting for fear of losing any implicit benefits in being of lighter skinned. Of its 180 million citizens, close to half claim to be of African heritage or racially mixed (Toplin, 1981: 91). This diversity of racial composition is unfortunately accompanied by a disparity in advantage and opportunity: Afro-Brazilians are the poorest, while white Brazilians or the lighter-skinned elites control the social, economic, political, and educational institutions—thus disenfranchising the black population in its entirety. Following the abolition of slavery and in order to mitigate the stigma of blackness on the idealized "white" Brazil, Brazilian elites created a concept known as "branqueamento" (whitening) by not only encouraging race-mixture but also incentivizing a wave of European immigration to help industrialize and "whiten" Brazil.

Economically and socially, Afro-Brazilians are still the worst-placed. Due to lack of access to education, they constitute the group with the highest level of unemployment, while their average individual income, mainly obtained through nonsteady menial jobs, may be as low as $75 a month. In terms of educational attainment, under 2% will make it to the university level (let alone graduate with a degree), with most dropping out of high school. This compares to over 10% of whites who obtain a university degree and more who enroll in university. Such an acute discrepancy of educational access and economic status clearly confirms the statistics that even in the political arena, the insignificant number of Afro-Brazilian members of Congress, ministers, governors, and mayors contrasts sharply with the millions of powerless workers who frequent the corridors of power only as janitors, drivers, domestics, detained criminals, or even helpless working women who have been sexually violated. The journey from the era of slavery in the eighteenth century to the current era of racial quotas and Affirmative Action policies in the twenty-first century has been a tortuous one. Though many colleges reserve 20% of their admissions for Afro-Brazilians, the record of retention is abysmal as these mainly older students must balance work and family life with educational opportunities that may or may not improve their lot in life due to the continuation of subtle racial discrimination practices in the marketplace. Though many policies to rectify past injustices against Afro-Brazilians are now legally in place, their implementation is a whole different challenge.

The Lula government did make some advances in the improvement of Afro-Brazilian life: (1) it declared November 20 a national "Black Consciousness Day" holiday to celebrate Zumbi dos Palmares, the seventeenth-century leader of the Palmares who resisted the Portuguese; (2) it approved a two-billion-reais program to revitalize the runaway slave communities ("quilombos"[11]) all over Brazil; (3) it enacted a law that sets aside 50% of university admissions for Afro-Brazilians, indigenous people, and all disadvantaged people; (4) it made the teaching of African studies (including African history, Afro-Brazilian history, and African languages) a requirement in national curricula; (5) it instituted, through the Secretariat for the Promotion of Racial Equality (SEPPIR), new legislation that supports the inclusion of Afro-Brazilians in political appointments such as in Itamaraty or the Foreign Service Academy. While skepticism is rampant about the specific gains in educational and political access for Afro-Brazilians in terms of equality in salaries when compared to whites, one can only hope that these concrete social and legal measures, which presuppose the falsity of Gilberto Freyre's problematic thesis of racial harmony and denial of racism, is at least the beginning of a different series of struggles and strides in the shift toward a more acceptable paradigm in bringing about racial equality in Brazil. It has been an arduous journey, no doubt, but the dividends of such a change in direction toward redressing retrograde social inequalities will come; it can only be a matter of time before Brazil can truly celebrate the veritable commonality and humanity of all races and restore human dignity, of which so many generations have been deprived, to the interactions among the new breed of Brazilians.

Against Slavery and Colonialism

Contrary to the myopic view that the enslaved and the colonized were willingly submissive to the machinery of slavery and colonial brutality, violence, violation, exploitation, and coercion, evidence indicates that the enslaved and the colonized resisted the bestiality of their "masters" through many veils and masked strategies of survival in which they may have appeared to be passive, collaborative, conformist, and subservient, but indeed, systematically worked out their freedom[12] in both clandestine and combative manners. In his rather dense study on the relationship between slavery, racism,[13] and capitalism, *Escravidão e Racismo* [Slavery and Racism] (1978), Octávio Ianni[14] advances five arguments for the continued and contemporary exploitation of Afro-Brazilians as informed by an understanding of the capitalist consequences of race and class. First, capitalism created and also destroyed slavery. Second, capitalist structures manipulated African cultures and conveniently turned them into black and brown cultures while creating alienation as well as the politics of racial and class antagonisms in the process. Third, Gilberto Freyre's *Casa Grande e Senzala* is an incomplete assessment of Brazilian social formation and history because it omitted the political and economic structures that underpinned its entire process as a movement and as a

reality. Fourth, in limiting his analysis to the typologies of accommodation and racial conflict through the perspectives, attitudes, opinions,
stereotypes, and individual and collective representations in religious and
legal archives, Gilberto Freyre betrays the so-called liberal democracy or
liberal citizenship, which remains elusive especially for Afro-Brazilians.
Fifth, capitalism complicates racial problems rather than resolves them
because the capitalist system exploits racial tension and violence with
no roadmap for complete equality in the social structure. While Ianni's
critique exposes the limits of Freyre's sociology of Brazilian slavery, it
is rather silent on the actions of the slave in terms of resistance and
rebellion.

The critique of Gilberto Freyre would be incomplete without adding
the unimaginable sufferings during the Middle Passage of Africans taken
to Brazil, which made rebellions quite rare but also easy to suppress. It
was not unusual for Africans taken as slaves to be malnourished. Walter
Hawthorne's *From Africa to Brazil* (2010) presents a seminal case study
of the rice-growing Upper Guineans who were taken to Maranhão and
Pará, where they were able to recreate their Upper Guinean culture
as well as transfer African technology to northeastern Brazil. What is
remarkable in Hawthorne's study is the revelation that African slaves
were starving, as food and water had to be rationed, thus creating an
enfeebling and unhealthy environment that may have not been condu-
cive to rebellion. The same was apparent on board slave ships: it was
remarked that a "certain number of slaves [were allowed] on deck in
chains . . . each day . . . to get some fresh air, not allowing more, for
their fear of rebellion."[15] The important issue for me in the critique of
the notion of African passivity is that even during the Middle Passage
when food and water were rationed to control Africans taken as slaves,
the Africans still rebelled. Hawthorne includes the account of ex-slave
Mahommah Gardo Baquaqua detailing the horrific punishment for resistance or disobedience: "when any one of us became refractory, his flesh
was cut with a knife and pepper or vinegar was rubbed in to make him
peaceable" (123). Freyre not only overlooked this painful transatlantic
passage from Africa to Brazil, he also minimized the sexual violence
against female African slaves who were raped and violated in the midst
of what Freyre advances as harmonious relations between races and the
creation of the ultimate Brazilian "family" and "cosmic race."

In the case of Lusophone Africa, Charles Boxer notes that the
ambivalent treatment of their colonized subjects was very rampant and

evident: "prejudice against Mulattoes and Mestiços certainly existed in Angola[16] [. . .] the ambivalent attitude of the white Portuguese toward their Mulatto kith and kin, comes out very clearly in the discussions which lasted intermittently for the best part of three centuries on the formation of a native clergy" (33). Though the Portuguese were said to have con-quered lusophone Africa in the sixteenth century, actual colonization did not start until the nineteenth century. In the case of Mozambique, it was rumored that abundance of gold deposits existed in the Mwenemutapa kingdom and the Portuguese had wanted to exploit these mineral deposits. They landed at Sofala on the Indian Ocean and proceeded inland. But the Portuguese colonizers were not efficient, as they were interested in their own personal gains. This led to the Portuguese Crown preferring the loyalty of the settlers called *prazeiros* or trustees of Portuguese Crown estate. These *prazeiros* were noted for indiscrete land-grabbing from the indigenes as well as forced labor and excessive taxation. The Portuguese colonial machinery also used Catholicism to pacify the natives, so as to control their minds, bodies, and souls. Despite these colonial efforts and strategies, some Afro-Portuguese *prazeiros* became rebellious and resisted the interference of the Portuguese in their indigenous political and religious structures; thus they formed armies that attacked Portuguese commercial centers and thereby resisted Portuguese power and control.

By the advent of the "scramble for Africa" in 1884, African king-doms had been successfully compromised and weakened by successive Portuguese invasions. As a result, the Portuguese started gaining better control of the African territories in 1885 by setting up an oppressive colonial system based primarily on taxation and forced labor; however, Africans resisted through many strategies: slow work ethics, feigning illnesses, sabotaging agricultural machines, and at times escaping to rural areas where the Portuguese could not easily reach and where they were protected by local leaders, with whom they conspired to launch attacks on Portuguese administrative installations. Examples of such rebellions included the Massingire of 1884 and the Cambuenda-Sena-Tonga of 1897. Though well organized, the rebellions were often, ironically, quickly subdued due to internal conflicts and lack of organization. Though the Portuguese exercised colonial control well into the twentieth century, sending thousands of Africans into South African mines as well as Rhodesian plantations, *assimilados* who included intellectuals and church leaders came together to form a national opposition movement against Portuguese oppression by starting the famed newspaper, O *Africano* (The

African). This newspaper became the dissenting African voice against Portuguese colonial oppression, especially between the 1920s and 1950s. These anticolonial resistances led the foundation for the outright armed liberation struggle (through guerrilla tactics) in the 1960s as launched by such movements of Lusophone African liberation as MPLA (Angola), FRELIMO (Mozambique), and PAIGC (Guinea-Bissau and Cape Verde), among others. These liberation movements saw the emergence of nationalist sentiments, the independence of lusophone African countries, and the emergence of such leaders and presidents such as Agostinho Neto of Angola, Eduardo Mondlane of Mozambique, and Amílcar Cabral of Cape Verde.

Yet the antislavery rebellions in Brazil were even more intense and dramatic than the anticolonial ventures that Africa[17] witnessed under Portuguese colonial control. Perhaps the sense that Africans who resisted and fought the Portuguese on the African continent were on familiar terrain may further explain the unimaginable burden placed on African slaves who were resisting or rebelling in an unfamiliar territory as was the case in colonial Brazil. Many were the strategies deployed for survival and freedom including but not limited to (1) running away from slavery to create a free settlement; (2) rebelling and taking capital risk in order to be free; (3) sacrificing through labor, financial, or even sexual arrangement to buy one's freedom in the form of the *carta de alforria* (freedom letter); (4) negotiating self-deportation as a form of self-imposed punishment after a capital offense; and (5) setting up black brotherhoods[18] as safe havens against Portuguese colonial intrusion. Of these different strategies toward emancipation, when it comes to rebellions and revolutions in Brazilian history as they relate to Africans under slavery, and with the exception of the *quilombos* (more the result of taking refuge on the mountains than setting off a local rebellion), the most pronounced is the Malê Revolt[19] of 1835. Although the "Quilombo de Palmares"[20] led by Zumbi dos Palmares is often evoked as a rebellion, it had to do more with resistance against the repeated Portuguese colonial invasions of the settlement that forced the *quilombolas* to defend themselves until the very end. Fragmentary studies of the Palmares resistance and Malê Revolt abound in journals and textbooks, but the most coherent and comprehensive book on slave rebellion to date remains *Slave Rebellion in Brazil* by João José Reis.

Reis makes a number of compelling arguments regarding this unique rebellion by African slaves, some of whom happened to be Muslims. First, that African slaves retained their African identities as a measure to envision coping strategies in dealing with social oppression. Second, the rebellion was not a *jihad* (a holy war), as some scholars[21] have suggested, as it required solidarity with non-Muslims to be successful. Third, the blend of African ethnicity, rebellion, and spirituality conspired to render this slave rebellion unique among those documented in the Americas. Fourth, the 1835 African Muslim rebellion was the culmination of a series of revolts already blooming against sociopolitical and economic disparities (even after independence from Portugal) that kept African slaves and freedmen as underdogs who could not hold it together and turned to anti-Portuguese sentiment, street riots, and military revolts. Finally, the unstable economic conditions that challenged governance facilitated the materialization of the uprising. From the foregoing viewpoints of Reis, the Yorubaness or Africanness of the insurgents is even more compelling than their Islamic affinity. The fact that Africans were able to be united under ethnicity and, to a lesser degree, religiosity, made for a well-coordinated, collective, and successful rebellion. Reis's rigorous methodology, which involves police archives and court documents, left no stone unturned, providing minute details on the rebellion even down to questioning the number of condemned insurgents as reported by certain researchers. For example, regarding the case of the death sentence pronounced on Pedro, Reis states: "No one knows why Pedro was singled out for the death penalty. I could not find the records for his particular trial" (216). Regardless of one's reservations about Reis's conclusion (epilogue), the rebellion would have succeeded if not for the internal betrayal of their cause to the authorities and the collaboration between the state and the freedmen, who also were united in repressing any forms of rebellion in order to maintain slave labor.

The religious factor is nonetheless significant. Despite the adaptation by slaves of Islamic rites and Islam's influence on divinatory practices within the Candomblé, one must also question the assumption that devotees of the Nagô (Yoruba) religion, which was how Candomblé was perceived, would willingly collaborate with Muslims, who belonged to a different ethnic group, known as the Hausa. Reis notes that the overwhelming participation of the Nagô in the rebellion often made scholars reduce it to a Nagô revolt (139–159). Reis argues convincingly that the insurgents did not want to be perceived as anti-Yoruba, and hence were creatively adaptive to not provoke any ethnic rivalry[22] or dissent. They even went as far as establishing intricate religious solidarity with the Yoruba:

The incorporation of Islamic elements into Yoruba religion is one more example of the latter's well-known malleability and tolerance. But the establishment of friendly ground for Muslims in the orisha universe was not without its own purpose. Power was at stake here. [. . .] Babalawos actually gained more power by incorporating Islam into their divinatory system, since it allied them with a successful religion that was becoming more and more popular among the Yorubas. (125)

Reis even goes further in establishing the solidarity of Muslims with the Yoruba by invoking the symbolic and ritualistic connections the two religions have in the sacred Ifa oracle in which African Muslims are considered the children of *Oxalá*, that is, Orisanla or supreme divinity. The use of amulets was not only common among the Hausa and Yoruba, but there was also religious syncretism between ethnic spirits and Muslim jinns. In a strategic sense, the rebellion played out as a political partnership between two major ethnic groups and two major religions hybridized by the accident of slavery. The differences in ethnicity and religion translated, through a complex interplay, into a shared hybridized culture that would spell success or failure for the rebellion. Had the rebellion succeeded, African and Afro-Brazilian relations in Bahia might have been changed forever. With Reis's inadvertent reference to the insurgents as "plotters,"[23] he insinuates that they were traitors and even committed punishable treason against the state. Regardless of how the incident is recorded in history, it unquestionably represents one of the most commendable efforts to seek freedom from social oppression, and indeed echoes the efforts of insurgents in the Haitian Revolution, which has now become a reference point for pan-African celebration against racial and colonial oppression.

Migrating Identities or (Trans)national Allegories?

The six case studies of protagonists selected for this analysis and exemplification of migrating identity (namely, Zumbi dos Palmares, Xica da Silva, Manuel Querino, Pedro Archanjo, Black Orpheus, and Cidade de Deus) embody what Fredric Jameson envisions as "national allegories." I extend that proposition by suggesting that in the era of globalization and transnationalism, these "foundational heroes," to borrow from Doris

Sommer, metamorphose into public discourse or what I term "transnational allegories" beyond their private, and to a certain degree, implicit national, narratives. While Jameson's use of "third world" to capture the totality of "underdeveloped" countries while privileging "first" and "second" worlds (being the developed and developing nations) is problematic and somewhat "Eurocentric," the centrality of his argument cannot be dismissed offhandedly when he states that "Third-world texts, even those which are seemingly private and invested with a properly libidinal dynamic—necessarily project a political dimension in the form of national allegory: the story of the private individual destiny is always an allegory of the embattled situation of the public third-world culture and society."[24] The transnational dynamism of historical and cultural phenomena may well be enriching for global consumption in that it provides a terrain for comparative dialogue and elucidation. The dialectical tensions between whiteness, blackness, and Afro-Brazilianness have at their historical root the primacy of slavery, the consequent economic, cultural, historical, spiritual, and psychological exploitation the complete narration of which is yet to be documented. Yet I argue that these national allegories have deeper significance as they resonate with realities in the African diaspora since the legacy of slavery is shared and is also a commonality of concern. The texts, the life stories, the theatrical and cinematic adaptations of these national heroes have been identified in this study as having archetypal significance and deserving of being considered as "transnational allegories" since these heroes have parallels in the pan-African world. While intertwining ambiguities are inevitable, especially from the viewpoints of the explication of the variances in identity formation in different historical contexts, there is a sense of commonality in the discourse on racial relations as they affect the migrating subjects in each case analyzed. Beyond the Jamesonian primary argument that a third-world text is "always already read" in relation to the colonial Other, the process of cultural production and documentation may be equally as important, hence the issue of versions and revisions of versions that constitute part and parcel of the shifting identity and significance of the given transnational protagonist. Colonialist binaries and logic are complicated when variables of cultural politics and interpretation are factored into the analytical frame of reference, since the perspective of the interpreter becomes even more significant.

As opposed to the elitist propositions of Gilberto Freyre and Paul Gilroy, an alternative paradigm may well be fashionable from what Stuart

Hall in "Cultural Identity and Diaspora" articulates as a "shifting" identity. The migrating identity of Manoel Querino in nineteenth-century Bahia stems from his dislocation from Africa, slavery in Brazil, and arduous efforts to re-historicize the distorted vision of Africa that had been provided by the European Other. The case of Zumbi dos Palmares, the leader of the Quilombo dos Palmares, is even more problematic, as he migrated first from Africa to slavery and then to the Maroon settlement from which he and his followers could have been recaptured and returned to slavery—but they resisted, opting for a transcendental battle with the different troops that invaded their newly found "free" or private space. In her own hyperbolic context, Xica (Chica) da Silva, an eighteenth-century slave who negotiated her freedom from slavery by using her body, migrates from Africa, to slavery, to the house of the Portuguese contractor, only to become almost as powerful as any European woman as his queenly "mistress" only to be abandoned and disillusioned when she was prohibited from entering a Catholic church and when the contractor returned to Portugal. But it is in the character of Pedro Archanjo, supposedly the fictionalized Manoel Querino, that one encounters the vicious migration triangle between Africa, Brazil, and the miscegenated world of spirituality that constituted one of the coping strategies of the quintessential migrating Afro-Brazilian subject. In the character of Black Orpheus is deposited the classical migrating subject who may be said to embody many worlds as his representation traverses the Yoruba/African, Greek, and Brazilian mythologies to become one of the most universal stories of love and of Carnival, where life and death oscillate in a dialectical tango and perpetual renewal. The final case study, that of the "City of God," an entire community of disposed Afro-Brazilians living under the pressure of survival amongst drug dealers and gangster culture, depicts a migration from Africa, to slavery, to the *favelas* or slums and the efforts of the marginalized to transgress as a form of escape, even if oftentimes, for these conditioned *favelados* (slum dwellers), the ultimate migration, sadly, is that which leads to death as a form of closure—not in the ideal sense but as an escape from the perpetual journeys of violence and violation that exasperate the spirit at every turn.

Whether national or transnational, allegories of identity as captured in Manoel Querino, Zumbi dos Palmares, Xica da Silva, Pedro Archanjo, Black Orpheus, and Cidade de Deus provide pertinent locations to problematize and resolve issues of racial tensions and elicit global dialogues that can begin to redress such conflicts. The choice of six sites or cases of such tensions as seen in the dramas of real and allegorized characters is meant to raise questions about the universality of racial oppression under whatever pretext and to propose that denying racial and social inequalities does not make the problem go away, but only through acknowledgment of the existence of such a human aberration can we begin to identify strategies of redemption and harmonization. No possessor of power who privileges himself at the expense of millions of others who are struggling to breathe at the bottom will give up that power or even share it as long as he can rationalize and blame the oppressed for their predicament. The issue is complex and demands resolution, and can be tackled only through painstaking, constructive, and productive dialogues. With the exception of Manoel Querino, who is not yet understood as the "Pedro Archanjo" in Jorge Amado's *Tenda dos Milagres*, all of the remaining case studies in this book have been cinematographically adapted for global consumption. The argument can then be convincingly made that by virtue of their morphing into the global diaspora of film production and dissemination, they have in fact become transnational allegories of the Brazilian nation. And it is in this sense that migrating subjects and cultures find a point of convergence and resolution of their private matters in the politics of transnational allegories that bring such issues to a larger public and thereby invoke empathy for their plights that are implicitly calling for outrage and intervention.

Chapter 2

Zumbi dos Palmares

Relocating History, Film, and Print

Comparing and contrasting dramatic and cinematic renditions of a socio-political icon, namely, Zumbi dos Palmares of Brazil, and highlighting some historical and biographical elements deployed to fashion these works, this chapter focuses principally on the dramatic text *Arena Conta Zumbi* (Arena Performs Zumbi) by the Teatro de Arena as authored by Augusto Boal and Gianfrancesco Guarnieri, as well as the cinematic adaptation of Décio Freitas's *Palmares: A Guerra dos Escravos* (Palmares: The War of the Slaves), titled *Quilombo*, as directed by Carlos Dieg-ues. It argues that Zumbi remains an enigmatic figure in the national psyche, whether as a "hero" or a "villain," and must be remythologized through carnivalization, which the Arena Theater directed by Augusto Boal, as well as his carnivalesque depiction in *Quilombo*, engender. In this holistic sense, Zumbi is critically relocated in historical, cinematic, and literary perspectives for better illuminations on his import to global cultural history and heritage.

The term "Zumbi," often written as "Zumba," or "Zombie," in English, has been so misused and misunderstood by unaware individ-uals that the original reverence associated with the name has equally been denigrated by unwitting association with zombification or a state of being temporarily hypnotized or under a spell, during which such a zombified figure is then under the conscious control of another individual such as a spiritually superior or colonizing being. Despite the efforts of Teatro de Arena to pay homage to Zumbi nationally, Zumbi remains a

37

mythical figure in the minds of many in Brazil. Since 1978, when Brazil started celebrating National Black Consciousness Day on November 20, Zumbi has become a national hero. In 1994, Brazil celebrated the 300th anniversary of Zumbi's death amidst celebrations and festivals. Zumbi is often portrayed officially as a Brazilian regardless of race while minimizing the racism, inequalities, and brutality he suffered as a child before creating the Palmares settlement and ultimately paying for his resistance against oppression with his life. This chapter seeks to correct this erroneous simplification of Zumbi's legacy and sacrifices for equality and citizenship.

A few recent texts attest to the foregoing "scientific-fictional," even "comical," portrayal of the "zombie" figure—one who is now considered a possible esoteric revenant who may invade the unsuspecting postmodern world.[1] The notion of the living dead carries with it a certain sense of ephemerality and suspension. When contextualized within the ideological significance of Zumbi in the Afro-Brazilian world, the need for critical relocation beyond the stereotypical image of Zumbi as a "weak," "subdued," "defeated," or "broken" leader goes beyond what history, fiction, and film can negotiate but locates itself within the moral responsibility of interpreting Zumbi as a heroic leader who defied the colonial assaults of European power in Latin America.[2] Perhaps by commission or omission, the authors of these works are ignorant of the significance of Zumbi dos Palmares in the larger frame of world literature and affairs—and hence portray his image as the generic rendition of the living dead. By virtue of Zumbi's indelible inscription in the memory of Brazilians through many statues and institutions dedicated to and named in his honor,[3] Zumbi dos Palmares must no longer be myopically denigrated as an embodiment of the living dead, even symbolically.

A conceptual framework that is even discursively challenging for a resolution in this chapter lies in the questioning of Zumbi as representative of all Brazilians in the context of desirable racial equality. If indeed racial democracy existed in Brazil, every Brazilian would be free to marry any race they desire without the *a priori* thesis that race mixture is a condition upon which the ideal of racial equality is possible. The question then is: what about equality *qua* equality without having to negate one race over the other? Why indeed should whiteness be the ideal or desired race while blackness is the undesirable or even problematic other that must be "erased" in the process of whitening? In the larger context of this book, these questions complicate the heroism of Zumbi who fought to resist European conquest, slavery, and domination. That life-sacrificing struggle that led to Zumbi's death and the destruction of Palmares would be unnecessary if, indeed, race-mixture were as viable a solution to racial discrimination as it has been proposed by its apologists. Zumbi may well represent the sacrifices of all marginalized and oppressed Brazilians, but primarily symbolizes the heroism required in the face of racial tyranny.

Brazilian History, Slavery, and the Place of Zumbi

Africans were transported to Brazil through the horrific Atlantic slavery the same way they were taken to the United States, and the Caribbean, among other diasporic locations. The Portuguese arrived in Brazil in the 1500s, a time when about 2.5 million indigenous Brazilians were already living in the land. The Portuguese attempted to colonize the land but faced resistance from the Amerindians. Much of the indigenous population suffered extermination, and others were forced to move into the more rural areas. The Portuguese settled on the east coast of Brazil in order to cultivate sugar, but the growing number of sugar plantations demanded more workers. Since the indigenous Amerindian population had become smaller because many of them had been brutally murdered, the Portuguese turned to the importation of slaves from Africa to work on the sugar plantations in the seventeenth century and later on the coffee plantations in the nineteenth century. In the context of the triangular slave trade, slaves were transported from Africa to Brazil, while European goods were taken to Africa; and in the process, African slaves were purchased and taken to Brazil to work on sugar and coffee plantations—thus making sugar and coffee stable exports from Brazil to Europe. When the sugar industry declined in the seventeenth century, the Portuguese felt compelled to move into the interior, where they found gold and diamonds. The resources from mining gold and diamonds provided the necessary financial surplus to intensify slave trading from the entire African continent—thus creating a diverse African population from the west coast, central Congo, southern Angola, and east coasts of Africa—all of which influenced Brazil tremendously as we currently know it.

Zumbi's significance cannot be told without telling the story of the Quilombo dos Palmares, the most famous of the free communities (*quilombos*) created by escaped slaves, located in Serra da Barriga in Pernambuco. It was at this very site that the ashes of the venerated

Afro-Brazilian leader (Abdias do Nascimento) and formulator of the *quilombismo* idea were spread when he passed to the world beyond in 2011. The name "Palmares" that Zumbi helped popularize is derived from palm trees associated with the province of Pernambuco. During the entire period of its existence between 1630 and 1697, this historical community resisted many attempts by the Portuguese and the Dutch to exterminate it. Contrary to the distorted colonial history that portrayed Palmares as separatist, Palmares had an organized cooperative style of government and had instituted democratic rules and laws. Members were responsible for cultivating the land and harvesting crops. Some cultivated corn, fruits, and other food crops while others fished and hunted. Some traded in gold and all lived in harmony with their neighbors, including some whites who willingly chose to join the community in good faith. All runaway slaves in the community lived in harmony and freely. Due to the need to empower the community through increase in numbers, slaves were captured from neighboring plantations, and were compelled to bring other captives in order to secure their freedom in Palmares community. It was considered a serious and punishable offense to run away from the Palmares community.

Zumbi was born in Palmares in 1655, and as a boy was captured during an attack on the community; he was consequently kept under the tutelage of Priest Antônio Melo, who kept detailed records about him.[4] Most of the historical works written about Zumbi come from Rev. Melo's archives. Zumbi ran away from Melo and returned to Palmares in 1670. Military accounts by the Portuguese describe Zumbi as a military strategist who fervently protected Palmares and the runaway slaves in that community. Finally, Palmares was attacked, defeated, and captured in 1694. A year later, going by official archives, Zumbi was captured and killed by the Portuguese. In today's Brazil, Zumbi is a popularly celebrated hero in Afro-Brazilian history, and by extension an undisputed national icon of resistance gradually getting his deserved honor in Brazilian intellectual history. Before the destruction of Palmares, the settlement was also home to Amerindians and poor whites; hence based on in the arguments advanced by Abdias Nascimento in most of his seminal works, Palmares was an example of the most democratic community in Brazilian history. At its peak, Palmares had about 30,000 inhabitants, who were divided into ten villages. As eighteenth-century writer Sebastino da Rocha Pitta (aka Pita) notes in his historical perspective of Brazil, slavery hindered the advancement of blacks in the same way that they had less chance of competing with whites or European immigrants after abolition of Brazil:

> Brazil was one of the last countries to end the slave trade and slavery. The end of slavery came with difficulty because the Brazilian economy depended on African slave labor. Brazil abolished the trade in slaves in 1850, and in 1888, all slaves in Brazil were emancipated, or set free. The slaves themselves took the lead in their fight for freedom by escaping slavery and organizing slave revolts. But after earning their freedom, slaves faced severe economic hardship and racial discrimination. They did not own any of the land they had worked, and immigrants who came to Brazil were often given jobs before black Brazilians.[5]

Despite abolition, the Brazilian government instituted certain policies that maintained ex-slaves in a second-class status. First, the white Brazilian elite officially introduced *branqueamento*, or "whitening," as a measure to make Brazil appear more white and less black. Likewise, Afro-Brazilian history is "whitened" by omitting significant episodes and by not recognizing Afro-Brazilian heroes in history books. Second, the Brazilian government sought to make Brazilians appear officially "whitened" and less black by encouraging blacks to marry Europeans in order to have social mobility or privileges. Third, the Brazilian government excluded race from the census in 1900, 1920, and 1970 so as to suppress data on black population. Finally, militants demanded the inclusion of race as a category in the census of 1980—resulting in the revelation that almost 50% of the Brazilian population is black, while less than 1% has college education. In spite of this alarming empirical data, the Brazilian government continued to deny racial discrimination. Only recently has there been any official admission of racism in Brazil; naturally, the brief intervening period has not yet resulted in concrete redress of its devastating effects on Afro-Brazilian communities. Rather, calculated efforts by the government can go only so far in repairing damage systematically perpetuated for 500 years. The absence of Afro-Brazilians from positions of power continues unabated, and the remedy of the situation continues on the level of symbolisms and tokenisms. Zumbi remains the ultimate symbol of resistance and advancement for Afro-Brazilians as well as for racial equality for Brazil as a whole.

Theater as Empowering Agency:
Teatro de Arena, Boal, and Guarnieri

Much of Augusto Boal's argument in favor of an empowering theater in which, borrowing from the theoretical principles of Paulo Freire's *Pedagogy of the Oppressed*, anchor on the assumption that the "oppressed" must be liberated through a combination of action and participation—in the sense that the actor must also be the spectator as well as the "act-spector" as the drama unfolds (un)consciously. A balance must be attained between active living and passive observation of one's own life.

The power of performance to liberate dates back to the ancients, as Roman and Greek deities were performed by humans in an effort not only to venerate them but also to humanize them—with their strengths and frailties or what have been called their tragic flaws. Yet Boal's *Poetics of the Oppressed* goes a step further through seeing less of flaws and more of strength in its characters by focusing on praxis as a way to generate applicable liberational ideology.

Unlike the earlier Teatro Experimental do Negro ("Black Experimental Theater," formed by Abdias do Nascimento in 1945), which focused on political themes related to Africa and African culture and history, and thus engaged primarily in anti-racist politics, Teatro de Arena (formed by Augusto Boal in 1965) revolutionized Brazilian popular theater as a whole. In his semiotic discussion of the Theatre of Gianfrancesco, Anderson alludes to Boal's *Coringa* (Joker) system, which was created during the performance of *Arena Conta Zumbi* but applied during the performance of *Arena Conta Tiradentes*.[6] Such a system allows not only for the democratization of theatrical principles but also the popularization of theatrical space in that such a space becomes more of a "public square" where participation is expected and maximized. With regard to *Arena Conta Zumbi*, the play attempts to represent the dynamics of Exu, the Yoruba deity of the crossroads and duality, thus suggesting a transformative essence for which Exu, as catalyst and interpreter of the zone of complexities, chaos, and divination, is revered:

> In this respect, *Arena Conta Zumbi* functions much like the Yoruba orisa Exu, viewed as the deity of transformation. Exu introduces chaos into a steady state, and conversely, helps new states emerge from chaos. Only those supporters of the established order need fear Exu. It is for this reason that slave

owners, founders and beneficiaries of plantation society, often
fearful of slave revolt, associated Exu with the Christian Devil.[7]

By organizing change within the realm of confusion, the open-ended paradigmatic shift allows for possibilities of change and alternative mediating
approaches toward such a desirable change. Anderson's critique of the
oppressors' association of Exu with the "Christian Devil" simply glosses
over the misrepresentation of the crossroads deity while failing to address
the power of duality in Exu's penchant for both enclosures and disclo-
sures, as in the manipulation of ambiguities to suit his own ambivalent
agenda. Locating the drama of Zumbi in the public space, for example,
a zone that represents the "crossroads" location of contact between many
possible paths, is not only inviting of conflict and resolution, but also
situates the hitherto "forbidden" subjects of violence, hate, and colonial
brutality that go along with issues of racial discrimination in the public
frame of analysis. The denigration of Exu, the revered Yoruba deity of
divination, and his interpretation as the "devil" is a lamentably ignorant
display of an African thought system in the Western world.

Considered one of the most important Brazilian theatrical groups
in the 1950s and 1960s, Teatro de Arena was founded in São Paulo in
1965 as an alternative to the theatrical scene of the time and with the
object of nationalizing and innovating Brazilian theater. Although it
ended production in 1972, its theater that seats ninety spectators, now
renamed "Teatro de Arena Eugênio Kusnet," has produced many plays
by significant Brazilian playwrights such as José Renato Pécora, Augusto
Boal, and Gianfrancesco Guarnieri. Against the international, expensive,
and sophisticated posture of the Teatro Brasileiro de Comédia, one of the
founders of Arena, José Renato, a pioneer graduate of the Escola de Arte
Dramática (School of Dramatic Arts), had wanted to stage plays with very
low budgets. The pioneering professional cast, consisting of José Renato,
Sérgio Britto, Henrique Becker, Geraldo Mateus, Renata Blaunstein, and
Monah Delacy staged Stafford Dickens's *Esta Noite é Nossa* (Tonight Is Ours)
at the Museu de Arte Moderna (Museum of Modern Art) in São Paulo.
After two years of performing in various improvised locations, in 1955 a
permanent home for the theater was secured downtown, in an adapted
garage on Theodoro Baima Street across from the Consolação Church.

With the arrival of a young Italian actor and playwright, Gianfrancesco Guarnieri, who had a precise vision of the type of theater appropriate for Brazil, the *Arena* was saved from extinction due to financial

constraints. Following the successful production of Guarnieri's *Eles Não Usam Black Tie* (They Do Not Wear Black Tie) in 1958, a theatrical "movement" finally took off with a series of Dramaturgy Seminars that sought to give exposure to new Brazilian playwrights such as Oduvaldo Vianna Filho and Flávio Migliaccio, among others.

Augusto Boal, who had recently returned to Brazil from the United States, became the group's director, and was a vital part of the transformation and professionalization of the group. In addition to searching for a national theater, the nationalization of classical plays was also encouraged. Following this phase was the addition of music as influenced by Brechtian theater, which led to the production of works such as *Arena Conta Zumbi* and *Arena Conta Tiradentes*, both written by Boal and Guarnieri—and with the application of the *Coringa* (Joker) system—in which all the actors play each other's roles without specific characterization. Due to the repressive regime of military dictatorship that took control in 1964, the *Arena* dream came to a permanent halt in 1972.

Arena Conta Zumbi:
From Colonial Myths to Dictatorial Realities

Beyond the social focus of the "new theater," *Arena Conta Zumbi* in form and content questions the myth of Zumbi as a "black" rebel defeated by European enslavers while elevating his reality to that of a national hero, indeed an embodiment of every human who stands tall in the face of racial tyranny and oppression. In this sense, myth and history collide in the theorization of oppression, especially in a context of censorship where cultural performers are obliged to mask their ideological intentions through aesthetic innovations and deviations from the norm. In the case of *Arena Conta Zumbi*, which was performed in 1965, a year after the inception of Brazilian military dictatorship, the myths of the brutal destruction of the members of the Palmares settlement led by Zumbi are countered by the analogy of the realities of military repression of the day. In so doing, Arena Theater succeeded in merging the seventeenth century's Portuguese-Dutch attack on Palmares with the twentieth century's military dictatorship that wreaked havoc on the majority of the Brazilian population, by bringing social inequalities issues of the past to bear on the social oppression in the present. With the overthrow of the liberal President João Goulart in 1964, and the inauguration of autocratic

President Humberto Castelo Branco, the *Arena* was obliged to move from its "nationalizing of classics" model to addressing contemporary issues by devising an alternative theatrical language that could bypass the stringent restrictions imposed by military censorship. Oscar Fernández (1967), Augusto Boal (1970), Margo Milleret (1987), and David George (1995) have each commented on the significance of this leftist theater or protest musical that highlights some of the defining characteristics of a social revolution through theater. What they have in common, as Milleret notes, is a new musical performance that combines Brazilian history with Brechtian distancing and new social realism.[8]

In his rather extensive survey of what he calls "Brazil's New Social Theatre,"[9] Oscar Fernández historicizes and theorizes on the trajectory of Brazilian theater from the influence of Portuguese *autos*, credited to Padre Anchieta, to José de Alencar's indigenist theater, through the emergence of dramatic companies such as Oficina, Opinião, Comédia, Arena, and Black Experimental Theater, as well as individual geniuses such as Nelson Rodrigues, Plínio Marcos, and Dias Gomes. The dramatic critic opines that despite the challenges of moving beyond "a theatre generally detached from the problems and tribulations of its day" (15), protest theater in which the stage serves as a pulpit for political expression has become the new wave in Brazilian theatrical and social reality. For him, "after a somewhat unsteady and generally undistinguished history the Brazilian theatre is giving signs of coming of age. In recent years its dramatists have become more daring, more *engagés*, more socially-minded" (15)—in other words, since the 1960s especially, and despite censorship, social theater has become integrated into Brazil's cultural life. Commenting on *Arena Conta Zumbi*, Fernández notes that "the theme is evidently the struggle for liberty, for it is the historical revolt of Negro slaves and their refuge in Palmares which climaxes a documentary-like exposition of Negro slave life in Brazil" (22), thus demystifying the historical myth of Zumbi as passively defeated by his attackers or murderers. By exposing the horrific slave conditions under which Zumbi lived, Arena Theater challenges society to better appreciate the totality of Zumbi toward the redressing of social inequalities in Brazil. Augusto Boal adds to this social perspective by insisting on a "neo-realist" theater that exposes reality as it is while creating what Anatol Rosenfeld calls "philanthropic empathy," or the feeling of observing a miserable situation and feeling responsible for that same condition.

Analyzing the processes through which *Arena Conta Zumbi* "is transformed from a documentary into a political protest" (21), Margo

Milleret, in "Acting into Action: Teatro Arena's *Zumbi*," concedes the fact that the *Arena*'s version of Zumbi's history came about after a laborious research into historical documentation and astute interpretation.[10] Through a blend of existing realist models and Brechtian theater, Arena Theater devised a strategy to popularize the values, challenges, and way of life of the working class. Creatively provoking the audience to use music to rebel against the new military regime, the Arena Theater dramatizes the history of Zumbi and Palmares by "reorganizing and emphasizing several episodes as well as adding numerous politically charged terms" (21), thus collaborating with the audience to question the injustices meted against the Palmares settlement, and ultimately creating a "friendly land in which men help each other."[11] As a purveyor of historical allegory, Arena Theater played on the idealistic and politically left-centered student audience for the most part by drawing parallels between the brutal attack on Palmares and the violent instrumentalities of the dictatorial state.

Boal's technique as influenced by Brecht includes (1) breaking with the actor-character unity by having all the actors play all the characters together; (2) using collective narrative form by adopting the model of "Arena tells of . . ." that incorporates the audience as well; (3) combining many genres of farce, melodrama, docudrama, and music in order to keep the audience critically engaged; and (4) deploying music for overall emotional effect while reinforcing the ideological position of a protest musical. Beyond the focus on the analysis of structural and paratextual strategies deployed by Arena Theater in *Arena Conta Zumbi*, Milleret argues that *Zumbi* was popular essentially because it met the audience's expectations, who indeed went to the theater as a symbolic act of protest. Though the *Coringa* (Joker) system is said to have developed from the acting of *Arena Conta Zumbi*, David George critiques its effectiveness, since it is not only a "wholesome borrowing from Brecht's Epic Theatre," it implied a silent protest or "invisible theater" in which the actors gave the audience an illusion of reality.[12]

Yet Arena Theater's significance under Boal as well as in the acting of *Arena Conta Zumbi* cannot be limited to the creation of the *Coringa* system alone. Post-1964 Boal called for a dramatic interpretation in which the cast assumes the entire performance as a collective narration. In creating the *Coringa* system, Boal sought to make characterization fluid, with characters changing from one actor to another; thus several actors played the same character, while the master of the acts, the *Coringa*, commented on the fiction. Deploying Brechtian models of the musical theater, Boal created a lyrical allegory that often confronts the present through the reenactment of the past such as the reality of the brutal dictatorial regime and the challenge for the Brazilian intelligentsia to cope with the social reality in the face of tyranny. Boal references Brecht's dictum that "Sad is the country that needs heroes"; hence Brazil, being a "sad country," needs individual acts and heroes to liberate the social condition. And he would remind us that ours is sad because it needs liberating individual acts. Boal stresses the need to create new myths to counter old ones in a dialectical tension that produces chaos and resolution at the same time. *Arena Conta Zumbi*, in this sense, depended on three disparate individuals—Boal and Guarnieri who wrote the play, and Edu Lobo who created music for the lyrics. Collectively with the actors, they created and performed a system that theorizes the possibilities of social change through the confrontation of inaction with action toward resolution of social contradictions and upheaval. The *Coringa* system then may be perceived as a carnivalesque paradigm that sets in motion a series of provocative actions toward social revolution, consciousness-raising, and political liberation.

The ritual-musical performance that ultimately revises the Zumbi mythology takes for granted the primacy of the disorder-order schema subsumed within the internal structural dynamics of the play. Contained in what Frances Baggage calls the "aesthetic of seamlessness," which, according to Brecht, "reflects an ideological belief in the world itself as fixed and unalterable, the relationship between form and content is thus itself politically charged, not coincidental."[13] *Arena Conta Zumbi* unconsciously adopts the crossroads paradigmatic shift verifiable in the Exú figure in the Yoruba worldview. As Funso Aiyejina notes in "Esu Elegbara: A Source of an Alter/Native Theory of African Literature and Criticism," Exú is the ultimate diviner who must open the gates of knowledge to Orunmila, the Yoruba deity of divination, for "without Esu to open the portals to the past and the future, Orunmila, the divination deity would be blind. As a neutral force, he straddles all realms and acts as an essential factor in any attempt to resolve the conflicts between contrasting but coterminous forces in the world."[14] The point here is that confusion, chaos, and disintegration, as well as clarity, peace, and re-integration, are all part of the same coin when it comes to Exú.

Combining the reversal or carnivalizing aesthetics typical of Mikhail Bakthin (1990) and Roberto DaMatta (1979), the Exú dimension triangulates a structural crossroads in which (1) ex-slaves are presented as universally human, courageous, militant, noble, heroic, and ethical in their quest for an egalitarian society; (2) the Portuguese colonizers and enslavers are portrayed as cold, violent, artificial, egotistical, inhuman, racist, decadent, and unethical; and (3) the ambience of Carnival or of a popular festival creates a conflict and contradiction as both ex-slaves (people) and Portuguese aristocrats (oppressors) are antagonistic characters who cannot possibly reconcile their differences. Rather, by portraying the contradiction of the wickedness and destructiveness experienced by the ex-slaves in the hands of the aristocrats, an analogy between the past (Palmares) is made with the present (military dictatorship)—thus equating a colonial event with a contemporary one for dramatic effect. Through inversion, Arena Theater succeeds in calling attention to the similarity between colonial atrocities and those of the current military regime.

Even if the *Coringa* system was only experimental in *Arena Conta Zumbi* and later fully applied in *Arena Conta Tiradentes*[15] (Arena Narrates Tiradentes), that experimentation appropriately embodies the domain of the crossroads where fluidity thrives in the midst of uncertainty, unpredictability, and open-endedness. In his perceptive study on "The Muses of Chaos and Destruction of *Arena Conta Zumbi*," Robert Anderson explicates the structuring motif of the performance as the reenactment of the trickster figure or the Exu character in Yoruba mythology:

> In the world of mid-twentieth-century theatre, Exu, through *Arena Conta Zumbi*, threw a stone that killed a bird the day before—the realist theatrical code. It is interesting that Exu is sometimes called a Trickster deity. The later Joker System can be seen as a codification of that Trickster motif. (16)

Exú's predisposition toward change of fortune is equally embodied in his destructive force of agency—all of which are enumerated in Boal's destructive techniques as highlighted by Anderson as quadripartite destructiveness—namely, (1) separation of actor and character; (2) unification of the character's subjectivity under a singular narrative point of view; (3) eclecticism of genre and style; and (4) use of music and chant for defamiliarizing effect. In two main acts, *Arena Conta Zumbi* reenacts the founding and development of Palmares, the attacks by the Portuguese-Dutch forces, the conflicts of the Portuguese colonials in relation to Palmares, and the ultimate violent attack by Domingos Jorge Velho that led to the destruction of Palmares and the death of Zumbi dos Palmares.

Turning now to the application of Boal's chaotic techniques,[16] the first dealt with the realist code in which there is separation of actor from character since all actors play all characters. In this adaptation of the Greek theater to Brazilian popular theater, the actors become "social masks" represented through speech, gesture, and movement, thus creating in Brechtian aesthetics certain empathy for the character in question. Zumbi's actor would simultaneously portray his violence as a mask—likewise the severity of Governor Ayres, the youthfulness of Ganga Zumba (Zumbi's father), and the sensuality of Gongoba (Zumbi's mother), leaving the performance open to subjective interpretation by the audience. In the first act, the section on "Zambi no Açoite" (Zambi in Pain) seeks to pay homage to all those who sacrificed their lives in the creation of a free settlement in Palmares. Zumbi's grandfather, Zambi, invokes his son, Ganga Zumba, while at the same time instructing the son about their African warrior past that led to capture of slaves. This "historical" perspective should be problematized, for not all slaves were stolen from Africans fighting themselves but some from deliberate assault on African villages by European enslavers and merchants in order to capture slaves:

Vem filho meu, meu capitão.	Come my son, my captain
Ganga Zumba, liberdade, liberdade	Ganga Zumba, liberty, liberty
Ganga Zumba, vem meu irmão.	Ganga Zumba, come my brother
É Zambi morrendo, êi, êi, é Zambi . . .	Zambi is dying, oh! Oh! Zambi . . .
Feche os olhos e imagine	Close your eyes and imagine
Viver em mil e seiscentos	Living in the year 1600
Havia guerra e mais guerra . . .	There were wars and many wars . . .
É assim que conta a História	Thus History taught us (Act I, Scene 2)

This historical context, rendered in semi-darkness, suggests the horrors of capture in Africa and the consequent enslavement that began with the Atlantic passage, and sets the tone for future inversion and illumination when Palmares settlers would escape from slavery in order to create a free state. The movement from darkness to light is not without its moments of stage theatrics, especially when the actors throw themselves on the floor simulating a slave's ship. The "darkness" is accentuated by the somberness of the mood as the chants echo the pain of the Atlantic passage.

The second of Boal's chaotic techniques deals with the unification of the characters into a collective narrative viewpoint. While the performance is structurally dialogic as a strategy to expose polyphonic voices while the ex-slaves are either indicting their condition or praising the sacrifices and risks of flight to freedom, even in moments of distress, or of regretting having run away, they firmly exude a collective will to continue the journey until they reach the metaphoric Promised Land—the Quilombo dos Palmares:

ELES—É preciso de uma nêga . . .	MALES: We need our women . . .
ELAS—É preciso de um nego happy pra gente ser feliz.	FEMALES: We need our men to be happy.
(*tiros dos brancos em busca das negras roubadas*)	(*Shots fired by whites searching for stolen black women*)
—Que foi?	—What was that?
—É os brancos vingando o roubo das escravas.	—Whites are revenging black women
—Tomaram as vontade de nós.	—They robbed us of our own wills.
—Cadê Carengue?	—Where is Carengue?
—Morreu.	—He is dead.
—Salé?	—What about Salé?
—Morreu.	—He is dead.
—Que se faz, gente?	—What do we do, people?
—Sou pela volta. Melhor enfrentar libambo que sofrer assim nesse fim de mundo.	—I favor returning. Better to face corporal punishment than to keep suffering in this end of the world.
—É na briga que se pode ganhar.	—Only by fighting can we win.
—Que liberdade é essa se é preciso trabalhar?	—What kind of freedom is this if we have to work? (Act I, Scenes 21–22)

The unification of theatrical spirit here is betrayed by the evaluation of their present condition and need for decision making. Through the analytical dialogues, and despite some individuals' wish to return to slavery, the collective resolved that they needed to continue their quest for freedom even if it meant paying a heavy price for it. There is a high price for freedom, and they were collectively willing to pay it. This democratic process is telling, as they not only hear each other, they also reach the conclusion as men and women that they need each other. They have associated their ultimate happiness in the Palmares they are still looking for, with having their women with them, and thus resorted to stealing them away from whites as an act of courage and necessity. The antagonistic element is not missed, as it is betrayed in the shots fired by whites searching for stolen black women. These whites are portrayed in a negative light as they want to deprive fellow "human beings" (of course, slaves were not considered human) of their need to be happy and free and to procreate.

The third of Boal's destructive or chaotic technique deals with issues of style and genre, as in the mix of cinematic, theatrical, musical, and political measures to drive the message home to the audience despite the reality of censorship. Blending disparate genres and styles such as melodrama, docudrama, farce, and musical, the performance becomes seamless and fluid in the sense that the audience gets the idea that there are no uniform theatrical principles in the performance—whereas, the entire spectacle is deliberately structured to confound and compel the audience to see alternative possibilities of interpretation beyond the strictly "historical drama" that the story of Zumbi hitherto has engendered. This eclectic approach also diverges from the Brechtian aesthetic model in that Zumbi, as presented in *Arena Conta Zumbi*, ceases to be the linear and pre-read figure of black resistance who was not only defeated but lost his symbolic "kingdom" of Palmares in the process. Exu is simultaneously operating in this structure—for as an agent of confusion and then of divination or clarity, the initial alienation of the audience due to the novelty of this technical mask forces the audience to actually converge in an exploration of pastness-presentness duality between Zumbi's heroism and the need to echo such heroism in the consciousness of everyone who went to see the performance.

One such moment of chaos for the audience lies in the presentation of Zambi and the Chorus of a sarcastic litany requesting forgiveness for atrocities the ex-slaves have committed—when indeed, they are not apologetic to have to set out on the course of freedom by any means necessary:

ZAMBI: Perdoai os nossos erros.

ZAMBI: Forgive our

CORO: Ave Maria cheia de graça

CHORUS: Hail Mary, full of grace

ZAMBI: Perdoai, Ave Maria
Perdoai a morte que matamos
O assalto, o roubo,
Perdoai, Ave Maria, Olorum.

ZAMBI: Forgive us, Holy Mary
Forgive us for those we kill,
the attacks, the robberies,
Forgive us, Holy Mary, Olorum.

CORO: Ave Maria cheia de graça
Perdoai, Ave Maria, Olorum.

CHORUS: Holy Mary, full of grace
Forgive us, Holy Mary, Olorum.

ZAMBI: Perdoai o nosso orgulho.

ZAMBI: Forgive our pride.

CORO: Perdoai, Ave Maria.

CHORUS: Forgive us, Holy Mary.

ZAMBI: Perdoai a fuga do cativeiro.

ZAMBI: Forgive the flight of the slaves.

CORO: Perdoai, Ave Maria. Mary

CHORUS: Forgive us, Holy

ZAMBI: Perdoai a nossa rebeldia

ZAMBI: Forgive our rebelliousness.

CORO: Perdoai, Ave Maria.

CHORUS: Forgive us, Holy Mary.

ZAMBI: Perdoai a nossa coragem

ZAMBI: Forgive our courage

CORO: Perdoai, Ave Maria . . .

CHORUS: Forgive us, Holy Mary . . .

ZAMBI: Assim como nós perdoamos os nossos senhores.

ZAMBI: As we forgive our masters.
(Act I, Scene 26)

It is ironic that a revolutionary spirit represented by Zumbi and his followers would stop to think that they may have offended their oppressors. The structural dialectics of seeking forgiveness is indeed meant to produce comic relief as the ex-slaves craftily used the "forgiveness" pretext to list the strategies deployed to set themselves free even if it meant offending their abusers, exploiters, and oppressors.

In a dialogical twist, even the white slave traders also feel the need to rationalize why they are resolved to attack Palmares, using the Bible as their divine justification for a violent act:

O que aqui existe só a nós pertence,	Everything here belongs only to us
aqui trabalhamos, nosso sangue correu	We labored here and shed our blood
O negro trouxemos, o negro compramos	We brought blacks, we bought blacks
pagamos bom preço ao barão espanhol.	We paid good money to the Spanish Baron.
Negro que foge é negro rebelde . . .	Blacks who run away are rebellious . . .
Nós os brancos comerciantes, nos guiamos pela bíblia	We white traders Are guided by the Bible
o livro santo prevê este caso	The holy book foresaw this situation
no Evangelho de Ezequiel:	in the Gospel according to Ezekiel:
– Com a rebeldia não há concórdia.	"There is no place for rebelliousness.
Punir com firmeza é uma forma	Punishing firmly is a way
de demonstrar misericórdia...	of showing mercy...
Resolvemos sem santa união	We decided without any divine agreement
dar fim ao povo ao povo rebelde	to terminate rebellious people
exterminar a subversão.	Terminate subversion.
CORO:	CHORUS:
O negro destruiremos (3x)	We will destroy blacks (3 times) (Act I, Scenes 46–59)

The dogged determination of white oppressors as expressed by the repetition of their resolve ("we will destroy blacks"), coupled with their proud display of ownership of a land that they stole from the natives, which they colonized and populated with stolen Africans as slaves to cultivate, betrays the lack of conscience and abject indifference to the plight of the ex-slaves. By contrast, the blacks' own determination to set themselves free by any means necessary raises a sense of empathy among the audience as if to want to intervene in their quest for social equality. The arrogant self-confession by whites further alienates and turns the audience against the white oppressors, as structurally intended.

Boal's fourth chaotic technique deals with the use of music. The performance begins and ends with music—creating and sustaining an air of agitation and suspense as the audience seeks for more aesthetic pleasure that is robed in subtextual political protest. By its very nature, music is the language of the soul and has a special way of provoking our reactions to the extent that we feel the impact of its message even if we do not understand the lyrics. In the dialectical theory and praxis that Boal employs in conjuction with his co-playwright and Edu Lobo, the musician and lyricist, *Arena Conta Zumbi* succeeds in disfiguring that which may be familiar *a priori* through the chaotic power of music. Examples in *Arena Conta Zumbi* of this Boalian function of music, in which "reason-music" fuses to restore meaning to a rather trivial verity, include exhortatory songs such as "Venha ser feliz" (Come and be happy) (46), "O açoite bateu" (The pain got to me) (48–49), and "Tempo de Guerra" (Time of war) (49–50).[17] The musical scene of "Venha ser feliz" in the last segment offers a moment of catharsis in which Zumbi is caught between his will to live and the overwhelming pressure to make the ultimate sacrifice even as he feels weak but determined to continue. In an ancestral twist, he now becomes Zumbi and no longer Ganga Zumba:

CORO: Ganga Zumba é Zumbi (3 vezes)

GANGA ZUMBA: Eu vivi nas cidades no tempo da desordem. Vivi no meio da gente minha no tempo da revolta. Assim passei os tempo que me deru prá vivê. Eu me levantei com a minha gente, comi minha comida no meio das batalha. Amei sem tê cuidado . . . olhei tudo que via sem tempo de bem ver . . . por querer liberdade. A voz de minha gente se levantou. Por querer liberdade. E minha voz junto com a dela. Minha voz não pode muito, mas gritá eu bem gritei. Tenho certeza que os dono dessas terra e sesmaria ficaria mais con-tente se não ouvisse a minha voz . . . Assim passei o tempo que me deru prá vivê. Por querer liberdade. TODOS—Por querer Liberdade!

CHORUS: Ganga Zumba is Zumbi (3 times)

GANGA ZUMBA: I lived in the cities at the time of confusion. I lived in the midst of my people in the time of revolt. That was how I spent the time they gave me to live. I grew up with my people, with my food in the midst of battle. I loved recklessly . . . I saw everything I saw without time to see very well . . . just for wanting freedom. The voice of my people rose up in me. Just for the sake of freedom. And my voice joined theirs. My voice could not do much, but shout, I did. I believe the Owner of this Earth and the Holy Trinity would be happier if my voice were extinct . . . And so did I spend the time they gave me to live. Just for wanting Freedom! (Act II, Scenes 87–89)

By leaving the closing of the performance open-ended in terms of the "death" of Zumbi, Boal may have signaled a strategic ambivalence and ambiguity since it is not clear to the audience if Zumbi was killed by the white soldiers or if he committed suicide as rumored. To maintain the Zumbi mythology, the suicidal theory seems to prevail. Regardless of the true version, *Arena Conta Zumbi* calls attention to a colonial atrocity while drawing equal attention to the contemporary reality of dictatorial oppression. Through ritual performance, Zumbi ceases to be a weak and defeated figure, and becomes a hero that commands national respect from the viewpoint of collective resistance against the horrors of dictatorial repression. As the multivalent interpreter of situations, Exú reigns supreme in *Arena Conta Zumbi*, causing chaos and providing solace with ambivalent resolutions that allow for many possibilities of interpretation by the audience.

One other possible reading of the formalistic chaos in *Arena Conta Zumbi* lends itself to the carnivalization paradigm. Mikhail Bakhtin and Roberto DaMatta are often cited in this regard, but with respect to this performance, the arguments put forth by Bakhtin seem more applicable, in which "carnivalization" is not necessarily a negation of the status quo, but rather a reaffirmation of it. The implicit suicide of Zumbi, echoing the same discourse pronounced by Zambi, his grandfather, serves as a heroic and resistant gesture since he refused to surrender himself to the oppressor. Based on the plot structure of the novel *Ganga Zumba* by João Felício dos Santos, *Arena Conta Zumbi* narrates how Ganga Zumba arrives in Brazil and is immediately sold as slave. Following the escape of Zumba, other slaves start thinking of doing the same, but there is no unity in that wish since some slaves do not want to risk trading the reality of a known enslavement for an uncertain freedom. As Freitas notes in *Palmares: A Guerra dos Escravos*, the utopian Palmares region was quite rural, dangerous and impenetrable terrain with the risks of facing wild animals and other mortal challenges (16). Sequentially, Ganga Zona, Zumbi's father, arrives in Brazil on a slave ship with his wife Gongoba, Zumbi's mother, who was at the time pregnant with Zumbi. With the help of other slaves, Ganga Zona escapes to Palmares. In Palmares, Zumba talks about the value of labor as instrument of liberation, suggesting a Marxist orientation.

Still in Palmares, freed slaves trade with white merchants—a scenario that confounded the colonials, who saw blacks as dangerous and subversive. Once the merchants realize the value of the riches that Palmares holds, they connive with the then monarch Dom Pedro to approve of repressive expeditions, which often end in the defeat of the colonial troops. With Dom Pedro considered weak, Dom Ayres takes over governance of Pernambuco and intensifies the repressive expeditions. In one of these expeditions, Ganga Zona dies and Zumbi promises to avenge the death of his father. Ganga Zumba soon commits suicide, and Zumbi is crowned king of Palmares. Domingos Jorge Velho, the Paulistan hero, negotiates with the governor and the Church to pardon his own crimes and give his family landed properties and, in exchange, ensures the isolation and total extermination of Palmares by sending blacks with contagious diseases into Palmares, ultimately planning to set it ablaze. Once Zumbi gets wind of the imminent war, despite the preparations of venomous arrows by black women and reinforcement of black warriors, he comes to the conclusion that the odds are against him—and ultimately commits suicide after making the same speech his father had made. To what extent, then, is *Arena Conta Zumbi* carnivalesque?

First, *Arena Conta Zumba* as a political performance deviates from the historical order of things while enacting an inversion in form and content in order to eliminate the usual distance between actors and characters. Carnivalesque principles include the expectation that daily hierarchical structures are subverted or even replaced temporarily with familiarity among all social classes; permissible eccentricities that reveal hidden aspects of human nature; the co-mixture of the sacred with the profane, the high with the low, the rational with the foolish; and finally, deliberate profanation based on parodies and indecencies. In the same vein, the performance took liberty with the deviation from clarity regarding structural details as in the ambiguity of the "suicide" of Zumbi and the free trading between the white merchants and Palmares dwellers as if the erroneous portrayal of Zumbi in didactic books is being corrected by the Arena Theater. As a critic notes, "Playwrights Augusto Boal and Gianfrancesco Guarnieri openly admit to rewriting history in their portrayal of Palmares in *Arena Conta Zumbi*."[18] This raises a question about historical authenticity as well as political historicity since the modification has a place in the intentionality of the playwrights, thus suggesting an authorial carnivalization well beyond that of Zumbi's "real life" as opposed to invented life.

Quilombo, Carnivalization, and Zumbi Mythology

Qualified as the "Black Eldorado" of Brazil by Gilberto Gil's opening and ending music, *Quilombo* synthesizes the very quintessential force of Afro-Brazilian intellectual history in its many resonances with the Atlantic passage, the horrors of enslavement, and the vital memory of resistance against colonial oppression. Documenting one of the most brutal moments in Brazilian history, *Quilombo* is at once the story of Zumbi dos Palmares and of the larger history of Atlantic slavery. Besides the "carnivalesque" atmosphere that most soap operas emulate as a constant in Brazilian global cultural marketing—equally found in such recent films as *Orfeu Negro*, *Orfeu*, *Macunaíma*, *O Pagador de Promessas*, *Xica da Silva*, *Tenda dos Milagres*, and *Cidade de Deus*, among others—*Quilombo* transcends this ephemerally "festive" perspective by exposing painful colonial atrocities with the same violence of its ideological counterpoint represented by the Palmares ex-slaves. In its form and content, like *Arena Conta Zumbi*, *Quilombo* retells the story of Zumbi, not as a passive loser in the hands of the European colonizers, but as a proud, strong, and militant strategist who resisted the exploitative advances of the invading oppressor.

Although this cinematic rendition presents Zumbi's death as inevitable, as he is somewhat ambushed at a moment in which he was already wounded and weak, he could have escaped with the help of his loyalists, but he stayed on—reflecting simultaneously on the promise of Acotirene, the spiritual guide of Palmares, who had stated that "Palmares will never be destroyed." The symbolic image of his blood flowing over the mountain suggests ritual sacrifice, as if Zumbi had been offered on a high altar. Another symbolic gesture was the throwing of his spear into the air, commanding it back to where it came, as if returning his power back to the giver, the Supreme Being, or the spirit of the ancestors. Riveting and spellbinding, *Quilombo* "torments" the viewer in the same way the viewer travels back in time to see conditions of enslavement unfold before his or her very eyes. Somewhat racy, fragmented, and fast-paced, the documentary has its entertaining moments, such as strategies and deadly tactics used by the entire community to surprise the invaders and thwart their repeated expeditions.

In carnivalizing the official story that Palmares was easily defeated without much resistance from the ex-slaves, *Quilombo* reveals a few episodes that indicate otherwise: (1) the entire community was involved in the resistance: children, women, and men; (2) some whites collaborated with Palmares through negotiation and exchange of goods (arms for food, for example)—which shows that Palmares would collaborate with any race on an equal footing; (3) the children were taught an African language (Yoruba from Western Nigeria) as a strategy to keep African cultural-spiritual values and ties with Africa intact; (4) Acotirene served as the community's spiritual leader, warning of the danger of being fooled by the seemingly friendly gestures of the enemy (whites)—she was the one who divined the renaming of Ganga Zumba as Xangô (thunderous and fiery deity), the chosen one to lead Palmares; (5) though Zumbi at one point was stolen from Palmares by one of the soldiers and given to a priest to be cared for, thus renamed "Francisco" caricaturally, he escaped and returned to Palmares to assume his destined leadership role around the same time predicted for the appearance of the 1694 comet—a sign that Ganga Zumba, Zumbi's father, recognized and anticipated; (6) Ganga Zumba's ghost often appears to Zumbi to offer him spiritual strength and reassure him that Palmares will never be destroyed, in the same way that Acotirene was the spiritual guide for Zumba; in these apparitions, Ganga Zumba always speaks in Yoruba as an ancestral spirit or masquer; (7) the ultimate destruction of Palmares was very taxing and came at a considerable loss of lives to the white troops and only after many abortive expeditions.

It should be noted that the order of those on the battle lines indicates that captured blacks were carrying the canons (putting them in greater danger) with which Palmares was defeated, followed by the white troops, and then the merchants. Overall, the many levels of carnivalization ensure that the production is far from being subjective but seeks to encompass all the elements missing from the official version. Through carnivalization, *Quilombo* does not reinforce the mythical vision of the destruction of Palmares but adds some balancing elements of realism, while not completely eliminating the illusions of reality given the creative imagination of recreating a seventeenth-century historical event in a carnivalesque ambience of the twenty-first century. Robert Stam suggests that the film should be considered a didactic saga that blends fact, legend, and creative extrapolation. He goes on to assert that "*Quilombo* is part historical reconstruction, and part musical comedy" (315) through which the cineaste deploys a "poetic synthesis" approach rather than a "naturalistic production" geared toward a historical hypothesis that is "above all *poetically* correct."[19] Stam's astute observation is instructive in the sense that for *Quilombo* to be a "perfect" production, it has to be carefully worded so as not to offend anyone's political or cultural sensibilities. And that it cannot possibly be.

Despite Stam's critical invocation of "Nagôcentrism" with regard to the use of cosmetic Yoruba language and culture in *Quilombo* as opposed to the more factual Bantu, the consistent interpretation of the political impact of these magical-realist moments permits a crossroads or "*Exúesque*" analysis. The three moments in question—(1) teaching of the youngsters in Yoruba by a community elder; (2) the spiritual renaming of Ganga Zumba as Xangô (thunderous deity) and the renaming of Zumbi as Ogum/Ogun (warrior deity); and (3) the apparition of Zumba to Zumbi (in which he spoke in Yoruba) to encourage him to continue resistance because Palmares would never be defeated—all indicate a conscious approximation of African cultural value systems and the belief in reincarnation. If the youngsters learn to speak Yoruba and immerse themselves in Yoruba culture, they will be well grounded to invoke their deities without shame—an experience that will draw them closer to Africa and inculcate in them black pride and dignity. Likewise Zumbi's apparition will then be easily processed as the continuity ritual in which the world of the living and of the unborn coexist with that of the ancestors without any disconnection. Symbolically, Nagôcentrism represents Africans in Brazil without assuming that all Afro-descendants come from the Yorubaland. Although Exú may be a problematic deity, the divergent and convergent personality who can make or break an individual depending on their relative submission to his wiles, ultimately, the goal of *Esu* is to remind interpreters that he is the quintessential gatekeeper of knowledge systems and anyone who consults and pays homage will not be misguided. By paying homage to Exú through the inclusion of Yoruba culture and, by extension, African culture, Diegues pays homage to the deity of the crossroads through whom Africa meets Brazil in a synergetic reconfiguration.

While Exú operates structurally within the fast-paced production, Gilberto Gil's underlying musical cut in the film, "felicidade guerreira" (warrior-like happiness), operates emotively, synthesizing all the ideological bent of the Zumbi mythological phenomenon in that the qualities of a warrior, a militant, and a hero are all subsumed under this combative, contradictory, yet affable personality. As a commandant, inspired by the Yoruba warrior deity, Ogum, Zumbi is a natural leader as he prepares the road for others to pass safely. As Gil sings against the backdrop of the Palmares mount as the film begins and ends, "Minha espada espalha o sol da guerra / Meu quilombo incandescendo a serra" [my spear spreads the sun of war / My Maroon settlement cascades over the mountain], the viewer is reminded of the sheer challenge not only of leaving slavery to create a well-secured freedom settlement but of sacrificing in order to ensure that all efforts by the colonial intruders are met with violent death (done successfully until a military and more powerful reinforcement is sent by the adversary). The implication of Gil's song, which blends well with the motifs of the quilombo settlers, lies in the fact that an Afro-Brazilian must always be a warrior in order to be happy and nothing must be taken for granted: "A felicidade do negro é uma felicidade guerreira! / . . . Meu grande terreiro, meu berço e nação / Zumbi protetor, guardião padroeiro / Mandai a alforria pro meu coração" (Afro-brazilian happiness is a warrior-like happiness! / . . . My great shrine, roots, and nation / Zumbi my protector, fatherly guardian / Send a freedom letter to my heart). From Exú to Xangô and Ogum, the temperament of these deities is all about social justice—thus echoing the systematic transformation of Zumbi from a dislocated, wronged, and tormented individual to a relocated agent of change and restoration.

Ultimately, whether Zumbi is a "hero" or a "villain" depends on the question of his contribution to national discourse on slavery, resistance, emancipation, and integration. Regardless of the "roles" he is assigned from divergent perspectives, regardless of his travails in the hands of the oppressor-colonizer, regardless of the efforts to counter his negative mythology with an understanding of him as a positive chapter in Brazilian intellectual history, the fact that old and young, whites and blacks, men and women, are forced to recognize and critique this phase of Brazilian history is in itself an accomplishment. No longer is Zumbi absent from the annals of Brazilian history, and no longer will he suffer the fate of many other marginalized icons of Brazilian history. Through the efforts of such artists as the actors and directors of the Arena Theater who produced *Arena Conta Zumbi*, as well as the director of *Quilombo*, Brazil is determined to remove or mediate all the remaining vestiges of racism and racial tensions toward an improved dynamic of racial relations in a practically multicultural but disenfranchised society.

Relocating History, Film, and Fiction

By its very controversial nature, the subject of Zumbi dos Palmares raises questions of multiplicity of agencies and meanings depending on who is advancing a position or a critique. Even in the context of historical narration and historiography, there is no agreement or unified school of thought. Often labeled Brazilian "Black Eldorados," or "quilombos," the self-governing communities that flourished for many decades in the seventeenth century are dramatized in Carlos Diegues's *Quilombo*, capturing the most famous in Brazil under the leadership of Zumbi dos Palmares himself. In its weaving of the story of Palmares with that of Zumbi, the historical saga has been compared to Alex Haley's *Roots*, which narrates the trajectory of an African American family as they are forcibly relocated from Africa to the United States. In the case of Brazil's *Quilombo*, narrating the saga of an Afro-Brazilian family from Africa to Brazil, Diegues may have synthesized in one production (and I imagine within budgetary limits) and 114 minutes what took the makers of *Roots* six episodes of about 100 minutes each. When *Arena Conta Zumbi* (1965) and *Quilombo* (1984), which were both adapted at different periods from historical archives, are approximated and compared, their aesthetic and ideological commonality lies in the need to remove from the arena of invisibility a vital part of Brazilian history as well as integrate its generated debates within the contemporary political discourse of racial relations and the adverse economic conditions of workers. In each case, from history, to fiction, then to film, an agency is constantly in flux and not fixed nor locked into any *a priori* categorization.

As Olakunle George advances: "The self that acts does so on the basis of a knowledge that is at the same time a misrecognition. By pressing a conceptual distinction between reality and the real—we open up a space where knowledge becomes historicizable as *achievement* and *lack, agency* and *limit*."[20] For the viewing audience of *Arena Conta Zumbi* and *Quilombo*, to what extent are both productions a simultaneous representation of achievement and its lack, of agency and its limits? George's dialectical conjecture that for every achievement there is a lack and for every agency there is a limit speaks directly to the potential ambivalence of the "achievements" of both productions. On one hand, in using the Zumbi episode to challenge social repression under military dictatorship, the black community may be partly pleased that an analogy is drawn about colonial and dictatorial oppression but may be equally displeased that the historical and traumatic issue of slavery is "trivialized" and "blaxploited" as convenient, even if that was not the original intention of Arena Theater. However positive the light in which Zumbi is contextualized, for the black community questions remain: Why is Zumbi not being celebrated on his own merits? And why must Zumbi be a tool (similar to the colonial) of settling the score in the quest for legitimization of a redemptive mission? On the other hand, *Quilombo*, while a recuperative production of the "glory" of a national hero, may well be seen as a "carnivalesque" production since the saga popularized a rather dark moment in Brazilian history with the result that Brazilians are now more aware of the significance of Palmares and of Zumbi—and hence more likely to want to investigate the contributions of Zumbi to Brazilian cultural heritage. If the portrayal of Zumbi by either Arena Theater or Carlos Diegues amounts to a "misrecognition," such a relocation of "history, narrative, and film" becomes problematic as it may well be a case of dislocation—hence a paradox of reversal.

Carlos Diegues's cinematic adaptation of João Felício dos Santos's novel *Ganga Zumba*, filmed in 1963 but not released until 1972 due to military censorship, has all the elements of naturalism even if the quality of production is still experimental. Likewise *Quilombo*, also directed by Carlos Diegues in 1984, and based on Décio Freitas's *Palmares: A Guerra dos Escravos*, has all the elements of creative and political freedom and, when it was new, felt like a cinematic Carnival of sorts, since the subject had not been that popularized until then. Yet each original historical narrative requires revisiting in order to highlight specific adaptations and aesthetic *cum* ideological implications for the changes. Palmares was a stronghold of a determined group whose strength lay in warfare and military prowess, as well as a strong collective purpose to die for freedom. It was a well-fortified Maroon state of fiercely capable and determined people. Palmares resisted the repeated colonial assaults for more than a decade. Even when battle-weary and weakened Ganga Zumba accepted the peace accord proposed by the governor of Pernambuco, the granted sovereignty came with a condition, which was to return fugitive slaves and to subsequently relocate to the Cacaú valley, which would move the community closer to the governor. Since Ganga Zumba seemed to be softening his position through this agreement with the governor, a palace coup was staged by Zumbi in 1690, leading to the death of Ganga Zumbi through poisoning. Zumbi quickly re-strategized and consolidated all members of Palmares under his control and started preparing for a different act of war with the Portuguese.

Based on conventional standards of comparative evaluation, it is arguable that Diegues's *Quilombo* may be closer to Zumbi mythology than the Arena Theater's counter-dictatorship version, thanks to the more accurate historical documentation provided by Décio Freitas's *Palmares: A Guerra dos Escravos* (1982), a work that is simultaneously a critical reflection on one of the most disgraceful events in Brazilian history. The colonial economy depended on the slave culture, and the slavery industrial complex needed to be eradicated by the working class. Considered politically dangerous, Palmares was an example of ideological and practical resistance against the exploitation of slave labor, and even today resonates on the large estates farmed by peasant farmers. Though quickly silenced or brutally suppressed, the slave revolts have been omitted from Brazilian history for so long that it is as if there was never any resistance by the oppressed against slavery in the Americas. The Palmares insurrection episode is but one of many such upheavals in the quest for freedom.

Regardless of the specific adaptations and implications for Zumbi's memory and memorial, Gilberto Gil's music, "Quilombo: O El Dorado Negro" (Quilombo: The Black Eldorado), offers a synthesis of the tripartite relocation thesis of history, narration, and cinematic adaptation in which he conjectures esoterically as if reassuring all those Brazilians who still feel burdened by social oppression that the day of enforcing the elusive racial democracy in Brazil may well be around the corner through the symbolism of Zumbi and the Palmares revolution that will transform Brazil into, one hopes, a more racially tolerant nation:

Once there was a Black Eldorado in Brazil
There it was, like a shaft of sunlight that liberty released

There it was, reflecting the divine light from the holy fire
    of Olorum
And there it was, relieving the utopia of one for all and all
    for one
Quilombo—everyone built it, took all the zeal of the saints
Quilombo—all of the waters of all of their tears irrigated it
Quilombo—all fell, loving, and fighting
Quilombo—even today all of us still want it so much.

Gilberto Gil's utopian call further invokes Brazil as a racially "toler-ant" nation whereas *Quilombo*, though revolutionary and persecuted, has now succeeded in becoming a symbolic rallying gesture for all Brazilians to come together to create a future "Brown Brazil." The problematic possibility of Zumbi as the ultimate synthesis of Brazilianness comes as a welcome theory for racial equality even in its counter-oppressive pos-ture that then makes the claim of Afro-Brazilianness a limiting though inclusive notion of national identity. Since Brazil is made up of what has rightly been called "three sad races"—comprising the Amerindian, the Portuguese, and the African—other heroes representing these "races" must also be factored into the reconfiguration of Brazilian identity. Indeed, the proposal for the "browning of Brazil" or the miscegenation of Brazil is a racist proposition, for in order for all Brazilians to be accepted into the national melting pot, race mixture is expected as a necessity if not a given. The question is: what happens to the many neglected "quilombos" threatened by military occupation and commercial demolition in the whole of Brazil where these communities have always been traditionally black? What happens to Brazilians, who by virtue of their unique Amer-indianness, Europeanness, and Africanness, are now expected to give up their respective identity to become superficially miscegenated? In sum, such a proposition confirms Olakunle George's suggestion that Brazilians using what appears to be based on knowledge in an all-inclusive sense may well be a form of "misrecognition" of themselves.

Chapter 3

Xica da Silva

Sexualized and Miscegenated Body Politics

Beyond the significant place occupied by Zumbi dos Palmares, the iconic Afro-Brazilian consciousness-raising hero (who was as relevant in the seventeenth century as he is in the twenty-first), no other national figure has been the subject of such diverse versions, revisions, and adaptations[1] in Afro-Brazilian culture as Xica da Silva. As controversial as she is fascinating in death as she was in life, she is regarded with either indignation or reverence, depending on the school of thought assessing her legacy in Brazilian literary, cultural, and national historiographies. Drawing on a number of theories on subversion of power, gender, slavery, and the problematic dynamics of freedom, this chapter explores the shifting versions of the legacy of Xica da Silva as portrayed in history, film, and fiction, while focusing on the collateral impact of her sacrificial strategies to free herself from slavery and enjoin others to do the same. Scholars and general readers alike are curious about the historical facts of this narrative because the story itself is so unusual. During the colonial era, the bodies of slave women were considered to be their masters' property, and it is common knowledge now that slave women were frequently seduced or raped by their masters; what is uncommon is that Xica da Silva was able to reclaim her body and use it as a bargaining chip. In order to do justice to the various sociopolitical, racial, and economic issues arising from the Xica legend, this chapter is divided into five parts, namely, historical narrative, literary adaptations, cinematic adaptations, versions and revisions of history, and Xica as a multivalent allegory of

nationalism—including a critique of her sexualized, exploited, and mis-
cegenated body. Four main sources inform my cultural analysis: Júnia
Ferreira Furtado's seminal historical reconstruction in *Chica da Silva: A
Brazilian Slave of the Eighteenth Century* (2009), Antonio Callado's theat-
rical adaptation, *O Tesouro de Chica da Silva* (The Treasure of Chica da
Silva, 2006), Luís Abreu's theatrical version, *Xica da Silva* (1988), and
Carlos Diegues's cinematic rendition, *Xica da Silva* (1976).

I propose that the sexualized and miscegenated body of Xica da
Silva represents both the "body" of Brazil and its experience of slavery
at the hands of Europe, as well as the politics of resistance though the
manipulation of desire by the colonized female figure. While the official
representation of Xica da Silva is that of the sexualized mulatta-slave,
Furtado, in *Chica da Silva*, argues for what she calls the "other side of
the myth."[2] Far from being a facile presentation of Xica as a domestic,
Furtado's account painstakingly documents the morals of eighteenth-
century Brazil when it was permissible—however rare—for a slave to use
"matrimonial strategies" to subvert colonial power by using the luring
enchantments and seductions of her body to entice a colonial administrator with whom she bore thirteen children. The daughter of a West
African slave woman and a Brazilian colonial noble, Xica was presum-
ably no stranger to the arts of seduction and determination, or to using
her body as a tool. In a society that accepted as normal the practice of
concubinage across social, racial, and cultural borders, the narrative of
Xica da Silva presents a historical personality—one fused with gendered
and cultural agency since she represents both the negation and viability
of racial democracy or miscegenation. Despite the tensions between
the official perspectives that objectify her and the militant viewpoints
that herald her heroism, Xica da Silva is an iconic national figure that
subverts as well as reaffirms the problematic of racial democracy as used
to justify and contest racism in Brazil. Whatever version of her story is
told, what is evident is that in myth and reality Xica da Silva remains
a convergence of the stereotypical image of the mulatta, as well as the
political drama of an ex-slave woman who rose to power through profane
means—even if that power was ephemeral. Ambitious, sexy, and political,
Xica da Silva combines feminine wiles with the intelligence of appro-
priating the manipulative art of lovemaking to persuade the Portuguese
governor to grant her freedom from slavery. Of course, there was more
to it than sex: Xica knew the psychology of seduction and how to use
it to attain her objective of freedom.

Yet, this manipulated purchase of freedom by Xica da Silva was not so simple. In *Slavery Unseen*, Aidoo exposes a hitherto obscured reading of interracial sex and sexual violence when it comes to enslaved black men and women. The author persuasively argues that through the many representations of Xica da Silva, she became the embodied invention of miscegenation as well as the reversal of sexual violence by presenting her as the sexual aggressor and the white elite as the victim of her sexual aggression, thus exculpating the white from their guilt of sexual violence. In explicit terms, Aidoo suggests that "the sexual agency that some enslaved women used to secure their freedom concealed the victimization and sexual abuse they suffered . . . that were critical fundaments to the national miscegenation narrative and the myth of racial democracy" (189). Of course, slaves were not really in control and were forcibly raped and exploited, as were Xica herself in the cinematic version of 1976 and the male slave (Paulo) in the hands of José Maria in the Telenovela version of 1996.

Beyond the deconstruction of the sexual violence faced by Xica da Silva as advanced by Aidoo (2018), Black feminist scholarship as pronounced by Thaviola Glymph (2008), Deborah Gray White (1985), and Stephanie M. H. Camp (2004) offer a provocative counterpoint to Freyre's miscegenation thesis. The three works engage questions of agency and sexuality as they regard enslaved black women in the southern plantations in the United States. Unlike in the reality of the enslaved subject in the Brazilian northeastern plantation in which white masters were the ones in control of black women's bodies, these studies focus on gender and class struggles between black women and white mistresses. Glymph argues in *Out of the House of Bondage* that instead of the popular notion that both enslaved black women and white mistresses were suffering under same paternalism, black women were more frequently victims of violence perpetuated by mistresses than by white masters. White racial supremacy was thus challenged by black women's resistance to mistresses' power of domesticity during the Civil War and by juxtaposing enslaved women's politics of dignity.

In a further deconstruction of the perception of black women's agency under slavery, sexism, and racism, White's *Ar'n't I a Woman?* questions the miscegenation thesis that black women had little control over their sexualized roles as mammies and Jezebels. The life cycle of female slaves was particularly instructive as they evolved from serving as young nurses of younger children, fieldworkers, childbearers, protectors of family life to being old caretakers of children. But it is in Camp's *Closer to Freedom* that one comes to terms with a more elaborate challenge to power relations in the American southern plantations from the viewpoints of gender, space, and racial relations. Camp argues that enslaved black women were able to deploy truancy (while pregnant), illicit socializing (during nighttime social events), and migrations from slavery (during the Civil War) as strategies to challenge the control of their bodies during the Civil War. When Xica da Silva is read against these empowering events in the lives of the enslaved women, her mythology may well be comparable to the stereotypes of the black mammy and Jezebel, which she challenged and transcended as the famous black mistress and "wife" of a white elite in colonial Brazil. Xica da Silva in this instance disrupted white domination by using miscegenation as an instrument of her own liberation and not as perpetuation of her oppression.

Historical Context

Two fundamental questions deconstruct the mythology and historicity of Xica da Silva: (1) what specific historical and socioeconomic conditions permitted Xica da Silva, born a slave in the 1730s, to become a wealthy and free woman by the time she died in 1796? and (2) to what extent are the popular myths surrounding her life verifiable or deniable? Furtado states: "With the publication of Joaquim Felício dos Santos's *Memórias do Distrito Diamantino* (Memories of Diamantina District) in 1868, which dedicates two chapters to her life in the village of Tejuco, now the city of Diamantina, the center of diamond production during the colonial period, her story became a well-known and integral part of the history of the mining region in the eighteenth century" (11–12). Nevertheless, Furtado suggests that it was not literature that should be credited for the popularity of the Xica myth, but film. For her,

> Cacá Diegues's film was the vehicle by which Chica da Silva definitively embodied the stereotype of licentiousness and sensuality always attributed to the black or mulatta female in the Brazilian popular imagination. The art of seduction, so natural to these women, enabled them to invert the logic of the system and three-tiered discrimination of race, color, and gender to which they were customarily submitted. And once

turned on its head, it was they who became the dominators. As was the case with Chica da Silva, through her relationship with the white contractor, the inversion of the order revealed one of the facets of the Brazilian racial democracy, that which allowed some individuals of color, particularly women, to climb the social ladder and even "dominate" those who were once their masters. (12)

While crediting both literature and film with the popularization of the Xica myth, Furtado also considers new research on women and slavery in eighteenth-century Brazil significant for the novel interpretation of the slave society, especially with regards to women of color and mulattas. This gendered perspective filters through her entire narrative reconstruction using varied sources, from the anthropological, ethnographical, sociological, and cultural, to the historical.

Xica da Silva (also known as Chica da Silva or Francisca da Silva Oliveira) (1732–1796) was born into slavery in Vila do Príncipe (Minas Gerais) and was eventually known as "the slave who became a queen."[3] Daughter of Antônio Caetano de Sá, a Portuguese colonial master, and his enslaved black lover, Maria da Costa, Xica da Silva lived primarily in Arraial do Tijuco, known as the "diamond city."[4] Xica's first colonial master was Sergeant Manuel Pires Sardinha, with whom she had two sons, Plácido Pires Sardinha and Simão Pires Sardinha. Her second master was Priest Rolim (José da Silva Oliveira), who was coerced to sell Xica to the diamond contractor and mining governor of Arraial do Tijuco, João Fernandes de Oliveira, considered one of the richest men in colonial Brazil. Following a passionate romance between Xica and Governor Oliveira, she persuaded him to grant her freedom from slavery and eventually bore him a total of thirteen[5] children—during a controversial period in which they were not officially married but lived together like a married couple. After a series of investigations concerning Governor Oliveira's unscrupulous activities in the Portuguese Colony, he was ordered to return to Portugal in 1770. He took their four sons with him, while their daughters remained in Brazil and were sent to the Convent of Macaúbas. Even after Oliveira's departure, Xica retained most of her privileges and prestige. In addition to being buried at the church of São Francisco de Assis in 1796, an honor reserved for select wealthy whites, she was granted membership to a number of brotherhoods[6] during her lifetime after the departure of Governor Oliveira.

By virtue of her ultimate subconscious intentions, there is perhaps no question that Xica went beyond the immediate subversion of colonial power to ensure her own freedom. Indeed, it is deducible that through allowing herself to be "conquered" by Oliveira, using seduction and satisfying the carnal desires of the colonial master, she was well aware of the future benefits as well for her children and descendants, who would no longer be subject to her own slave status. Arguably, Xica may well be the colonial representation of the problematic "racial democracy," a concept of harmonious relations among all races as represented in Jorge Amado's *Tenda dos Milagres*. Subscribing to miscegenation by necessity or by strategic manipulation, she knew that in a racist colonial society such as was (and still is) Brazil, she had to willfully submit her body to the disposition of the colonial master as a way to escape slavery, for herself and for her children and future descendants, in order to escape racism and improve their social mobility. By securing her freedom through the "carta de alforria" (manumission letter), she set up a process of social integration for the survival of the black race in a hostile and brutal society based on slavery and its implied social, economic, and spiritual exploitation and dispossession.

Sex, sensuality, and carnality—to which the relations between Xica and Oliveira have been reduced—raise questions about the extent to which the colonizer dominates and the colonized submits to or subverts power relations. In this sense, sex becomes psychological as well as physical, especially when the act is obligatory. The "pleasure" of such an encounter is unilateral and not mutually fulfilling since the goal was to get Oliveira to the point of sexual ecstasy, which would then compel him to be at the service of Xica. The question could be raised: to what extent is sex determinant in the granting of freedom in colonial Brazil? A related question is, why was sex so vital to the normalization of concubinage with white men? Such arranged sexual acts are not so far from prostitution since the payment comes in terms of questionable freedom—which in reality does not mean leaving these white men but a guarantee that the ex-slaves are made sufficiently pleased by their newly found freedom and the guarantees it provides for their descendants. As scandalous as Xica's relationship with Oliveira was considered in colonial Brazil—because an ex-slave had managed to become one of the most powerful women in the Americas—it was not a unique exception to the rule. Furtado argues that the stereotypical portrayal may have been necessitated as a symbolic representative of the mulatta woman who, though treated as a sex object, was intelligent and astute:

While the whites and their customs emerged as awkward, cold, and almost ridiculous, Chica da Silva's sexuality and radiant energy portrayed a rich and complex African culture. As such, it undermined the stereotype of white domination over blacks in Brazilian culture and presented an alternative picture of this relationship. Chica da Silva is the vehicle of redemption in this movie: using her sexuality in her favor, she inverts the mechanism by which the whites ensured their dominance over her race, namely, the use of colored women to satisfy their sexual appetites. (302)

Despite being used as sex objects by their colonial masters or mistresses, slaves in colonial Brazil seized their opportunities, and used the situations to their advantage by improving the lives of their descendants. As a result, objectified sex, however negative, also became a means to an end for those in colonial and enslaved circumstances.

A few cultural critics and historians have argued for racial tolerance in the case of Brazil, using the myth of Xica and the problematic miscegenation thesis. On the surface, their arguments about interracial relations appear persuasive since Xica used her sensuousness and sexuality to "overpower" a powerful colonial administrator, and she, in turn, turned out to be a powerful woman by obtaining her freedom from slavery. Of these cultural critics, Júnia Ferreira Furtado appears to be the most contextually grounded and critically balanced in terms of sheer archival information, meshed with ethnographical conviviality amongst the descendants of Xica da Silva in Minas Gerais. In her seminal book *Chica da Silva: A Brazilian Slave of the Eighteenth Century*, Furtado seeks to reveal the true Xica, as opposed to the stereotypes and myths surrounding her character. While Carlos Diegues may be responsible for the popularization of Xica's mythology in the 1976 movie *Xica da Silva*, Furtado is surely responsible for her de-mythologization. The central arguments of Furtado's book can be summed up as follows: (1) that the stereotypical image of Xica as a sensual mulatta who synthesizes the notion of integrated Brazilian identity is subverted by the verification of her empowering real-life narrative and that of her free-born miscegenated descendants; (2) that Xica represents an agency for other women of color who made a case for the historical facts as opposed to popular mythology by emphasizing the "other side of the myth" (19); (3) the mining boom brought many men to Minas Gerais, creating a five-to-one ratio imbalance between men and women, compelling men to have sexual relations with enslaved women, and thereby creating freed descendants afterward (65); (4) that João Fernandes Oliveira's sexual relationship with Xica was typical, thus creating a society of legitimate Afro-descended concubines who recognized their status of double exploitation, in racial and sexual terms (xxiii); (5) that Diamantina was a community noted for female-headed households and for a high rate of births outside wedlock; (6) that since Catholic marriage was meant for social equals in the colonial era, João Fernandes Oliveira never formalized his union in marriage with Xica, although she realized her wishes of miscegenation as a vehicle for social mobility; (7) that Xica herself owned a hundred slaves after obtaining her freedom, but was never recorded as freeing any of them (154); (8) that the analysis of Xica's house and the sheer amount of jewelry owned by her daughter, Quitéria, in Diamantina, reveals the extent of material possession, influence, and charity displayed by Xica's elitist legacy as one of the most affluent in the city; (9) that many of Xica's daughters were benefactors of local religious brotherhoods and married members of the white elite, while João Fernandes Oliveira's four sons were educated in Portugal and became influential within the Portuguese court; and (10) that in presenting the biography of Xica, the author equally exposes the limitations and possibilities of reconstructing the eighteenth-century history of Minas Gerais, not only as it relates to Xica's and Oliveira's lives, but also as it concerns broader Brazilian colonial history and the implicit place of the negotiation of hierarchies concerning race and gender in transatlantic or even world history.

Literary Adaptations

Xica's story has been literarily adapted or retold by at least five different authors and in four genres: short story, poetry, novel, and play. While these efforts differ in their perspectives and focus, the essential thrust remains that a uniquely powerful black woman, an ex-slave, rose to become influential and significant in Brazilian colonial history. What these narratives also have in common is the notion that Xica was an exception to the rule, endowed with extraordinary sensuality that allowed her to seduce the Portuguese contractor of mines, João Fernandes de Oliveira. Each genre deviates slightly from the master narrative, enriches the plot to suit its own purpose, exaggerates where necessary for comical effect, or expands on issues where they illuminate the local color or reinforce the mythology or mystification of Xica da Silva. In Viriato Corrêa's "Chica da Silva" for example, a short story published in 1955, the narrative does not delve into the details of her idiosyncrasies except for the lavish way she dressed, her extravagant demeanor, her attitude toward visiting Portuguese in Tijuco, and the opulence in which she lived, coupled with the powerful control she had over Oliveira and the decisions he made for the colony. The story starts with, and maintains, an air of mystery for the way Xica swept Oliveira off his feet, since she was not particularly beautiful. Beauty, of course, is in the eye of the beholder. Yet, when the narrator describes Xica as "gross," "ugly," "uneducated," "distasteful," and "vain," before meeting Oliveira, he is suggesting that beyond her sensuousness and the luck she had to have seduced the most powerful man in the colony, Xica had no positive attributes, only liabilities as a slave. The narrator, however, recognizes other challenges facing Xica, such as the issue of racial discrimination: "racial discrimination at that time must have been very profound and terrible. She succeeded in minimizing the effects, though. In the churches (and there were churches in those days in which only whites could enter), she was always an honored guest. The mulatta, whenever she was around, was treated with all royalty; adorned from head to toe with the most exorbitant jewelries that gold could buy" (22).

Viriato Corrêa seems to treat the story with incredulity, constantly reminding the reader of the uncanny manner through which Xica seduced Oliveira. Belittling her reputation, the narrator reminds readers that Xica was not even a virgin when she met Oliveira, as she had had two sons with the previous colonial master, José da Silva, before having twelve[7] children with Oliveira. A more salient display of Xica's power is revealed in the following admonition: "Chica da Silva was the most extravagantly odd woman that ever lived during the Pombal era. An absolute lady of the mineral contractor's heart, she ruled over Tijuco with the magnificence of a queen. There was desire of her, however strange, that was not immediately fulfilled" (21). Such was the powerful influence Xica had on Oliveira, and perhaps, vice versa. Even when Xica felt like traveling to Europe, Oliveira ordered the construction of a ship and an artificial sea so she could simulate a leisurely sailing to Europe. This example confirms a persistent startling eccentricity on Oliveira's part because he does not genuinely love Xica beyond her being his officialized mistress. Otherwise, Xica would have been allowed to accompany Oliveira to Europe under any circumstance. Interestingly, as a reference for his own source for recreating the story of Xica da Silva, Corrêa invokes Joaquim Felício dos Santos's *Memórias do Distrito Diamantino*, considered the most accurate of the historical records on Diamantina and from which the author extracted some of his anecdotes. Considered the most opulent and happiest woman of her time, Xica was described as "swimming and dying in gold" (25), as if wealth became her undoing. According to the short story, Xica is an embodiment of contradictions: she is ugly and beautiful, poor and rich, powerless and powerful, colonized and colonizing, comical and ultimately tragic. From the perspective of the narrator, she is saddled with the guilt of having provoked Oliveira to his own uncontrollable seduction and submission to the most controlling woman in the colony.

Crediting Cecília Meireles for "breaking into the traditionally male territory of history and the epic," Luiz Valente suggests that the Meireles "goes against the grain of most early Brazilian Modernism."[8] Her *Romanceiro da Inconfidência* (Poet of the No-Confidence Affair)[9]constitutes an innovative literary adaptation of the famed "Inconfidência Mineira,"[10] referencing political conspiracy against the colonial government and necessitating the capital punishment for the leader (Tiradentes), and condemnation, imprisonment, or exile for others. Of the seven-part epic narrative, containing forty-five poems, or "romances,"[11] the first part, titled "Fala Inicial" (Initial Speech), which has nineteen "romances," contains seven episodes (romances 13–19) specifically related to Xica's saga, namely, "Contratador Fernandes (XIII)," "Chica da Silva (XIV)," "Cismas da Chica da Silva (XV)," "Traição do Conde (XVI)," "Lamentações no Tijuco (XVII)," "Velhos do Tejuco (XVIII)," and "Maus Presságios (XIX)." These episodes, like the rest, evoke events in the historical life of Minas Gerais, seeking solidarity in the ideas of patriotism, independence, and eternal archival memory. Luiz Valente argues against the critique of *Romanceiro* not only as claiming "objectivity" but also as an "unfortunate characterization of the work as a narrowly patriotic, mindless and ultimately alienated celebration of official Brazilian history" (100), which makes it unsurprising that "*Romanceiro* would become a major reference for left-wing leaning artists during the military dictatorship" (100). Rather, the critic suggests that "*Romanceiro* acknowledges its self-conscious dialogic exchange between the raw material from past and the present where its subjective poetic voice, understood both as the poet herself and as a spokesperson for the Brazilian people" (100). One can surmise that Meireles could neither resolve the social issues faced by Brazil when the work was written in 1953 nor the colonial event itself—a time when Brazil had not completely forged itself as a national entity. Valente could not have expressed the contradictions between the progressive claim of Brazil and the reality any more convincingly, whether during the colonial or in the modern era: "*Romanceiro* shows Brazil to have been founded on predatory, savage capitalism. Despite the appeal to the *inconfidentes* of democratic political philosophy, such enlightened ideas failed to penetrate and transform the fabric of Brazilian civil society" (103). These seven episodes are reflective of the decisive moments in the life of Xica da Silva. One can even argue that Meireles's perspective paints Xica not as a victim of Oliveira but as a well-positioned black woman, especially in the persuasive phrase: "Chica-que-Manda!" (44) or "Chica-in-Charge!" Even in sarcastic terms, there is power in those words.

Though poetically rendered, these episodes are, to a certain extent, realistic and objective and capture a historical moment when the implications of what is said or not said, done or not done, may not be as unbiased as they may seem, as during the colonial era they would not have been subject to the same outside critique as would have taken place at the time *Romanceiro* was written. "Contratador Fernandes (XIII)" speculates on the mission of the royal representative in Tijuco, whether he was in Minas Gerais simply to oversee, or to exploit the colonized and enrich himself in the process: "The Count listened unconvinced, / evaluating voice, manner / and attitudes of Fernandes, / Suppressing his desires, / exploiting gold and stones / like any petty criminal" (41). While there were doubts about Oliveira's agenda, much of what pertains to Xica in "Chica da Silva (XIV)" are praises and admiration for this rich, beautiful, powerful, and controlling black slave: "there goes Chica da Silva / there goes Chica-in-Charge! [. . .] / In round, the night rotates, / golden dances / by Chica da Silva / by Chica-in-Charge" (45); to which the poetic voice responds in "Cismas da Chica da Silva (XV)": "Lord, forgive me, but the Count / must have come for his own hidden agenda" (45). In the "Traição do Conde (XVI) episode, Oliveira reacts to Xica's complaint about the Count, giving Oliveira reasons to want to "save" her from him, even if for his own personal reasons of infatuation and desire: "João Fernandes did not answer: / he hears silently / what Chica had told him / in a resenting voice" (50). Only in the last episodes, "Lamentações no Tijuco (XVII)" and "Maus Presságios," do we sense a critique by Meireles, not only of slavery and slave labor, but also the premonition of the abandonment of Xica when Oliveira was called upon to return to Portugal: "Accursed the Count, and accursed /

this gold extracted by slaves [. . .] / Gone are those days / of Fernandes the Contractor. / Where is Chica da Silva now / Is she still covered in shining gold?" (51–53). Such is the precision of language with which Meireles renders the epical poetic outpourings contained in the *Romanceiro* about Xica da Silva. From her precise exposure of the burden of slavery, to the wonderment of the plight of Xica after Oliveira leaves Tijuco (Minas Gerais), Meireles documents the essential dramas of the Xica mythology as representative of the plight of a black slave, and as subjective as the realities of the time.

Based on the film script upon which Carlos Diegues's cinematic adaptation was equally inspired, João Felício dos Santos's novel *Xica da Silva*[12] (2006) reinterprets the classic historical text *Memórias do Distrito Diamantino* (1978), written by his uncle Joaquim Felício dos Santos, which focuses on the life and times of Xica da Silva in select chapters. A seasoned historian turned novelist, with an eye for historical details and penchant for dramatic intensity, the younger Santos creates a balance between necessary narrative details and pertinent dialogues. The result is a novel where humor collides with pathology as the drama of Xica unfolds—transcending the life of a slave to incorporate a significant period in Brazilian colonial history, especially of Minas Gerais. With artistry and pageantry, the Xica who was portrayed as ugly and "witch-crafty" by many historical records is transformed into a lively, human, beautiful, and legendary black icon who not only survived slavery but reconfigured it through sexuality—in order to appropriate its economic exploitation into her own inheritable assets. Without falsifying historical facts, Santos systematically orchestrates the life of a fascinating Brazilian historical figure: one who is ultimately transformed into a national heroine, regardless of the controversies and mythologies surrounding her life. In a total of 148 unusual, cohesive, and expansive chapters, or what may well appear to be filmic scenes, *Xica da Silva* translates Xica's humanity. She is portrayed to the reader as a complex, multidimensional personality who could have lived yesterday and who appears to continue to live amongst us. A credible character by all conventional standards of historical fiction, Xica is reinvented to challenge some of the contradictions and accomplishments of the era—embezzlement of public funds, stifling bureaucracy, festivals, road constructions, the mining industry, social inequalities, music, literature, conspiracies—during a period when Portuguese colonizers were characteristically looking for silver and found gold, were searching for emeralds but found diamonds. Ultimately, the extreme mineral richness led to brutal violence and power struggles instead of a civil society.

Representing one of Brazil's major historical figures, Santos's textualization of Xica in *Xica da Silva* redeems the ex-slave understood in the minds of many historians as the "Xica who likes to be in charge." Unlike the many stereotypical "Xicas" created for denigrating and distasteful reasons in popularized samba songs, film, or theatrical forms, the redeemed character created by Santos lends an intriguing and carnivalesque perspective to Xica the heroine, Xica the queen, and ultimately, Xica as an emblem Brazilian cultural history. Structurally, the novel can be divided into five main parts, which follow a linear and chronological plot structure: (1) historical context, main characters, and arrival of Governor Oliveira (chapters 1–42); (2) "acquisition" of Xica da Silva by Oliveira and implications for both Xica and Oliveira as well as the larger colonial society (chapters 43–69); (3) limits of Xica's "power" and symbolic interdiction to enter the local Catholic church despite her official freedom (chapters 70–91); (4) Oliveira's redress of Xica's humiliation with other material compensation (chapters 91–120); and (5) corruption of Oliveira through contraband dealing, his departure to Portugal, and the consequent humiliation of Xica da Silva (chapters 121–148). While some themes may overlap due to historical reconfiguration within a systematic narrative, Santos was essentially faithful to the history, while embellishing the narrative with compelling dialogues that later became the hallmark for Diegues's cinematic adaptation.

Santos's stylistic strategy, which echoes the life history of Xica, lies in building her expectations from the moment she is set free by an official letter, only to be disillusioned when she is prevented from entering the church building. The novel itself begins with the humiliation of Xica as a slave at the hands of the first master: "Dubious Xica, where are my trousers?" (9); "Black woman! Xica! Vagabond! . . . Xica! Xi . . . ca!" (10); "Xica, daughter-of-a-bitch, more unfaithful than an overheated milk" (20). She longs to change her condition by meeting Contractor Oliveira when he first arrives in Tijuco. As Xica performs why she wants to leave her present master, she betrays the Count by exaggerating her ordeal in front of Oliveira. This embarrasses the Count to the extent that he confuses his own defense: "Your Excellency, kindly forgive me . . . yes, the black woman is my property . . . No question, your property, my Lord! I no longer know what I am saying . . . the black woman is mine . . . of course . . . But, not really my Lord! Yes, some beating, that is true. I have lost my judgment since she went home with me, my Lord!" (68). It took a more intensified sensuous performance to convince Oliveira that Xica needed a new master: "As a result of the pink button I gave him, he hurt me here . . . bit me here . . . pinched me here . . . stepped on me here . . . Finally, in wildly orchestrated dancing and gracious moves, Xica started tearing her clothes piece by piece until she became almost nude" (69). Such a public and strategic display of nudity obliges the Count to warn as well as discourage Oliveira based on his own assess-ment of the risk of acquiring Xica: "God forbid that I sell her to Your Excellency! Or even to give her to you as a gift which is going to be the case. She would be something like an earthquake besetting Lisbon! Your Excellency, Xica would kill you! Simply kill you!" (73). It did not take long for Oliveira to experience what the Count means. Shortly after acquiring Xica, Oliveira is overwhelmed by her sexual prowess:

> "Goodness! Xiquinha, my God! My love . . . You finish me, quite knowledgeable little thing! This style of yours, not even in France, believe me . . . Tell me something, how did you learn all of this stuff? Who taught you to do what you do? Neither do I know . . ." Xica smiled, self-assured and having fun with everything. She insisted: "Nonsense, mister! Once again . . . just one more time, come on, you fool; let me have you once again . . ." "No! No! Xica! Enough! No more for me! You want me dead, little girl . . . No! No! . . . Please . . ." (80)

Such are the passionate sexual transactions that will eventually buy Xica her official freedom from slavery. Both Oliveira and Xica, though not officially married, have finally signed a business contract in figurative terms. Xica gains her most desired freedom and goes on to become a force to be reckoned with in Tijuco.

One of the most dramatic moments in the novel, beyond Oliveira's departure and Xica's lamentations, is when she is barred from entering the church. From grace to fall, Xica becomes a subject of ridicule amongst her own newly acquired "slaves" (mucamas), with whom she had danced amidst fanfare and pageantry across town on her way to the church. It is an epiphanic moment for her—her expectations are dashed and her entire world comes crashing down when she realizes that the "freedom letter" she's been issued cannot guarantee all freedoms and rights accorded to whites or even mulattos. She later tells Oliveira that the letter she was given is worthless: "João Fernandes . . . João Fernandes . . . your letter . . . is nothing but worthless shit!" (105). The dialogue between the Priest and Xica about the rules of acceptance offers multiple vistas to assess the contradictions of colonialism when intersected with a romantic adventure that was bound to cause emotional distress for both Xica and Oliveira:

> PRIEST: Unfortunately . . . Unfortunately, Xica . . . Madam Xica . . . I cannot let you in! It is about the rules . . . rules, you know? You cannot come in! . . .
>
> XICA: First, good morning Priest. As far as I know you and I don't sleep together . . . Good morning also, Madam Hortên- sia! Damn, in this chapel no one can save us?
>
> PRIEST: The rules . . . all about the rules . . . unfortunately . . .
>
> XICA: Open up Priest! Do me a favor! Read this letter with your very own eyes . . . Open it up . . .
>
> PRIEST: Well, as I said, the rules . . . there must be some misunderstanding, Madam Xica da Silva, I am sorry . . . Con- gratulations on your well deserved freedom letter! In fact, all of us are grateful to the Contractor . . . It is not my own making, please understand, but not only slaves are barred from entering . . . you see! Only light complexioned people can enter, you understand? You understand, my daughter? Whites! That is it! The rules . . . (104)

This episode serves as the anticlimax as it prepares the reader for the departure[13] of Contractor Oliveira from Tijuco—a clear signal that the protection and privileges that Xica once enjoyed around Oliveira are coming to an end. It is remarkable that the priest emphasized "light complexioned" as a euphemism for whiteness. Santos, the author, may well be critiquing the racism of the era since the only barred person in this instance is the black woman.

Xica's tragic end is not without struggle, as Xica laments, suffers, cries, queries, wonders—wishing that it was some nightmare that will soon pass and that she might relive her newly found freedom all over again in the arms of Oliveira. But as she later finds out, Oliveira is gone forever. All that is left her are memories as she tries to reconcile her disbelief with the reality that it is all over: "'What! Where did João Fernandes go? Tell me now! I want to know once and for all . . .' Thus Xica knew for sure one thing that could no longer be novelty for her: João Fernandes was irreparably lost!" (221). But Xica is not the type to give up easily; she continues her fantasy quest for Oliveira's lost love, holding his legs while he is mounted on his horse, crying and begging: "'My love, no! My love, don't go! Never! No one lays hand on my love! I doubt it, nasty bunch! . . . Don't go my love. It is me . . . your Xica who is begging you . . . You will never come back . . . you will not come back again'" (223–224). But the dice are already cast—all Xica has left is humiliation: "'João, my João, where is my life?'" Xica cries quietly on the floor: "'Where is my life? João, my João?'" (227). The novel might have ended on this melancholic tone, but Santos sought comic relief in the remaining chapters by invoking the "redemptive" sexual power of Xica as she returns, one more time, to her first master's son, who has become a priest but lacks the moral strength to resist Xica's advances. In this sense, Xica's relative sexual power seems to come full circle, even if intended stereotypically by Santos, or for the purpose of counterbalancing her not-so-victorious end.

While Santos in *Xica da Silva* sought to recapture a chronological plot structure, Antônio Callado in *O Tesouro de Chica da Silva*, a play in two acts, only recreates episodes in the life of Xica da Silva. *O Tesouro* inverts the chronological order, and presents Xica as already free and influential in both acts. In fact, Callado's focus on the most glorious and powerful moments of her life, as opposed to when she was a slave, seems deliberate.

In this telling of Xica's story, Valadares, an auspicious royal representative of the terrifying Portuguese monarch, the Marquês de Pombal, disrupts the tranquility and lavish life of not only the ex-slave, Xica da Silva, but also her lover, Oliveira, the diamond contractor, who had been sent to oversee the finances of the colonial state of Minas Gerais. Upon discovering evidence of embezzlement and corruption, including Oliveira's illicit sexual escapades with an ex-slave, Valadares proposes a challenging compromise by urging that Xica be sent back to the slave quarters while imposing some "sanity" on the social order of Minas Gerais. Oliveira refuses to succumb to the pressures, and ostentatious gifts from Xica cannot soften the visitor's position. As a result, Oliveira is compelled to return to Portugal while Xica suffers psychologically from this abandonment. Behind this seemingly simple story line, Callado exposes varied social questions about avid racism and abject corruption in colonial Brazil, providing the reader a taste of life in colonial Minas Gerais from the perspectives of Xica and the Portuguese court. Ultimately, *O Tesouro* posits Xica as a powerful black woman who rose from slavery to freedom—but not without ironic twists, such as the fact that Xica herself owned slaves and treated them no more humanely than the Portuguese colony treated black slaves in general.

In choosing to dramatize Brazilian colonial history in Minas Gerais, not from the viewpoints of the elites such as Oliveira, Valadares, and the Priest, but from the perspective of Xica, Callado is making a statement about the need to consider Xica a national heroine rather than the victim that she has been portrayed as by historians and cultural critics. Details surrounding the life of Xica reverberate throughout the play as we follow her actions and intrigues—whether in her own private chambers, in Oliveira's palace, in meetings with foreign dignitaries, or in the behind-the-scenes plot to subvert Valadares's mission to end her relationship with Oliveira. Xica must deal with the central threat against her position once Oliveira leaves, and even before he leaves Valadares is scheming to have her returned to the slave quarters. With this imminent threat, Xica puts a counter-scheme into action—once again, through her sexuality—using her body as a powerful tool of manipulation and subversion. By choice, Callado omits the moments of weaknesses and vulnerability that portray Xica as human and subdued. Rather, we see Xica orchestrating a military strategy to defend herself against a declared enemy by setting the son of Valadares up for suicide. The real tension created between Oliveira and Xica, the threat of Xica losing her newly found privileges, the prospect that Oliveira may be sent to Portugal, among other tensions, all signal to Xica that the issue boils down to self-preservation, resistance, and self-defense. As a result, compelled by his love for Xica, and in trying to express that love, Valadares commits what may partially be called "patricide" by killing his father's captain in order to protect Xica from being banished to the slave quarters. Although she found out rather late in the process, or perhaps she feigns ignorance of his identity, it is moving to hear him denounce his own father and submit to Xica:

CHICA: Son of the Count? . . .

D. JORGE: Or perhaps used to be . . . I no longer consider myself his son. I came to Brazil to give him support by using my sword in any great enterprise, and he almost killed me in anger because I refused to stay on in Portugal to marry a rich old woman. I would have pardoned every sin committed by this greedy hypocrite if not for his persecution of Your Excellency . . . (156)

By implicating Valadares's son in a criminal venture, Xica succeeds in securing Oliveira's absolution from all charges of moral turpitude and corruption. Instead, it is now Valadares and his son who are at the mercy of Xica da Silva—thus forcing Valadares to negotiate with Oliveira. In so doing, Xica saves not only herself but also Oliveira, while making a fool of the Count. Valadares has no choice but to release Oliveira from prison in order to secure the freedom of his own son—who is now a criminal by default. In this sense, the Count's power is carnivalized (subverted) by the sexual and conspiratorial astuteness of Xica.

Creating a European theater within a Brazilian colonial theater, Callado seeks to ridicule European tradition from the viewpoint of Xica, who ridicules the Portuguese theatrical group. Callado finds in Xica a powerful counterpoint to colonial oppression as well as the superiority complex used to justify colonial domination. Unlike Madam Hortênsia, whose role as Portuguese "senhora" is often grotesque and laughable—given the many occasions she faints or behaves in an unsophisticated way even during formal, ceremonial settings—Xica artfully plays the role of a Portuguese senhora with her Victorian outfit and wig, constantly taunting the guests with her sarcastic comments and creating tension between the cultures. In order to corrupt Valadares, Oliveira and Xica prepare a banquet and invite Valadares and members of Tijuco's high society as guests. Following the banquet meal, Oliveira contracts three actors to perform parts of *Comedia Eurfrosina*, a comedy by Jorge Ferreira de Vasconcelos. Callado notes (58–59) that the script has been extracted from Act I, Scene 3—a deliberate choice that is meant to be confusing to both the performers and the banquet audience. Everyone is so petrified and lost in the act that even Valadares leans forward to better gauge what is going on. Xica taunts him by asking that he explain the scene—to no avail. At some point, Xica stands to applaud the performance, provoking Valadares to action. He queries Xica as follows:

VALADARES: So, what did you think of our Coimbran theater, Madam Chica?

CHICA: I confess I prefer the actors of *Encantos de Medéia* than the actors of Tijuco.

VALADARES: You prefer that better than the royal theater?

CHICA: It is not without reason, Mr. Count. Just that I would like to understand what they are saying. At least once in a while. I can tell when I see a good theater. I realize a good performance needs not be understood but it is just my personal thing.

VALADARES: Oh, what can one really *learn* from a work such as *Comédia Eufrosina!* Especially people who are not quite enlightened, Madam Chica . . . It is a matter of application: Even we did not understand the whole drama. But as Zelótipo said, "there is no gold without sweat."

CHICA: I prefer my own gold without any hassles. (68–70)

The tension between colonial and counter-colonial forces is unmistakable. Valadares wants to get rid of Xica, and she wants to preserve the status-quo that protects her privileges, including the interests of Oliveira, her lover. It is remarkable that Xica steals the entire banquet show with her sarcasm, through which she deconstructs colonial power. The metaphorical "treasure" that Xica promises Valadares is nothing other than his own son, whom Xica has held as ransom for the freedom of Oliveira. Through miscegenation and sexual savvy, Xica not only saves herself and her loved ones, she saves an entire community from colonial manipulation and excess.

As emerging as the critical reception on the Xica da Silva mythology is, the reality is that not much has been written on the works of known literary adaptations, as emphasis has been placed primarily on the cinematic tradition. Even in the case of theater, Luis Alberto de Abreu's *Xica da Silva* has no known published critical analysis to date, while criticism of Carlos Diegues's film *Xica da Silva* is significantly on the increase. What is it about Abreu's version that is a radical departure from Antônio Callado?

The answer is not simple. The selective episodes of Callado serve their purpose in the same way that the ideological rendition in Santos's *Xica da Silva* (the closest to the cinematic rendition) fulfills the dramaturgic and popular intentions upon which it has been oriented. One critic has invoked the notion of a "chess-game"[14] to qualify the dramatic paradigm adopted by Luís Alberto de Abreu in his plays, but has not included the playwright's *Xica da Silva* in that critical analysis. Still selective, no doubt, Abreu's *Xica* differs from Santos and Callado in the sense that beyond being fairly chronological, it omits certain known episodes while emphasizing others that may or not have been as critical in previous versions. In the first instance, instead of using "acts" as divisional, dramatic units, and "scenes" as subdramatic moments, Abreu favors only "scenes" throughout—suggesting a certain fluidity and spontaneity. There are fewer stage directions; rather, each scene begins with a defined theme, as well as a consciousness of multiple linguistic registers that differentiate, for example, a slave from a priest, or a colonial administrator from visiting Portuguese royalty. The conflicts are also abridged—as in the central ones between slaves and the colonial representatives: Xica and racism, Xica and the church, Xica and the Count, and Xica and Oliveira's departure to Portugal. Of the omissions, one notes the sensuous dancing of Xica, encounters with D. Jorge (Valadares's son), corruption dealings with Teodoro (black dealer in diamonds), which now seem replaced with the priest for dramatic intensity.

It is remarkable, for example, that the priest (Bento Cruz) is openly a diamond dealer—as if the playwright desires to showcase the collision of corruption between the Church and the State. In terms of chronology, Abreu starts the play with a revisitation of the Portuguese colonial adventure as D. Sebastião emerges in the exploitation of gold and diamonds, as if to put Portugal on notice as a colonial exploiter who could not have Brazilian interests in mind. Ideologically, it appears that Abreu sets up the play against the logic that Portugal is not in a position to question the morality of Xica and Oliveira when its own colonial mission and enterprise are based on moral turpitude. By and large, this central motif runs through the play as corruption is exposed at all levels of human interaction—among colonizers, as in Bento Cruz and Xica (interdiction in entering the church), or between Xica and Cabeça (betrayal of Oliveira's "extra-conjugal" escapades by informing Xica under pressure). The celebration of Portugal's past glory and present colonial exploitation is clearly under attack and ridicule.

Some of the forgoing questions or speculations are more cogently answered by the playwright himself. He notes: "How was it that black Xica da Silva, for more than twenty years, maintained herself as the absolute queen of Tijuco? Beyond her folkloric sensuality, it could only be through her intelligence . . . Xica da Silva was our queen; the same way that Macunaíma was our uncelebrated king." Abreu's formulation goes beyond a chess-game strategy at which Xica was adept, and speaks to the heart of the playwright's thesis—that, contrary to stereotypical assumptions, Xica is a national heroine who must be celebrated as such, not demonized nor sexualized, as she has been to date. From the very poetic "Prologue" (3) in which she is referenced as an "exemplary woman" whose history is worthy to be told in a dignified manner, the reader gets the sense that Abreu has set out to do a revisionist project in his *Xica da Silva* by attributing positive values to her character. Although he tells the story in a generally chronological fashion, Abreu avoids presenting Xica to the reader as a common slave.

Instead, Abreu de-emphasizes her moments of vulnerability and chooses to focus on her moments of glory while turning Portuguese colonial adventure upside down through caustic critique. For example, in the fifteenth scene (ironically titled "Xica Cannot do Everything") about Xica entering or not entering the church, Xica is very assertive and torments the priest as if exercising power over him, instead of vice versa:

XICA: Good day, everyone. I have come to worship.

PRIEST: Here?

XICA: Why not! Where else could it be? Don't we all worship in the church?

PRIEST: Of course, but blacks worship in a different church.

XICA: Well, I am tired of going there. I want to meet new people; I want to worship here; they say this church is beautiful.

PRIEST: The Carmo church is meant for whites only and you are well aware of this.

XICA: Are you suggesting that blacks have no soul, my Priest?

PRIEST: You can only come in here with the order of the Pope!

XICA: You know who gives orders here! I can have you expelled from Tijuco!

PRIEST: Who do you think you are?

XICA: I am Xica da Silva! (Abreu 48–49)

Although she is not allowed to worship, the tense encounter conveys Xica's power, even if the priest ultimately has the ultimate power to deny entrance. Yet, in this passage, Xica has the last word. Many other instances of resistance or subversion of power occur as well, such as the conversation between Oliveira and Cabeça, his oldest slave, at the end of the play. As Oliveira reflects on his impending departure for Portugal, wondering if he is going back home or going into exile, he asks his oldest slave in the collective if "our land" was not worth the adventure? Cabeça retorts: "Your land. My land is Angola, is Cabinda!" (89). Such a direct rejoinder by Cabeça highlights the contractor's loss of power; such a remark would have been unthinkable beforehand.

Cinematic Adaptation

Critical reception[15] of Carlos Diegues's 1976 film *Xica da Silva* has been mixed. Some have complained that the film popularized her stereotypical image as a sex object, while others applauded its putting Xica da Silva on the world stage, as it were. The main plot in Diegues's interpretation seems chronological but also embodies an air of gaiety, fanfare, and carnival—which then situates an eighteenth-century event into a popularized memory for generations yet unborn. From the arrival of the diamond contractor, João Fernandes de Oliveira, his "discovery" of Xica da Silva, who basically sought him out as the most powerful man in town, to the passion that developed between them, to Xica's astute manipulation of the relationship between them to her advantage, through Oliveira's departure to Portugal, Xica comes to terms with the persistence of racism in Brazilian society, and the viewer gets a sense of grotesque comedy. In this version, the character of the Priest is disturbingly clear in the interdiction scene. He tells Xica that only blacks who have been free from slavery for "five generations" are allowed to enter the "white" church. Otherwise, she is condemned to the "black condition" of the colonial era, which saw her as nothing but an object of the state to be used and abandoned at will.

Oliveira may have intended to show his fellow Portuguese that love between the races—and classes—was possible. Yet, when it came to testing the miscegenation hypothesis, Oliveira failed; instead of challenging the racism of the Church, Oliveira ordered the construction of a black chapel solely for Xica's use. Such a separatist model contradicts the claims of racial democracy and may well be an attempt by Oliveira to prove it. Oliveira also never married Xica, but treated her as a well-loved and truly respected mistress. The miscegenation thesis falls apart in this instance. How can there be racial democracy when Oliveira did not marry Xica, not even to make a political statement? While Zezé Motta, the acclaimed black actress, was up to the task of portraying Xica in Diegues's movie in 1976, one must note that in the 1996 Brazilian soap opera (based on the same Xica legend), Zezé only got to play the roles of Xica's mother and an older Xica—an ample indication that even in the twentieth or twenty-first century social ascension for blacks may still be closely connected with miscegenation since racism is still a social reality in Brazil, however subtle. Xica may have been successfully portrayed as clever, witty, vibrant, colorful, rich, affluent, and full of political control; yet her rise to fame and fortune is burdened with the stigma of having been achieved through the exchange of her body. Brazil's military dictatorship was still in place when Diegues's film was made, and the film is careful to avoid revolutionary undertones. By giving the film an air of fantasy, Diegues inadvertently undermines what could have been a revolutionary portrayal of a black woman in Brazilian society: one who siphoned power from the whites and claimed her own life for herself. The colonial society of Xica's time and even Brazil in 1976 did not see blacks beyond the color line. The colonial system continued to bar blacks from churches, even after they had been granted their freedom based on old age. Women were often accused of witchcraft, which gave the colonial system an excuse to order interdictions against them. Xica's successes are truly legendary, but through deliberate exaggeration, Diegues reinvents the myth of Xica by giving it a popular flavor at the expense of the real woman. Diegues's Oliveira could not be a better colonial contradiction—representing the Portuguese colonial government in the diamond-rich colonial state, he was tasked with ensuring the successful operation of the diamond operations, which he did from 1739 to 1773. Instead of maintaining the distant colonial posture required of such an office, he is lured into sexual passions by the charismatic Xica, who practically turns him into her puppet. But the fantasy and political manipulation of the colonial state do not last. Xica is finally expelled from her palatial abode and finds refuge with her former lover, José, son of the town's Sergeant Major. Reminiscent of Hollywood "Blaxploitation" movies of the 1970s in which sensational black issues are misrepresented and exaggerated for commercial appeal, Diegues's portrayal of Xica reduces her to little more than a skilled prostitute and downplays her extraordinary accomplishments. The theme song, while evoking the significance of Xica, also seems to mock her. The chorus "Xica da . . . Xica da, Xica da Silva!" creates a duplicitous homage given her background and rise to fame and fortune.

The process of adapting *Xica da Silva* for the cinema must have been wrought with deliberate cultural and political ambiguities. The moral and political authority to question social inequalities through film was undermined by the dictatorial dispensation of the moment of production—thus making the rendition more of a *samba enredo*[16] (samba theme or plot) couched in fantasy and hyperbole to avoid military censorship. Taking excellent advantage of the baroque architecture of Diamantina in Minas Gerais, Diegues recreates an eighteenth-century ambience of slavery and its challenge for a black woman who subverted colonial subterfuges in order to assert her own freedom and charismatic sexuality. Not only did she seduce the wealthiest man in the region, she spent a total of forty-three years with him (according to historical records) and bore him thirteen children. Xica became so powerful that she had her own palace, servants (or slaves), a ship, and the material wealth of a royal. Confined to a corporeal power, fulfilling what Stam calls "the fantasy of the sexually available slave" (293), she is limited in her exercise of any moral authority since her authority is defined in the context of sexual favors and manipulation. A Bakhtinian reading of *Xica da Silva* offers a parodic questioning of European rigid "high" culture as opposed to the fluid popular "low" culture in which the culture of indulgent merrymaking subverts all rigidity and formality embedded in the brutality of slavery and the economic exploitation of the slave's body. While "cultural victories mask political defeats" (296), Xica da Silva has performed what the Unified Black Movement could not even fathom, which was to turn history upside down by staging a performance in which blacks were in control through the prism of Xica (even cosmetically) in the governance of Brazil. Stam puts it cogently in his assessment of the fact that despite carnivalesque inversion, Xica is still subordinated to Oliveira. In the final analysis, Xica's power was symbolic and ephemeral: "If Brazil's soul is black, its power structure is white" (296), to the extent that "the many instances of appreciation of Afro-Brazilian culture are projected into a social conjecture in which blacks are excluded from the centers of political and economic decision-making" (296). *Xica da Silva* lends itself to a paradigmatic dialectical invocation in which black cultural vitality is predicated upon white political intelligence. When Xica uses her body—and Afro-Brazilian culture—through frenetic dances to hypnotize Oliveira, such maneuvers are deemed less savvy since their politics are conditioned on the extent to which the colonial authority wants to cede power. Yet, despite the tragedy that befalls Xica at the film's end, she can be said to have skillfully made the colonial power look less forthright and intelligent than previously thought.

While the section on literary adaptations has addressed the racial and religious confrontation between the Catholic Church and the state and Xica as representation of black exclusion, the episode of the banquet provides a case study in the reversal of order through Xica's ingenuity. Other episodes, such as the significance and plight of Teodoro as a rival to Oliveira who often buys back diamonds from Teodoro as an independent and defiant black "contractor;" the confusing relations of Xica with José; the wild sexual escapades recurrent throughout the film; Xica's humiliation at the end of the film; Xica's iron-fisted treatment of her own slaves (*mucamas*); and the vengeful treatment of whites (mostly servants) and authority figures once she became free, wealthy, and powerful, are equally worthy of critical analysis but speak to the political tensions between bondage and freedom—a central problematic that the carnivalesque banquet set out to redress through sarcasm, humor, and ridicule (if not the actual disempowerment of the visiting Count).

As soon as Xica achieves her "social ascension" by becoming Oliveira's lover, she puts herself in an empowered position to ridicule the society's elites and their assumption of superiority over the indigenes. Xica appears to thrive in every way and gets all her wishes met by Oliveira. Through her exaggerated sexual control over all men, the viewer participates in a series of orgasmic screams as if Xica overpowers them with her almost pornographic lovemaking. From the Sergeant Major who regrets being obliged to sell her, to his son whom he blames for Xica's excuses to warrant such a sale to the contractor, to even the sympathetic "rescue" by Oliveira, who then becomes her benefactor by showering her with expensive European silks, a palace, and even an artificial ocean where Xica and her slaves have a good time, Xica is completely in charge in the colony. But her vindication of past abuses comes during the banquet when, as an act of retaliation for the Count's debasement, she seasons the lamb with excessive pepper and paints her face white, as if performing "whiteness"—to the annoyance of Count Valadares. Unwilling to offend, the white elites feign that all is well by forcing an air of contentment during the banquet while they suffer from the meal's unpalatable mix of pepper, excessive salt, and sour eggs. In ridiculing those she sees as her adversaries, Xica sabotages (at least temporarily) Valadares's mission.

The banquet may be seen as a two-step enactment of Xica's inner conflict: she is at once conscious of the intentions of the Count and determined to avenge moments of insult not only from the Count, whom she suspects has come to investigate Oliveira, but from the entire elite class. As a result, the mischievous food preparation enacts the point of departure of settling the scores with those she considers her past and present enemies and oppressors. As soon as Xica realizes the Count's power, she sets out to dislocate him through some culinary tactics and by preparing a humiliating banquet in his honor:

XICA: Don What's-his-name . . . ? We are receiving an aristocrat, hurry up; this man is a real nobleman.

MUCAMA: Do you want to try a little of this chicken stew?

XICA: Hmmmnnn

MUCAMA: Is it according to your taste?

XICA: Even better. And what's that?

MUCAMA: Lamb, madam.

XICA: But you know that I don't like lamb at all.

MUCAMA: It's for Dona Hortênsia.

XICA: Why doesn't she eat at her place? [spitefully adding excess of seasonings to the lamb . . .] . . . a little pepper, salt, a rotten egg, and the eggshell. It'll do him good. A little pepper, and more pepper! [spitting on the lamb mischievously and vindictively . . .] It will all be very delicious. Now it is all quite flavored, now.

MUCAMA: What about the Count?

XICA: Not to worry, I'll tell him it's a little too spicy . . . and that he'll better have the chicken stew . . . I'll find a way around it. (Diegues, 1976)

Xica delights in setting the Count up for digestive difficulties as a prelude to making him lose his balance and, hopefully, give up on his investigative mission. Following this, Xica gets the opportunity to formally welcome the Count in an elaborate white gown, but instead of complimentary words from the Count, she feels slighted by his negative remarks about her dark complexion, as if drawing a sharp contrast between her "royal" white gown and her inner darkness. The Count's racism is unmistakable, by the name-calling ("negress") and the condescending beckoning as if she is less than human.

Diegues transits from food preparation, the Count's official encounter with Xica, and the beginning of banquet without Xica, to Xica's "arrival" at the banquet—only that she has been present all along but unnoticed from a distance until someone asks about her as if formally asking her to join them at the table. This may be a deliberate technique to allow the Count to express his impressions about Tijuco with his fellow elites before the anticlimactic moment in which the banquet turns quite sour—as Xica has intended:

PASTOR: What about Madam Xica, I mean, Francisca?

XICA: Here I am; I cannot miss this event [sitting at the high table opposite to Oliveira with two guards at her side] . . . Gentlemen, serve yourselves; come on, serve yourselves, gentlemen . . . [emphasizing the fact that she is no longer a slave who serves anyone.] Don't wait for me for I am on diet. No,

Count, no. Don't touch this chicken. It is very tasteless. Let them serve you the special one for you . . . specially made for me and João Fernandes who are sick in our guts.

PASTOR: For sickness of the guts?

XICA: Yes, sick in the guts. Awful burning gasses; fat to the stomach, like the rancidness of rotten eggs . . . The only thing that helps a bit is taking castor oil. Have some lamb please. It is a regional specialty done with much taste. Besides, when the chicken is done, it turns brown. Brown, Count! [with a hilarious laughter!] [The overspiced, overpeppered lamb is then passed on to each one with catastrophic consequences.]

MAJOR: I choked, didn't I?

PASTOR: That's very good! Really delicious! I have never eaten a comparably delicious lamb in my entire life.

Quite noticeable, and sitting behind Contractor Oliveira's chair, are three black children, acting or looking like they are hungry and wishing for any leftovers passed to them. This is a clear demonstration of power dynamics between the oppressor and the oppressed, but also clear is the exploitative use of these children as props or local color. The children are not only displayed as helpless, but also mirrored against the black slaves serving at the table of the elites. Although they pretend to be having a good time, they too are suffering from the peppery lamb, for which they are drinking whatever they can lay their hands on: water, wine, anything to alleviate the pain. The viewer can easily see the concern of Contractor Oliveira, who passes on his chicken to the children, suspecting that Xica is up to some embarrassing mischief. In the end, Xica gets her revenge and the Count retires to his room in complete disarray. In the final analysis, the Contractor attempts to pacify the Count by sending him a gift of silver cups, to no avail. The Count saves the letter from the Portuguese court, ordering the Contractor back to Portugal.

Diegues's *Xica da Silva* shifts scenes very quickly in order to cover essentials in the history of Xica da Silva, and in the process inadvertently leaves out certain episodes. Some of these are not as obvious as others, yet are noteworthy. Beginning with the scene of Oliveira playing flute with black slaves and white wardens on the outskirts of Minas Gerais, the society is erroneously presented as less racially tense or polarized. In so doing, although Oliveira eventually arrives in Tijuco in a messianic mode (reminiscent of how Jesus rode a donkey into town on the first Palm Sunday), Diegues's *Xica da Silva* evokes the Christmas *autos* (morality plays intended to entertain in the spirit of rebirth in December), and thus conflates a rather complex issue of the portrayal of Xica with a larger religious concern, as if the movie were also geared toward pacifying the Christian audiences who might not only find the "pornographic" nature of the film offensive, but might not appreciate the exposure of the Church's racism. A few other episodes have been deliberately exaggerated in order to paint colonial administrators in the worst light, as a way to critique the social inequalities of the 1970s. The most humiliating of Xica's cinematic portrayals comes after the departure of Oliveira to Portugal, when children shower insults on her by calling her "Chica-da-Bunda," which translates as "Ass-Adept Chica" or "Ass-Made Chica," suggesting that she is only savvy when it comes to "ass business." Despite having obtained her freedom, Oliveira's departure strips her of the protection she has enjoyed. Xica may have been popularized by Diegues's *Xica da Silva*, but to a problematic degree it may also have inadvertently reinforced the stereotypes about Xica in the Brazilian imagination.

Versions and Revisions of History

Any attempt to conceptualize the totality of "Xicaness" and judge any deviation from that mythic state of being must begin with the examination of diverse versions and revisions of the grand historical narrative and subsequent alternative narratives. For this purpose, I conceive of this segment as a critical triangulation of "ritual archetype" or redemption, "mythical version" or enslavement, and "popular version" or the sexualized mulatta stereotype. The tripartite conceptualization intersects within the centrality of Xica as a dramatization of Afro-Brazilian women's aspirations (in their anti-patriarchal stance) as well as the larger national integrationist sentiment betrayed by Xica's alternative political exploits. Elisabeth Wesseling, in *Writing History as a Prophet*, argues for a series of models involving historical narratives, beyond the general mutability of the genre as a social institution. The first, the classical model, is didactic, imitative, and emulative. The second, the modernist model, questions objectivity of historical knowledge while making a case for subjectivity and transcendence such as is illustrated by detective narratives. The third, the historical fiction, is the utopian model defined by parodic counterfactual conjecture. The fourth, the negational counterfactual model, refers to the construction of alternative histories, in which historicity is subjected to analytical rigor, while counterfactual shifts are favored within the narrative. In the modernist experimentation involving "self-reflexivity" and which concerns the case of Xica da Silva (given the colonial time of the events narrated), it is deducible from this model that "modernist experiments with historical fiction were intent on inventing alternative modes of character portrayal that could present history as a mode of consciousness rather than an objective process" (82). The extent to which even the "master narrative" was faithful in the minutiae is debatable, for every historical account is bound to be altered by the individuality, subjectivity, and perspective of the historian or narrator. In this regard, a comparative summation and critique of the alternative histories found in the versions and revisions is worth considering.

Joaquim Felício dos Santos's *Memórias do Distrito Diamantino* is considered the master narrative in this context, followed by many alternative narratives: Júnia Furtado's *Chica da Silva: A Brazilian Slave of the Eighteenth Century* (2009), Cecília Meireles's *Romanceiro da Inconfidência* (1975), Antônio Callado's *O Tesouro de Chica da Silva* (1976), Luis Alberto de Abreu's *Xica da Silva* (1988), and Carlos Diegues's *Xica da Silva* (1976). Even a cursory analysis of the 1996 soap opera by the same name provides ample proof of the longevity of Xica's fame in Brazilian imagination. The comparative analysis reveals a commonality, a convergence, and a divergence. The commonality lies in the significance of Xica as a national heroine regardless of the limits of her representation by any school of thought. The convergence stems from each author's attempt to "correct" what is perceived as a myopic representation of Xica, while the divergence captures concrete structural and ideological shifts from the normative historical representation. Wesseling does not believe that historical narrative is impossible; she opines that what is deemed "historical" is subject to debate since different writers would have certain biases or convictions about the episodes they choose to emphasize and those they choose to be silent about. As Barbara Christian notes, "every text is silent about something,"[17] and as a result, each alternative narrative articulates other things that a given author may have deliberately silenced for their own ideological purposes. The variation in poetic license stems from the individuality of each author and provides certain clues as to the motif of representation.

Of the forty-two chapters comprising Joaquim Felício dos Santos's *Memórias do Distrito Diamantino*, only chapters 14 and 15 concern João Fernandes de Oliveira and Xica da Silva. Despite the details of the daily activities of the colonial royal representatives in the diamond-mining region of Minas Gerais (Diamantina, formerly Tijuco), the lives of Oliveira and Xica are summarized, as the focus is more on the accumulation of wealth for Portugal in the Brazilian colony. In chapter 14, Oliveira is described as follows:

> João Fernandes was the happiest of all diamond contractors. No other extracted diamonds in such abundance. He was a celebrity: seemed like a special destiny was guiding his path. In all his business transactions, he made extraordinary profits; he gained great riches in lands abandoned and thought to be poor and useless by his predecessors; he completed projects once thought impossible with superior efforts and determination. (Joaquim Santos, 165)

As for the only woman with whom he shared his power, Francisca da Silva, vulgarly known as Xica da Silva: "This woman was famous, the only woman who could make the proud contractor acquiesce to any of her demands; her wishes were blindly executed, while her frivolous and capricious requests were equally promptly approved" (169). Given the brevity of these two chapters (nineteen pages total), one can easily infer that the details of the life of Xica da Silva as described in subsequent alternative narratives were derived from more in-depth colonial historical records, such as Júnia Furtado offers in her more focused work on Xica. As Diamantina was a state within a state, its records could only be about how colonial wealth was accumulated and how such wealth was protected and administered by the designated governor or contractor, and would not have been concerned with the details of their lives.

Furtado's *Chica da Silva* (2009), an eleven-chapter, elaborate, and extensive overview of the life and times of Xica da Silva, details "Chica da Silva in the light of the times in which she lived rather than from the perspective of the present" (304). And therein lies the main contrast between the other portrayals of Xica, and this one by a historian. Furtado seeks to counter the mythology of racial democracy by using the myth of Xica da Silva as a case in point:

> The myth of Chica da Silva has been used to suggest the the-
> sis that, in Brazil, the bonds of affection between free whites
> and colored women that concubinage established somehow
> mitigated the exploitation inherent in the slave system. How-
> ever, we must not forget that, despite the economic benefit
> it brought to many of these women, this practice disguised a
> dual exploitation—both sexual and racial—as these women
> were never elevated to the condition of spouse. (xxiii)

Whether Furtado is historically explicating the economic context of the formation of the colonial village of Tijuco, the ancestry of Xica da Silva as a mulatta slave, the previous diamond contractors before the advent of Oliveira who fell in love with Xica, the central significance of Xica in her romantic love with Oliveira, Xica's rise to fame, fortune, and slave ownership, the social networks and brotherhoods created by Xica, the apogee of diamond mining, the separation between Oliveira and Xica, the conflicts that ensued between the different estates left by Oliveira, the destinies of Xica's descendants who stayed on Minas Gerais, or the historical and mythical memories invoked by Xica's legend, Fur-tado painstakingly portrays Xica not as an exception to the rule but as a normative subject who could have risen to greatness just like any other freedwoman of color if properly loved and empowered. Problematically, the conformist character of enslavement remains a one-sided argument of narrative history; likewise the nature of the *quilombolas* (those who believe today in the spirit of slave rebellion as in the seventeenth-century maroon settlements) in rebelling against slave oppression is a limited perspective. Furtado does provide a balanced perspective—demystifying the stereotypical image of Xica and replacing it with that of a compre-hensive and elevated national heroine and symbol.

Unlike the two previous historical accounts, Cecília Meireles's *Romanceiro da Inconfidência* (1975) is at best a poetic rendition of cer-tain episodes from life in Minas Gerais, especially concerning the famed "Mineira Conspiracy," and including some highlights about the life and times of Xica da Silva. By its very poetic form, clarity is replaced by ambiguity for only through poetics can we uncover the many layers of metaphor in Meirelesian poetry.[18] Constantly extending the limits of poetic sensibility and possibility, an intellectual poet in spite of herself, and dubbed the "sylph of poetic imponderability,"[19] Meireles cultivates the historical through the epic immersed in issues of love, gold, freedom, and betrayal as the episode of Oliveira and Xica unfolds. In the midst of reconfiguring the mission of the Count, Meireles psychoanalyzes Xica's mindset, who intuits The Count's real motives:

E diz a Chica da Silva	Then says Chica da Silva
Ao ricoço do Tejuco	to the richest man in Tejuco:
—Eu neste Conde não creio;	—In this Count I trust not,
Com seus modos não me iludo,	with his manners I am not fooled;
Detrás de suas palavras,	Behind his words,
Anda algum sentido oculto.	Lurk some hidden meaning.
Os homens, à luz do dia,	Men at dawn,
olham bem, mas não vêem muito:	Be vigilant, but look not too far:
dentro de quatro paredes,	within the four walls
as mulheres sabem tudo.	Women know everything.
Deus me perdoe, mas o Conde	God forgive me, but this Count
Vem cá por outros assuntos.[20]	Has come here for other motives.

In this poetic piece, Meireles paints the caring, affectionate, and sensitive side of Xica, endowing her with characteristics befitting a noble military strategist and not the stereotype of the sexualized mulatta with which she has been associated in popular imagination. Thus Xica is re-humanized and elevated to the status of a power-broker and intellectual.

Though only 7 of 85 poems, or "romances," concern Xica and Oliveira in *Romanceiro*, these episodes are as poignant as the rest of the cultural and historical landscape of Diamantina.

If Meireles romanticizes the life of Xica da Silva, Antônio Callado's *O Tesouro de Chica da Silva* (1976), in its two-act structure, critically dramatizes it with an emphasis on her dynamic relations with the men she was associated with at different levels: D. Jorge, Contractor Oliveira, and Count Valadares. In this triangulation, each encounter is an opportunity for each man to state their "case" in relation to Xica's destiny. D. Jorge is a mere lover turned antagonist, especially through jealousy of all Oliveira had done for Xica to win and maintain her love. In his tormented and quasi-delirious moment of epiphany, D. Jorge realizes his limitations and begins to express frustration and confusion as he keeps promising better gifts to Xica while unveiling his now interdicted "true love," given that Xica is with the most powerful man in Diamantina. In reaction, Xica warns him of her power and influence:

> CHICA: Mr. D. Jorge, don't force me to call on the Governor to punish your insolence. The Governor General, Count Valadares and his entire entourage (of which you are a mere soldier) are guests of the Diamond Contractor. The Count is staying with the Contractor. And I am his wife.
>
> D. JORGE: Your honor is the diamond of the Contractor.
>
> CHICA: Kindly leave now, especially if there is any love in your peaceful demeanor.
>
> D. JORGE: When love is born, peacefulness is the first thing to die. I lost my peace a few days ago, when I saw your honor for the first time. (Callado, 22)

It is curious that the loving encounter between Xica and D. Jorge comes early in Act I. This is a structural device to economize time and space by putting one of the members of the Count's entourage, who is simultaneously in love with Xica, in conflict with both Governor Valadares and the Diamond Contractor. To resolve the love triangle, Xica makes an impossible demand: send away the Count from Diamantina or starve of love; once again, Xica deploys her sexuality to manipulate Oliveira:

> JOÃO FERNANDES: [holding her by the arms with passion] Chica . . . Please . . .
>
> CHICA: No, João Fernandes.
>
> JOÃO FERNANDES: You are my wife.
>
> CHICA: Your wife is in Lisbon, I am your lover.

JOÃO FERNANDES: No longer will you be if you don't let me love you.

CHICA: [violently] Love, love as you will. But you are not welcome in my bed until you send this Count away from Tejuco! (34)

Even when she cannot change the departure of Oliveira, with all the men with whom she had had relations in both Acts I and II, Xica is dynamically in charge, including during the banquet.

The process of re-humanization and de-mythification of Xica by different writers takes a different turn in Luis Alberto de Abreu's *Xica da Silva* (1988). In addition to not having a traditional "act" division (rather, named thematic scenes), the structural fluidity conforms more with African oral tradition, while the language of characters is customized to their "ethnic" background and social status. The language is also more poetic, precise, and emotive. Of a total of twenty-nine scenes, the first five focus on Portuguese colonial incursion and settlement in Minas Gerais, while the sixth and seventh scenes deal with the "catechism" (or conversion of Xica by the Catholic priest). In scenes 9 through 14, the reader is acquainted with the arrival of Oliveira and the financial queries given to the local administrators about diamond mining, to give a sense of the riches of Diamantina. As to be expected in the chronology of the master narrative, scenes 15 through 17 expose the frustration of Xica based on her prohibition from entering the church, while scenes 18 to 22 expose the emotional weaknesses of Xica as she copes with aspirations and even prophesies concerning her uncertain future; scenes 23 through 27 concern the arrival of the Count and the disarray that puts both Oliveira and Xica through even more emotional distress. The final two scenes document the paradoxical lamentations of Oliveira about Portugal (as exile or as home) as well as Xica's humiliation upon the loss of her co-dependent source of power: Oliveira. Many of these scenes have been created by Abreu as a measure to re-invent the mythology of Xica in order to include aspects that put her in touch with Afro-Brazilian mythology and dignity. Of these creative scenes, both normative and deviational, Xica's frustration and questioning of the value of her freedom letter is worth analyzing as appropriately captured by scene 16's title, "Of what value is a manumission letter?":

XICA: What is it worth? What is the point of the freedom you gave me? Tear it up, Cabeça, tear it!

João: No! You need to understand that no one can have it all.

XICA: Xica is neither the same as the black miner who spends many years looking for precious stones, nor is she the black woman of the slave quarters who is saving up copper in order to buy just her manumission so as not to be a slave. That is way too little for Xica.

João: I gave you well more than that, Xica. Be fair. (Abreu, 51)

Abreu has painstakingly recreated Xica's life with an ideological focus on her representation as a conscious strategist, not as a victim of her exploited sexuality.

Of the many versions and revisions of the grand historical narrative about Xica da Silva, Carlos Diegues's *Xica da Silva* (1976) is unquestionably the most widely known, and follows Xica's trajectory from slave, to colonial power-broker, to public disgrace. Citing an allegory used by Diegues himself, Randal Johnson notes that Xica da Silva is "a multi-colored glass butterfly resting on a solemn wall of a colonial church,"[21] evoking at once the "fragile" and fragmented nature of Xica's being in relation to acceptance and rejection by the ultimate symbol of colonial repression: the Catholic Church. The question is: will the "glass butterfly" fly, or will it fall from the church wall and be crushed underfoot? Regardless of the interpretation, Diegues's *Xica da Silva* is a political satire that ridicules the excesses of colonial Brazil while exemplifying a case of love in exchange for freedom. In the Afro-Brazilian context, the notion of a heroine glorified for only a short moment is counterproductive in the final analysis. The achievements of Xica may be compared to those of the Afro-cultural social movements that organize events such as Carnival and Capoeira dances as a reversed ideological response to the repression in their daily living. Lavished with palatial homes, ships, and even a number of her own slaves, Xica's possessions are actually Oliveira's; when her lover leaves for Portugal, she loses his love and the position that has given her life meaning. Filled with symbolism and allegories such as the Carnival pageant that ushered her only to the gate of the church, where she was ultimately barred from entering; the banquet prepared in honor of Count Valadares which, while successful as a statement of "revenge" over colonial oppressors, ultimately failed to save her from tragic humiliation at the end; and finally, her reduction to a community nuisance—all attest to the "farce" that the life of Xica was. Xica's reality is a love-hate relationship that betrays the contradictions of Brazilian colonial system. Ultimately, Diegues may have reinforced an unhelpful stereotype of black women in the process of popularizing the drama of Xica da Silva even if overall it makes a larger statement about race relations and power dynamics in both colonial and contemporary Brazil. Diegues's version may have been intended to embarrass the military dictatorship by suggesting that even the most powerful and oppressive systems can be manipulated by a clever woman with nothing to lose. If this was a message directed to the minority of Brazilians in 1976, the filmmaker may have achieved some ambiguous political point.

The 1996 soap opera about Xica went a little further by popularizing Xica in Brazilian households, but tainted her with the same stereotypical images of a simultaneously beloved and wounded heroine.

Allegory of Brazilian National Identity?

By her subversive and heroic acts, Xica inadvertently established herself as a symbol of Brazilian national identity. This critical appraisal is based on her actions in the face of oppression in the colonial Brazilian state of Minas Gerais. Despite using her body, she transcends the limits of power established for black women, and most especially for slaves who lacked power over their lives or their bodies. The black body of Xica was sexualized and miscegenated for the sake of freedom. Could it not represent a larger allegory of Brazilian nationalism? In this context, Oliveira represents the colonial authority, and Xica is an object of colonial desire, just like the gold and the diamonds of Minas Gerais. When all is said and done, Xica is both a victim and a villain in the perpetration of overarching sexuality and proactive submission to the will of the other, subconsciously or otherwise. In conceptualizing Xica's body as miscegenated tool in the hands of the colonial human machinery, we have unveiled the masks of history in order to understand the apprehensions of Afro-Brazilian identity before and after abolition of slavery.

Chapter 4

Manuel Querino

African Contributions to Brazil

"To speak the truth, the development of Brazil depended primarily on the backs of blacks."

—Manuel Querino

Of Preambles and Dislocations

The Yoruba proverbial saying that "*odo ti ko ba mo orisun re, yi o gbe laipe ojo,*" that is, "the river deprived of its knowledge source will dry up swiftly," speaks to the undeniable fact that Africa is inextricably linked to the formation of Brazilian identity in all its manifestations and ramifications. Yet the discourses on Latin American hybridity have minimized the significant impact of Africa in that cultural contact zone by encouraging the propaganda of racial harmony, a mythological state of racelessness, and nonracism while fundamentally masking the contentious terrains of struggle for institutional, economical, and cultural equality among different races. In this chapter, through the analysis of select works of Manuel Querino and the questioning of hybridity as a political and cultural construction, I propose that the reversal of perpetual dis(locations) in African diaspora discourses that emanate from myopic rendering and simplification of complex cultural realities and contexts must begin with a close examination of the contributions of each racialized group in order to better understand the extent of the strategic contribution of every race, and the deliberate marginalization of African diaspora voices in Brazil's continuously problematic racial democracy.

Manuel Querino was a formidable Afro-Brazilian asset and a neglected abolitionist in terms of Brazilian intellectual history and cultural reclamation, and I argue that the neglect of this intellectual by Brazilian mainstream intelligentsia is deliberate and racist. Recent efforts to reverse this unfortunate state of affairs (for example, by commemorating the 160th anniversary of Querino's birth in 2011) suggest that the Brazilian intellectual elites of the nineteenth century would rather see Manuel Querino's works as "folkloric" manifestations than rigorous academic inquiry and historical documentation of Afro-Brazilian life, letters, culture, and customs. While a few scholars[1] from virtually distinct academic spheres (anthropology, history, literary criticism, cultural studies) have attempted to "rescue" this erudite scholar, an interdisciplinary and more rewarding approach is yet to be deployed in order to recuperate the lasting legacies of Manuel Querino, whose contributions are indeed comparable to those by such leading and contemporary African-American intellectuals as W.E.B. Du Bois, Booker T. Washington, and Martin Luther King Jr., even if they are not contemporaries.

A rather peculiar aspect of Manuel Querino's afterlife lies in his expert fictionalization by Jorge Amado in *Tenda dos Milagres* (Tent of Miracles). Through an interdisciplinary approach, this study overlaps intellectual history with the literary and the cultural in order to re-historicize Brazilian culture from a miscegenation prism. While Manuel Querino did in fact exist in historical terms, Pedro Archanjo, the fictional character created by Amado in *Tenda dos Milagres*, is an invention of the foremost Latin American writer. Although African contributions to Brazil have been documented by colonial and contemporary authors, Jorge Amado remains the most persistent curator of such African relics in his regionalist works. Amado's knowledge of Afro-Brazilian religious rites has equally been reflected in such works as *Jubiabá, Mar Morto* (Sea of Death), *Capitães de Areia* (Captains of the Sand) *Tenda dos Milagres* (Tent of Miracles), and *Os Pastores da Noite* (Pastors of the Night) where aspects of Candomblé and religious symbolic actions are woven into the daily fabric of the people. Despite persecutions from the police of the colonial and post-abolition era, Amado proves in these works, especially in *Tenda dos Milagres*, that the miscegenated figure is rather a myth than an accepted model of Latin American or Brazilian identity.

The dislocation of "captive" souls from mother Africa, the subsequent displacement and recuperation of cultural values in the New

World, and the attendant confusion and reconstruction of fragmented selves form part of the history of the African continent (within and without its immediate shores) that has been reconfigured by the very reality of the horrendous process of the Atlantic Middle Passage and enslavement. Beyond the traumas of slavery and the gradual process of dehumanization and marginalization, the balance sheet of African diaspora discourses—from Pan-Africanism, Double Consciousness, and Afrocentricity, to Black Atlanticism—lies in the necessity to form a progressive coalition of recuperative identities that does not hesitate to confront the past and embrace the present while critiquing both past and present, and ultimately formulating a cohesive mindset despite differences and further disjunctures that have been created as a wedge that encourages things to "fall apart" rather than for them to come together. Any conscious peregrine African researcher in the Americas and the Caribbean can easily note the air of solidarity and dismay with which the dislocated African (diasporan) eyes a fellow brother or sister, as if first to lament why we were separated in the first place and then to wonder quite frustratedly if brothers and sisters could ever come back to be united again in the midst of mounting challenges that keep us divided, alienated, confused, and untrusting of each other. Despite this odd opposition of mutual suspicion with fraternal and unconditional love, we must look beyond appearances and reach out into what I call "lasting monumental legacies" of resistant minds and souls.

Manuel Querino was one such lasting monumental legacy, mind, and soul in his quest to document the place of Africa in Afro-Brazilian arts, cultures, and history. He not only sought to leave an indelible imprint on his era through scholarship and intellectually rigorous historicism, he also endeavored to reach out to the white establishment by educating them, through his research and publications, on the extensive contributions of Africa to Brazilian culture and civilization. Born in Santo Amaro in the Recôncavo Baiano in 1851, and dying in 1923, Manuel Querino was an active participant in the struggle for better conditions of black workers as well as for the institutionalization of workers' rights generally in the nineteenth century. As a "neglected" abolitionist, Manuel Querino's legacy is yet to be adequately appraised, though he fought tirelessly to guarantee freedom, equality, and justice for all Afro-Brazilians of his time and beyond. As an activist, educator, fine artist, painter, politician, anthropologist, and ethnographer, Querino has to his credit over forty publications on Afro-Brazilian affairs, embracing history, artistry, cuisine, religion, archeology, folklore, and theater, to highlight just the most obvious. He wrote on virtually every subject matter of note in Afro-Brazilian history and letters, and deserves the special place he received in the fictional world of Jorge Amado, who dedicated an entire creative work, *Tenda dos Milagres*, to Querino's life and memory.

Querino took issue with Eurocentric bias of Brazilian history and identity. His contributions can be summed up as follows: (1) he narrated Afro-Brazilian history from the perspective of the subject and not as an object defined by the Other; (2) he consciously exposed and documented the cultural values, customs, traditions, aspirations, frustrations, and hopes of Afro-Brazilians in their multifaceted perspectives; (3) he rescued the voices of prominent local intellects and community leaders whose knowledge base is fundamental for the archival repository of historical data for future generations; (4) he questioned and ridiculed the persecution of Afro-Brazilian religions by the power of the state (as represented by the police) by restating the validity and relevance of Africa-derived religions in Brazil; (5) he bridged the many races, classes, and belief systems by explicating the value in coexistence and mutual respect of value systems; (6) he demanded that mainstream Brazilian elites recognize the huge debt owed to Africa and acted to restore and quantify this debt toward possible redress; and (7) he insisted on rewriting Brazilian historiography by embracing African contributions as part of national heritage and cultural patrimony. These summations are just that—icing on the cake of the wholesome relevance and significance of Querino's monumental legacy as the very first Afro-Brazilian historian of note and a perceptive cultural critic. To date, no historian, Afro-Brazilian or otherwise, has given Querino's wealth of archival information and perspectives the adequate attention it deserves in order to better understand Afro-Brazilian life, times, and culture. Writing at a time when Africa was not only a source of persecution of the remaining relics of memory in Brazilian history, Manuel Querino represents the thorn in the flesh of the Brazilian intelligentsia of the nineteenth century.

Manuel Querino's investigations sought to be abreast of political and cultural matters, including issues regarding labor disputes and civil rights, with a recurrent focus on African contributions to Brazilian thought, culture, and identity formation. Beyond the documentary value of his historical research and writing, Querino succeeded in exploring the myriad layers of interest regarding Afro-Brazilian affairs—from ethnography to the biography of Bahian artists, he inadvertently ensured that his work was lasting and that no research could be conducted on any of Afro-Brazilian subject matter without consulting his works. In so doing, Querino may well be a cultural archivist and art curator of the Bahian and, by extension, Brazilian intellectual landscape of the nineteenth century and early twentieth century.

As an ethnographer and cultural researcher, Querino was meticulous and systematic. A cursory look at his scholarly corpus reveals a pattern: his seminal works started out as reflections on a given subject matter, and progressed via presentations at scholarly meetings and shorter publications before finally culminating in book-length publications. *A Raça Africana e os Seus Costumes na Bahia* is a good example of this strategic methodology. First published in 1918 under the above title and later expanded as *Costumes Africanos no Brasil*, a quick comparison indicates that the contents were not only revised, they were thought through in order to develop the topic even further. By adjusting the title from a focus on Bahia to one encompassing all Brazil, Querino suggests that the whole of Brazil shares the experience of being black by virtue of Afro-Brazilians living anywhere in Brazil and being conscious of their African roots.

In no other discussion is mention of dislocation more appropriate than when it concerns displaced Africans in the diaspora who seek to recuperate what shifted from a concrete experience before enslavement to an abstract idea after enslavement. For Doris Kearns Goodwin,[2] displacement is the act or process of dislocating or the state of having been dislocated. She elaborates by suggesting that by dislocation she refers specifically to "the severe emotional dislocation experienced by millions of immigrants who were forced to separate themselves forever from the circle of people and places on which they had depended." In this context, Querino reverses the historical dislocation and disempowerment of Afro-Brazilians by using the power of research and dissemination to confront the white racist establishment of nineteenth-century Brazil. The process of reversing dislocations is, however, laden with various structural hindrances that often sabotage efforts at re-vindication and reparation by the very power of the hegemonic and white minority establishment, be it in Brazil or elsewhere in Latin America.

In his bibliographical essay on Manuel Querino, perhaps the most precise in the English language to date, E. Bradford Burns notes that Querino's contribution lies in his "efforts to assess the role the Africans played in the formation of Brazil" because it would be impossible to understand Brazil without this significant aspect of Brazilian history.[3] Along those same lines of praise, Maria das Graças de Andrade Leal, in her recent work *Manuel Querino: Entre Letras e Lutas—Bahia 1851–1923* (Manuel Querino: Between Words and Struggles, Bahia 1851–1923), argues that Querino's background as a black Brazilian man and laborer gave him a firsthand appreciation of the situation of the arts in relation to education as well as artists in relation to the new republic that claimed to be in favor of civilization and progress. For Leal, Querino "opened four major fronts of struggle and debate by articulating issues of labor, education, active party politics, and intellectual production."[4] Beyond these four lines[5] of struggle, Querino also expressed his indignation against the contradictions of republican ideals, especially regarding issues of race and class that affected workers who were primarily blacks and biracials in nineteenth-century Brazil. Drawing on empirical data, social memory, and ethnography, Querino argues that while African descendants contributed to the formation of Brazilian identity, they were often excluded from political participation and power. For Querino, the game of negation and negotiation was inevitable in order to dialogue with an establishment that was at worst hostile, racist, and uncompromising, and at best only sympathetic to the extent that Afro-Brazilians knew and were content with their second-class position in the society. Singlehandedly, through scholarly dissemination, Querino researched and defended Afro-Brazilian life and culture at a time when doing so brought the risk of being stigmatized for challenging the official position about Africa and its descendants. Querino thus made a name for himself as the first Afro-Brazilian cultural historian.

Manuel Querino did not escape critiques and criticisms alike, despite a worthy political and academic career that placed him side by side with eminent Pan-Africanists and civil rights activists who came much later. In a sense, Querino was a pioneer Pan-Africanist and civil rights activist *avant la lettre*. Considering him as a journalist and politician in his occasional paper *Manuel Querino: O Jornalista e o Político*[5] (Manuel Querino: The Journalist and the Politician), Jorge Calmon provides a balanced perspective on the legacy of Querino as a political analyst and public intellectual of his time. Citing Querino's most authoritative work on the African retention/contribution thesis later developed by Melville Herskovits,[6] *O Colono Preto como Fator da Civilização Brasileira*[7] (The Colonized African as a Factor in Brazilian History), Calmon argues that although Querino did his best within the circumstances he confronted, the odds against him were such that he could have done even better had he emerged at a time when the political climate was less hostile to his revolutionary ideals about workers' rights and racial equality. Querino's

legacy may be tainted by the very context of institutional and intellectual racism in the sense that what he had to say was an affront to the
establishment. He was the anomaly, the black intellectual exception to
the rule of African backwardness and mediocrity. Some of the critiques
leveled against Querino are rather flimsy and far-fetched, such as the
controversy about his claim that blacks were the major developers of
Brazil in terms of national unity and identity. Without the free, skilled,
and unskilled labor provided by the black race, there would have been no
so-called cosmic race, the misleading concept of a "racial paradise," or the
misplaced theory of "miscegenation." Regardless of the reservations, the
works of Querino are undoubtedly monumental and seminal, and paved
the way for further illuminations and insights in Afro-Brazilian studies.

     Edison Carneiro, in comparing Querino to Nina Rodrigues and
Arthur Ramos, inappropriately labeled Querino as an "insignificant little
public functionary,"[8] thus betraying subjective judgments that must have
been influenced by the fame and visibility already enjoyed by these Brazilian thinkers. Needless to say, Edison Carneiro saw, in both Rodrigues
and Ramos, models for Brazilian cultural anthropology that did not align
with the ethnographic methodologies of Querino. Carneiro may well have
dubbed Querino a "folklorist" through his critique, but the issue extends
beyond intellectual rigor, to racist bias. According to Carneiro: "Worse
than Nina was Manuel Querino, who did not even know about these
divisions among blacks from Africa. He just went around announcing
everything he saw with his characteristic lack of intelligence [. . .], and
juvenile explanations in the ethnography and social psychology of blacks."[9]
The question for the curious mind is not so much the validity of the
methodology deployed by Querino but whether his contributions are
lasting and worthy of study. While criticism is part of intellectual debate
and growth, it does appear that the critics of Querino simply wanted
to see him silenced and marginalized. Without the sheer volume of his
seminal essays, some of which have now been edited and compiled into
a book, potential researchers would have nowhere to start in regards to
Afro-Brazilian studies in the nineteenth century.

Reversing (Dis)locations

Afro-Brazilian thought has been marred by a mix of myths, stereotypes,
and misrepresentations based on the perspective of a white establishment bent on discrediting black contributions to Brazilian intellectual

history. From the erroneous myth of black backwardness and ignorance as propagated by enslavers, to institutional racism propagated by the white intelligentsia that sought to minimize black contribution, as in the Lusotropicalist myth of Gilberto Freyre, much disservice has been done to the legitimacy of Afro-Brazilian thought. Manuel Querino, in the company of such eminent theorists as Nina Rodrigues, Edison Carneiro, Florestan Fernandes, and Roger Bastide, adopts an ethnographical model in order to comprehensively document Afro-Brazilian thought systems. In so doing, his scholarly corpus, in quantity and in quality, represents an undeniable contribution to the elaboration of the Afro-Brazilian way of life. It is interesting that dislocations have emanated not only from white Brazilian intellectuals but also from black or mulatto sources as a measure to divide and conquer, such as the allegation of the "insignificance" of Manuel Querino credited to Edison Carneiro. Despite these fragmented reflections on a state of affairs that calls for redress rather than for continued negation of African contributions in the broader scope of Brazilian identity formation, in challenging these dislocating hypotheses it is rewarding to highlight the essential contributions of Manuel Querino to Afro-Brazilian thought.

Unlike cultural theorists who came to prominence after his death (such as Brazilian Gilberto Freyre and Cuban Fernando Ortiz), Manuel Querino sought to preserve African cultural essences, consciousness, practices, and sensibilities by systematically documenting the Afro-Brazilian way of life within a rather denigrating, racialized, and hostile context. As a pioneer ethnographer and "cultural anthropologist," Querino faced the odds of educating an intransigently racist society, even in the nineteenth century, the so-called post-abolition era. By the time Freyre and Ortiz emerged in the twentieth century, the Latin American intelligentsia had had time to assimilate shifting liberal ideas from Europe such as those contained in the discourses of modernism and modernities. While Freyre and Ortiz sought to explicate the insignificance of race in the larger context of national identity, hence creating more ambiguities than solving social problems, Querino pragmatically engaged issues of racial polarities and inequalities while exposing African contributions in order to appeal to a need for inclusion and confrontation of a dilemma toward concrete solutions in racial relations. Querino sought to empower descendants who, to date, have been subjected to the horrors of enslavement and its aftermath by insisting on workers' rights, including access to educational opportunities, access to political participation, organization, and representation through the prism of African-derived values geared toward challenging the white hegemony and status quo. Querino saw in Africa a concrete possibility to conceptualize power and pride as the basis to recuperate a lost sense of Afro-Brazilian self and historic past. Undaunted by the label of "folklorist" of Africa in the Americas, he forged on to greater heights by producing a vast ensemble of works that will remain fundamental to the understanding of Afro-Brazilian cultural history in the nineteenth century and beyond.

By all conventional standards of historical and empirical evaluation of Querino's works, his contributions are primarily connected to the struggle for emancipation, the labor movement, and the quests for individual autonomy/self-empowerment and social development. His own life story resonates with the lives of many Afro-Brazilians. His parents were manual laborers (his father was a carpenter, his mother a laundress) who lost their lives to the cholera epidemic of 1855 when he was barely four years old. Adopted and trained by historian Manuel Correia Garcia, who founded the Provincial Institute of History, Querino was recruited by the Brazilian army at the age of seventeen to serve during the Brazil-Paraguay war. It was then convenient to serve in the army, as slaves were offered their freedom in exchange for military service. In 1871, Querino returned to Salvador where he started studying the humanities and the arts in general at the Liceu de Artes e Ofícios at night while working during the day as a painter of churches, theaters, and buildings. Querino was exposed to ideas on abolitionism and republicanism and was later to become active in and leader of the Bahian Liberation Society because he was disillusioned with lack of social change in the post-abolition era. He was particularly troubled by the Brazilian policies of miscegenation and whitening, which led to the immigration of Europeans from Europe while freed slaves were treated with disdain and impunity. Querino gained some political experience by serving as city councilman from 1890 to 1891, serving the interests of the labor movement. He was reputed for fighting political corruption, and some of his measures to fight for the poorly represented resulted in the establishment of a number of institutions, including the Centro Operário (Worker's Center) and Instituto Geográfico e Histórico da Bahia (Geographical and Historical Society of Bahia) in 1894. Overall, Querino challenged the pervasive provincial notions of "high" and "low" cultures by focusing on popular expressions of African culture in Brazil as valid and integrative parts of Brazilian civilization.

In his discussion of Querino's contribution to Afro-Brazilian thought, Antônio Sérgio Alfredo Guimarães suggests that the gap between North American and Brazilian scholarship in the social sciences dates back to the nineteenth century, in the sense that African American thought had been established by the 1880s, whereas in Brazil, it would not be until the 1950s before such a field could be considered fully formed.[10] As a consequence, based on the quality and quantity of his ethnographic Afro-Brazilian studies, Querino can be considered a social scientist well ahead of his time. Elevating Querino to the level of W.E.B. Du Bois, Guimarães saw in his works and academic trajectory the capacity to understand Brazil as a mixed-raced country through which blackness or negritude could be better appreciated as compared to the French Caribbean notion of negritude, or even that of the "New Negro" in the United States—all of which are further differentiated by the "Negrismo" of white Latin American intellectuals. In addition to exploring Querino's engagement and rejection of *branqueamento* (whitening), Guimarães takes the position that Querino used his emphasis on ethnicity as a strategy to make integration more inclusive. Questioning the tendency at the time to see all black intellectuals as "journalists" as a reductionist way to suggest they were less than sophisticated, Guimarães sees in Querino a competent scholar whose issue was primarily civil and labor rights. The author sums up Querino's republican ideas as follows: (1) expansive and popular autonomy; (2) respect for constitutional rights; and (3) regrouping of the members of the Old Regime to demand equality and citizenship. In the final analysis, Querino must be seen as a pioneer in the legitimization of the significant role of Africans in the formation of Brazilian identity.[11] In his daunting scholarship and oppositional political agitations, Querino clearly made it a point of duty to humanize Afro-Brazilians with all their limitations and contradictions.

Querino may be seen as a precursor to Abdias do Nascimento, the foremost Afro-Brazilian statesman whose concept of *Quilombismo* has garnered volatile reactions from many intellectual quarters, especially with regard to the blatant rejection of the myth of racial democracy in Brazil and a call for a more inclusive paradigm that does not negate or denigrate blackness. Yet it is quite curious that Nascimento would not engage Querino in his seminal article, "African Culture in Brazilian Art."[12] Nascimento has been the erstwhile champion of Afro-Brazilian civil rights in the twentieth century and in his body of works, on everything from political thought to artistry, theater, and poetry, the grandfather activist embodies the most cogent and the very best in the defense of the rights of Afro-Brazilians. One cannot but wonder about the motivations and implications of this omission of Manuel Querino in the discussion of Afro-Brazilian art and the place of Africa in it—a subject well-engaged and documented by Querino. That Nascimento was more interested in twentieth-century artists or did not find any merit in Querino's work is neither here nor there in the sense that the essay was a historical analysis that reviews works from the Portuguese "discovery" of Brazil in the 1500s through the present day.

Nascimento's essay, published in 1978 in one of the foremost learned journals in black studies, *Journal of Black Studies*, had the opportunity to champion the contributions of Manuel Querino—in fact no other rationale for his omission exists other than the fact that Nascimento was a Pan-Africanist and was, even as early as the 1970s,[13] considered an Afro-Brazilian icon and hero. The main thrusts of Nascimento's essay may be summed up as follows: (1) arguments against the assimilationist policy of miscegenation that in practice veiled racial discrimination, exclusion, and racism itself; (2) incisive invocation of Candomblé (Afro-Brazilian religion) as the main source of Afro-Brazilian arts; (3) recognition of Afro-Brazilian dances as a continuum of African rhythms, rituals, and ceremonies brought to Brazil by slaves; (4) recognition of the place of music in the Afro-Brazilian daily experience of reenacting "stylized suffering" as a measure to ultimately free the body of the trauma of slavery; (5) recognition of Yoruba influence in Afro-Brazilian literature based on works by Afro-Brazilian writers such as Jorge Amado and Antônio Olinto; and finally (6) a self-portrait of sorts, given his own personal investment and involvement in Afro-Brazilian theater (Experimental Black Theater) as well as film—thus completing the trajectory of the essential contributions of Africans to Brazilian literary, religious, and cultural history.

In critically assessing these cogent overviews of African contributions to Brazil as competently articulated by Nascimento, it is still puzzling that Manuel Querino is neither a footnote nor a significant entry but a symbolic passing mention, despite the abundance and quality of his artistic/ethnographic legacy and accomplishments. In view of Nascimento's esteemed position, I can only assume this unusual omission was simply inadvertent and not deliberate as in joining the biased white establishment to minimize Querino's contribution.

From African Contributions to Querino's Legacy

Any discussion of African contribution to Brazilian civilization is confronted by a counter-argument that such a quest for the Herskovitsian retention thesis usually leads not only to an "essentialist" argument, but also to a "separatist" orientation. When discourses of racial democracy, racial paradise, racial harmony, and miscegenation are advanced in different contexts, little attention is paid to the "essentialist" argument that all Brazilians are living an illusion of a harmonious society where racial tensions are minimal if not nonexistent. Yet much evidence abounds that the myth of racial democracy is far from being eradicated from the official and unofficial quarters of the Brazilian intelligentsia. Manuel Querino may have been marginalized and neglected, but his contribution to correcting the myopia of Brazilian intellectual elites of the nineteenth century, and even today, is far-reaching and must not be minimized.

In his fascinating, yet ultimately disappointing, study "After Racial Democracy,"[14] Antônio Guimarães offers a refreshing perspective on "racial democracy" in Brazil by putting forth the thesis that although Brazilians recognize the failure of "racial democracy" to adequately represent the reality of social inequalities, black political organizations are also not equipped to reverse the state of things even when empowered by the state to do so. While Guimarães's essay is provocative, it fails to move beyond the ambivalences and ambiguities that end up confounding, rather than providing, solutions to social problems. In this regard, Manuel Querino's contributions are unparalleled in the hostile nineteenth-century context. An in-depth analysis of some of his seminal works reveals a seasoned and methodical intellectual who sought to disprove the a priori thesis that Africans had no culture and could not have contributed anything to Brazilian civilization. Rather, according to the racist argument, Africans should be "grateful" for being uprooted from their motherland and brought to Brazil to be enslaved.

Within this expository exercise, I limit myself to five works by Querino, namely, O Colono Preto como Fator da Civilização Brasileira (The Colonized African as a Factor in Brazilian History), A Bahia de Outrora (Bahia of the Past), A Raça Africana e os Seus Costumes na Bahia (The African Race and their Customs in Bahia), Artistas Bahianos (Bahian Artists), and A Arte Culinária na Bahia (The Culinary Art in Bahia). Written at different phases of Querino's career, these works speak to the dynamism of African descendants in Brazil as they negotiate racism and education in order to liberate themselves from the fangs of slavery and capitalist exploitation of mind, body, and soul. For most of the African descendants documented by Querino, all they had left was their resolve not to be mentally enslaved and to use their intelligence to combat the stereotypes and mythologies that had bound them physically and psychologically for many centuries. And this is the crux of the legacy of Querino. By not only showcasing the African descendants as laborers, but also exposing their skilled and unskilled areas of productivity, he presents a balanced perspective of African contributions to the making of Brazil, from colony to nation-state. In fighting to correct the eronneous claim that it was Brazil who "saved" Africans from Africa through slavery, Querino went a long way toward exposing this hypocrisy by intellectually and evidentially challenging the government of the time. E. Bradford Burns observes that Querino resented the deterioting state of African descendants as the Brazilian government diverted funds to European immigration at the expense of the newly freed slaves who needed help to adjust to the new dispensation of freedom and subsequent economic and social dependence. According to Burns:

> Always aware of condition in Africa, Querino noted ironially that Edward VII treated his subejcts in the distant African colonies better than the Brazilian president did his fellow black citizens. The lack of educational opportunities in Brazil figured as a constant theme in his writing. He attributed the lowly status of the black in Brazilian society to that lack. In short, he concluded, only education could bring about the final, the definitive, emancipation of the black.[15]

It goes without saying that Querino's contribution or legacy would not be an issue for debate if not for the continued racism in Brazilian society that has now regressed back into the intellectual arena from which it originated.

In six systematic chapters (with a preface written by celebrated Brazilian cultural anthropologist Arthur Ramos), Querino offers the reader in O Colono Preto como Fator da Civilização Brasileira (1918) an intimate portrait of the African descendant, not as a passive individual in the course of history, but as an active agent of Brazilian development and nation-building. One must note a strategic posture of theoretical carnivalization at work in this seminal treatise. First, Querino portrayed the African descendant as the "colonizer," not the "colonized." Second, Querino saw in the African descendant a "civilizing" agent, not the barbaric figure that he had been portrayed to be. The first chapter, "Portugal no Meado do Século XVI" (Portugal in the Mid-Sixteenth Century), invokes the works of such eminent writers of the time as Latino Coelho, General Abreu e Lima, Guerra Junqueiro, and Rocha Pombo to suggest that the Portuguese were pathetic colonizers despite their so-called achievements in Asia and Africa. For Querino, the Portuguese were not only incompetent colonizers, they failed to develop the arts, sciences, and industry-intense areas such as agriculture; rather, they were apt at enslaving unsuspecting populations—an endeavor facilitated by bringing criminals and mediocrities to administer their colonial machinery. Consequently, their so-called "colonized" turned the tables on them by their sheer intelligence by ending up craftily colonizing Brazil, strategically, culturally, and spiritually.

If the first chapter is provocative, the second, "Chegada do Africano no Brasil, Suas Habilitações" (Arrival of Africans in Brazil, Their Skills), is even more daring. Querino advances a few more theories, citing expatriate scholars such as Stanley, Capelo, and Ivans[16] who suggest that Africans, well before being uprooted from their comfort zone, had been well-equipped workers in hunting, sailing, cattle rearing, salt extraction, mineral mining, and ivory marketing, among other pursuits. Consequently, it is arguable that contrary to the colonial portrayal of African descendants as "lazy" and "unskilled," one could conclude they were in fact skilled and proud laborers content in cultivating high working standards and ethics in managing their own land—unlike the Portuguese adventurers who were more freeloaders, parasites, and conquerers, and who left a catalog of brutality, oppression, and exploitation during and after their (un)successful colonization of Africans and their descendants in the New World.

The work's remaining three chapters detail how African descendants reacted to the brutal colonial-enslavement state of affairs characterized by torture and total disregard for human life in the process of economic exploitation and dehumanization. Chapter 3, "Primeiras Idéias da Liberdade, o Suicídio e a Eliminação Violenta dos Senhorios" (First Ideas of Freedom, Suicide, and Violent Elimination of the Masters), addresses the frequent outbursts of violence against the masters by the slaves as a normal reaction (counterviolence) to a primordial violence perpetrated by the European colonizer. In addition, slaves were prone to suicidal impulses as a form of resistance and protest in which death was preferable to suffering and humiliation. To demonstrate a typical oppressive situation of the slave, Querino observes: "A slave who is hand-chained and at times even neck-chained without any food or water, while these nutritious elements are deliberately placed in front of himso that rodents eat at his feet, is compelled to seek a form of revenge to alleviate his victim status."[17] Such a succinct description confirms that the slave was not merely a passive participant but a rational, thinking, and calculating participant, looking for every opportunity to set himself free by any means necessary.

In chapter 4, "Resistência Coletiva, Palmares, Levantes Parciais" (Collective Resistance, Palmares, Partial Upliftment), Querino invokes a different model of resistance—steering away from violence to a more mutually strategic essence of collaborative freedom, as captured in the *quilombo*[18] model. Drawing on the writings of Oliveira Vienna, Rocha Pombo, and Caldas Brito, Querino presented the *quilombo* as a far more sophisticated form of governmental organization than any colonial structure had believed Africans and African descendants capable of. The resolve of freedom is further accentuated in chapter 5, "Juntas para as Alforrias" (Freedom Juntas). In these juntas slaves actually raised money to buy their own freedom through organized labor, ethical imperative, and unparalleled perseverance. In the final chapter, "O Africano na Família, Seus Descendentes Notáveis" (Africans in the Family, Their Notable Descendants), Querino pays homage to African descendants who not only resisted slavery but also paved the way for a possible thesis on nation identity. Whether Querino believed in the concept of miscegenation or not, it is clear that he was particular about unreservedly recognizing African contributions to the construction of Brazilian identity in all its manifestations.

In A *Bahia de Outrora* (1946), volume three in the Livraria Progresso Press series on Brazilian Studies, Querino brings together a number of short stories, essays, and anecdotes about daily life and African traditions in Bahia of the nineteenth century, particularly in Salvador. Comparable to yet different from Jorge Amado's later cultural landscape book, *Bahia de Todos os Santos* (1977), Querino appears to be interested in the workings of society from the many perspectives of family, work, social gatherings, spirituality, and cultural expressions. In a catalog of popular festivities, from Christmas, Capoeira, "Noite dos Reis" (Kings' Nights), Bonfim, Carnival, and Yemoja (sea goddess), to family traditions and rituals such as special dinners and police patrols, coupled with mundane observations on such varied topics as the Business Association of Bahia, superstitions, and lithographs and engravings, Querino details an expansive range of subject matter that makes for a rich encyclopedia of Salvador's way of life in the nineteenth century. Despite the appearance of folklore, the lives of the people are intertwined in these popular events so much that the observer becomes a participant as well. Querino may lack the poetic finesse of Jorge Amado, but his observations are incisive and detailed.

In his description of a Christmas day, for example, Querino compares the preparations for the event to the genius of *Auto de Natal* by Gil Vicente. Even today in Salvador, Bahia, I personally have witnessed Christmas plays staged by common folk, students, workers, and children throughout the month of December in Pelourinho—a central cultural industrial location for tourists and researchers. The air of celebration is mixed with the spirit of harvesting captured in the coloring of fruits as if making an sacrifice in recognition of the blessings of the passing year. The excitement is captured in one of the stanzas that punctuate Querino's narration:

> Sky decorated with little stars
> Stars made of paper
> White clouds invented
> With cotton wings
> Angels hanging in the air
> Fish popping out of the sea.[19]

While Christmas is not particularly an ethnic event, Querino must have noted the overwhelming presence of blacks in these public performances. Even when the actors are not blacks, they paint themselves black, which resonates with the blackface mistrelsy tradition in African American culture. Querino appears to have found his scholarly or vocational niche in his documentation of these African traditions that indicate an African way of life and the adaptation of African descendants in Brazilian culture and tradition.

Comparatively, *A Raça Africana e os Seus Costumes na Bahia* (1918), published three decades before *A Bahia de Outrora* (1946), provides a far more incisive depiction of African-derived customs and traditions in Bahia. A quick review of the contents reveals the following fascinating themes: "In African Backlands," "Fetish Religion," "The Orixás," "New

Yam," "Ifa Divination," "Foretelling or Divining," "Rumors," "Offering to One's Head," "Santa Barbara's Stone," "Trading One's Head/Destiny," "Sacrifice," "A Candomblé Initiate," "Legend," "Characteristics of Diverse Tribes," "Funerals," "Muslim Fasting," "Caboclo Candomblé," "The African as Colonizer," "Initial Ideas of Freedom," "The African Family," "Arrival of Africans in Brazil," and "Colored People in History." By virtue of the diversity of topics touching on African rites and ceremonies, some of which were later developed as occasional papers, such as the ones on the African as a colonizer and on the African family, it is evident that Querino was a pioneer in the use of ethnography for African studies in Brazil. The compilation includes about forty photographs illustrating some of the traditions explicated by Querino.[20]

Querino appears to have heeded the call of Reverend Father Camilo de Montserrat, who in the mid–nineteenth century called on professor Nina Rodrigues and his anthropology friends to pay serious attention to the documentation of African practices in Brazil. In his appeal, he stated: "Before the total extinction of African race in Brazil, and above all, before the different interesting and less known African cultures disappear, it would be prudent to retrieve these cultural relics from those individuals who embody these cultures that would soon be difficult to access."[21] Father Montserrat was obviously concerned that the best ethnographic information could be collected only from the very mouths of African descendants and those living in close proximity with them as opposed to travelers, prone to personal bias and error of observation and interpretation.

As a matter of methodical principle and philosophy, Querino used authentic materials such as photographs to contest and combat negative and "scientific" images of Africa and African descendants. He sought to represent the African descendant as a sophisticated and dignified human being. The book's photographs can be categorized as follows: African types or "tribes"; singers cloaked in complete African garb despite their seeming "slave" status; Felisberto Couve (an ex-king and Ifá diviner) symbols of royalty from various parts of Africa; *iyalorixás* (priestesses); women dressed in overflowing African textiles; and other miscellaneous subjects. While the captions are laconic and sometimes condensed, they offer a rare window onto the world of African descendants that may now indeed be "extinct," to use the words of Father Montserrat, except for ritual practices and ceremonies still being practiced. It is in this regard that the work of Querino needs a re-evaluation and recognition for its lasting documentary value and legacy.

In *Artistas Bahianos* (1909), Querino sought to defend the cultural and artistic patrimony of Bahia by documenting the biographies of the state's most distinguished artists. Another text, which would ideally be an accompanying one, *Artes da Bahia* (1909), equally provides essential reading for the understanding of Bahia's art history from the perspective of Querino. For our purposes, we limit this study to the artists themselves, as in *Artistas Bahianos*, in order to uncover the motivations and rationales for Querino's having chosen them (he also included himself in the compilation).[22] Methodologically, he seems to be at ease with documenting the lives and times of artists and must have been exposed to organized orders such as sisterhoods and brotherhoods. His primary method was to use oral interviews as a form of documenting historical memory, within the expected limits. Of course, there are issues, such as his being unable to identify all the artists as black or mulatto given the incompleteness of his data. While oral history is not always reliable or precise because of the passage of time, memory serves as a means of recollecting information. In each of the biographical entries, Querino provides us with rare information that may not be recovered again about parentage, lineage, patronage, and apprenticeship. Querino identified at least twenty-seven major artists and their disciples.

Through his aesthetic judgment in selecting the artists, Querino gives us a look at the way scholars handled artistic documentation during the period. Through details about artworks, Querino demonstrates his training in art hsitory at the Liceu de Artes e Ofícios and the Academic de Belas Artes in Salvador. His enthusiasm for the arts and the lives of the artists may have carried over into value judgment about certain aspects of the lives of the artists. For example, when he speaks of Cândido Alves da Souza, he states: "Troubled by not having been able to complete works entrusted to him such as the works of the Third Order of São Domingos, he lost his mind and was remanded in the João de Deus Asylum."[23] Querino's discourses reveal pertinent information that can no longer be recuperated in modern times. The Afro-Brazilian ethnographer has the facility to represent the most pertinent details of the life of an artist, such as the cases of Bento Sabino dos Reis and João Carlos do Sacramento,[24] whose works of sculpture were supposedly exhibited in Rio de Janeiro, Pernambuco, Amazonas, Pará, Ceará, Aracaju, Santa Catarina, and Rio Grande do Sul, and even abroad in England, Portugal, and France. Querino did not limit himself to the traditional but also included such nontraditional artists as inventors, medical doctors, literati, and musicians from all epochs and nationalities.

Referencing fine arts as the "touchstone of a people's civilization,"[25] Querino sets the book up as an invaluable resource for Afro-Brazilian arts, especially at a time when the biases against representation of Africa were immense. In an effort to provide a realistic representation of the period, Querino championed the representation of African descendants and Africa as if making a statement about the construction of the image of Africa in the Americas in which a counter-image was necessitated to balance the negative images. Through the gallery of artists and their works, Querino reminds us that indeed African descendants contributed to the physical, cultural, and intellectual development of Brazil.

Any casual visitor to Salvador will be fascinated by the presence of *baianas* (women wearing white African-derived garb typical of a religious rite) and similarly dressed women selling *acarajé* (bean cakes fried in palm oil and originally eaten by Yoruba-speaking people of Nigeria). Yet this is not the only delicacy that reminds one of Africa. In *Arte Culinária na Bahia*, Querino lays out a tapestry of Bahian cuisine as a gesture of recuperating African influence in Brazilian culinary arts. From drinks and plates used to venerate Orixás in the Candomblé shrines, to exotic appetizers that transport one to their origins in West Africa, Querino's manual details the preparation and significance of each item. Whether it is okra used to honor the *ibejis* (twins), *jenipapo* (a fruity alcoholic drink) used to celebrate Santo Antônio, popcorn to celebrate Omolu or Obaluaiê, Mingau, and Tapioca, Vatapá, Carurú, or Abará, among others, Querino provides an Afro-Brazilian culinary history that will remain a cogent statement on the African influence in Bahian cooking for many years to come.

Conclusion

While we cannot claim to have exhausted the issues raised by Querino in his works on African contributions to Brazilian civilization, culture, and history, we can at least surmise that in the era of constant denigration of African culture on the continent and in the diaspora, the revisitation of the relevance and legitimacy of Querino's legacy is a point of departure to reversing political and theoretical dislocations that have sabotaged the study of Africa and the African diaspora as complementary sites of contestation and convergence. The shifting dynamics of culture in the broader discourses of ownership and identity allow for a constant inter-rogation of those areas of human endeavor in which Africans and their descendants are relegated to the margins, though their true contribution is central. We cannot continue to validate alien discourses, myths, and stereotypes as we engage and recognize African culture not as an appendix of Euro-America but as a significant part of the global knowledge system.

Chapter 5

Jorge Amado's Poetic License

Fictionalizing History

In works of historical fiction, the line between verity and inventive-
ness is usually blurred to the extent that the author's intentionality is
predicated upon the value placed on contextual historical accuracies
in conjunction with that placed on such author's creative license. As
the extensive list of historical fictional works by Jorge Amado testifies,
fictionalizing history is indeed an art by itself—in which the writer
deliberately seeks to defamiliarize that which is supposedly familiar but
dislocated by the passage of time and the limits of memory. In order to
rescue fiction from history, the writer is burdened by the responsibility
of documenting without the constraints of real characters or historical or
factual events, and by the need for creative credibility and precision. In
the case of *Tenda dos Milagres* (Tent of Miracles), where Amado delves
into analogies between history, biography, and authorial license, our
challenge is to ascertain the extent to which the process of inventing
Pedro Archanjo as the alter ego of Manuel Querino in *Tenda dos Milagres*
is as easily predictable or decipherable as the complexity of writing itself.
In this chapter I argue that Amado invented Pedro Archanjo as both a
synthesis of Afro-Brazilian character as well as a political strategy to pay
homage to Manuel Querino for his contributions to the documentation
of African legacy in the formation of Brazilian identity, especially in the
context of Bahia—the same way that Amado paid homage to Castro
Alves dramaturgically in *Amor do Soldado* (The Soldier's Passion).[1] Dis-
cussing issues of the creative construction of Pedro Archanjo, specific

parallels and changes within the Amado text, Pedro Archanjo as fact and fiction, and comparative perspectives between history and fiction, this chapter sheds some light on the significance of *Tenda dos Milagres* as a historical fiction as well as a parody of Manuel Querino in order to complicate and correct the facile miscegenation image hitherto associated with him beyond his veritable perspectives as a seasoned intellectual, anthropologist, painter, militant, and community leader.

In "Manuel Querino's Interpretation of the African Contribution to Brazil," Bradford Burns notes that Amado's account is an integrated rendition of Querino's life as well as a creative deviation from that historical context: "The novelist Jorge Amado has written a fictionalized account of Querino's life entitled *Tenda dos Milagres* [. . .] It has been translated into English as *Tent of Miracles* [. . .] The novel is brilliant. In certain aspects, the book follows the basic outline of Querino's life, but Amado liberally elaborated the known facts and altered the time period."[2] As a historian, Burns did not consider it necessary, perhaps, to delve into more concrete evidence of such creative elaboration and alteration of time period that Amado deployed to achieve his brilliant masterpiece. Linda Hutcheon, in "The Politics of Postmodernism: Parody and History," would however argue that fictionalization through the power of parody can produce an aesthetic confrontation between fiction and history. For Hutcheon, then, "it is precisely parody—that seemingly introverted formalism—that paradoxically brings about a direct confrontation with the problem of the relation of the aesthetic to a world of significance external to itself, to a discursive world of socially defined meaning systems (past and present)—in other words, to ideology and history."[3]

Arguing against a repressed history of forms and citing iconic historiographic metafictions such as Salman Rushdie's *Midnight's Children*, E. L. Doctorow's *The Book of Daniel*, and metafilmic historical movies such as Peter Greenaway's *The Draughtsman's Contract*, among others, Hutcheon suggests that the success of these works is predicated on their historicity and political-ness as facilitated by the parodic narrative mode. Essentially, Hutcheon insists that postmodernism is a "fundamentally contradictory enterprise" (181) in which art forms deploy and subvert established conventions in parodic ways, thus acknowledging self-consciously the need to be inherently paradoxical and tentative in order to perform a critical re-reading of the past by subjecting that past to ridicule or contradictions. In this contextual sense, the historical past for Amado is nothing but a creative pretext to question and affirm history at the same time. Such a premise cannot but lead to us a series of questions about the motives, intentionalities, and mediations of Jorge Amado's 1969 historical fiction, *Tenda dos Milagres*. To what extent did Amado set out to represent, contradict, or question the historical past? To what extent is Pedro Archanjo a faithful or distorted rendition of Manuel Querino? What strategic criteria were set forth by the author to achieve these goals? And in the final analysis, how successful was the (mis)match between fiction and history? It is instructive that beyond the fictionalization of Manuel Querino's life, Amado had a more political agenda—which was to point out the racist outlook of the historical period in question (post-abolition) while praising the efforts and conquests of Pedro Archanjo in combatting the denigration of the African worldview in a gradually miscegenated nation that consequently sought to obliterate its own Africanness by historical design.

The Creative Construction of Pedro Archanjo

Jorge Amado must have gone through an extensive review of a series of popular stories, legal documents, testimonials, and newspaper editorials to arrive at this fragmented character better defined by the ambivalence in his assigned name: Pedro Archanjo. Combining the symbolism of "pedro" (biblical rock or foundation upon which the Church is built), and "Archanjo" (biblical Archangel, referencing the fallen angel or Lucifer), Amado may be playing with ambiguities and symbols with regard to the complex and fallacious characterization of the original Manuel Querino in a racist society. Providing a balanced perspective of the fictional Pedro Archanjo as "good and evil" was as important as portraying the implications of the innuendo and gossip in the larger context of Brazilian racism or even of racial democracy mythology. In a circular plot structure, Amado begins the narrative with the death of Pedro Archanjo, followed by an elaborate funeral procession and the subsequent arrival of the Columbia University professor, Dr. Levenson, who indeed must be read as the alter ego of Gilberto Freyre based on the fact that Freyre returned to Brazil soon after he completed his graduate studies at Columbia University—a time that also coincided with the death of Manuel Querino. These parallels are no mere fictional coincidences but ample evidence that Amado was following a pre-established timeline even if he altered some of the facts and the time period. Whether these altered details are a matter of poetic license on Amado's part or, as Hutcheon posits, a deliberate parody of historical fact, is less materially relevant than the final product in which Manuel Querino's once-neglected name is regenerated in order to dialogue with past and present mythologies about his significance and relevance to Afro-Brazilian history and culture.

Dr. Levenson's pretext in going to Brazil is to investigate and pay homage to Pedro Archanjo, a Bahian intellectual who had written a lot about Afro-Brazilian culture, remained unknown, and who, sadly and ironically, died very poor. Like Manuel Querino's many ethnographic works, Amado invoked a number of historical figures in the novel, such as Nina Rodrigues (Professor Nilo Argolo in the novel), Arthur Ramos, and the notorious Police Chief Pedro Gordilho (fictionalized as Pedrito Gordo), who was celebrated by the elites of the time for repressing Afro-Brazilian temples (*candomblés*). Many scenes in the cinematic adaptation also echo these repressive moments in Afro-Brazilian religious resistance again state oppression and police brutality. Employing the research services of a local poet and journalist in the figure of Fausto Pena, Dr. Levenson seeks to know everything possible on Pedro Archanjo. Using flashback techniques, the reader (along with Dr. Levenson) discovers many rumors and myths about Pedro Archanjo, such as the stories that he was simultaneously a hustler, drunk, intellectual, poet, womanizer, and great community leader. Creatively, Amado succeeds in bringing the complex issues of racism, police brutality, and state oppression of Afro-Brazilians to the fore by suggesting that even in death Pedro Archanjo was a hero of not only Afro-Brazilians but of all Brazilians given his demand for justice and equal rights. Amado describes the crowds that turned out to honor the funeral rites of Pedro Archanjo in the following lines, implicitly arguing for a more inclusive Brazilian society: "sing, dance, and make way: master Pedro Archanjo Ojuobá is coming through [. . .] not one but several, many, multiple: old, middle aged, young, adolescent; vagabond, dancer, fine talker, hard drinker, rebel, radical, striker, street fighter, guitar and *cavaquinho* player, wooer, tender lover, writer, sage, sorcerer. And every one of them mulatto, indigent, native of Bahia."[4] Parodying the state position on racial democracy via the position of Gilberto Freyre, Amado critiques the duplicity of the Brazilian government in sponsoring Africa-influenced popular events such as Carnival and Samba, while at the same time supporting post-dictatorial policies that repressed African culture in Brazil.

Arguably, Amado sought through the construction of Pedro Archanjo a critique of the violence leveled against African rituals and values by the white establishment represented by the police. As the text clearly shows, the protest is not only against racial mixture, but Amado also ambivalently defends religious syncretism. From the perspective of Amado or Archanjo, racial or religious mixture was not a problem per se—what was problematic were but the attitudes of the white minority system that sought to assault Africanity as a pretext for maintaining racial purity masked under the contradictions of racial democracy. On the one hand, the system preached racial democracy, while in reality only whites had full citizenship status, given that both browns and blacks must justify their inclusion through denial of their blackness. The archetypal figure of race-mixture and victimization is located in Pedro Archanjo himself, since even as a biracial he is not fully accepted as an equal. Poor, unable to afford an education even if he had aspired to study medicine, he had settled for the position of a janitor in the Bahian Faculty of Medicine, where through his interactions with the professors he began a passionate study of Afro-Brazilian culture that led to the publication of four chapbooks. Often criticized by Nina Rodrigues (Professor Nilo Argolo in the novel) for favoring miscegenation, he would suffer this embattled status all his life, as Rodrigues considered biracials as less than human, or even "degenerates," thus putting Archanjo's social theories at loggerheads with his own.

In his "Postface" to *Tenda dos Milagres*, João José Reis notes that "In *Tent of Miracles*, Jorge Amado pits Archanjo's ideas against those of Argolo in a celebration of miscegenation, folk traditions and Negro culture. The novel attacks the colonized posture of accepting the early twentieth-century European racial theories and takes a swipe at the tardy appreciation of the Negro intellectual, whose work is only recognized on the initiative of a foreigner."[5] In this summation lies the fundamental pretext of Amado as he creates Pedro Archanjo in order to dialogue with a racist society—not to condemn it totally but to suggest that the solution to racial conflict lies in problematic miscegenation. The sheer details of Archanjo's involvement with Africa-derived Candomblé rituals, his leadership as the *Ojuobá* of a Candomblé temple or the "eyes of Sango," in homage to his adherence to the volatile Yoruba god of thunder, further attest to the iconic image Amado associates him with as the resistant figure against all the vestiges of racial discrimination and religious intolerance. Referencing Arthur Ramos's "Preface" to Manuel Querino's *Costumes Africanos da Bahia*, an anonymous author notes that

Querino was deeply disillusioned by the political and social changes (or lack thereof) that took place after emancipation in 1888, and the declaration of the Republic in 1889. He was particularly disturbed by the federal government's "whitening" policies that subsidized European immigration and set up social services for immigrants in Brazil, while at the same time there was a lack of such infrastructure organized or funded for ex-slaves.[6]

It is commendable that even if Amado shared some of the whitening ideals in terms of the notion of Brazil as a miscegenated society, he nevertheless did not embrace racism. Instead, his approach to equal justice was to portray Afro-Brazilian culture and religion as valid "signs and signatures" of an emerging pluralistic Brazilian culture that needed Africa as much as Africa needed it. Pedro Archanjo's character, in this sense, is a cultural bridge, a mediator and an embodiment of that which makes Brazil Brazil. The irony is that the novel *Tenda dos Milagres* is full of moments of persecution of the ideals of integration—thus making Pedro Archanjo both a protagonist in favor of racial tolerance but also a victim of that same principle of racial democracy since he was not accepted by the same society that preached racial equality. And this is where Linda Hutcheon's notion of the parody of history is instructive as a reminder that all the claims of postmodernism do have their contradictions. What is "post" in postmodernism and postcolonialism is but an illusion, for in the final analysis the likes of Pedro Archanjo in society perceive the reality very differently.

Pedro Archanjo's world can be seen as multiply binding; he is the quintessential Bahian prototype, and by extension, the classical Afro-Brazilian found in the corners and centers of society by virtue of his ability to crisscross the highs and lows of that same society with ease. He is at once the intellectual, the writer, the hustler, the womanizer, the drunk, and the cultural historian and anthropologist. From the Candomblé temples to Capoeira dances and popular Bahian festivals, he is at ease in all the real and symbolic rituals of Afro-Brazilian identity. He is a lover of music and connoisseur of the best *cachaça*, like another of Amado's creations, Quincas Berro d'Água in *Morte e a Morte de Quincas Berro d'Água*[7] (The Two Deaths of Quincas Wateryell), determined to challenge the racist ideals of his time, became a self-appointed sociologist, walking and combing the corridors and corners of Salvador in search of cultural mementos that would negate the stereotypical images of Afro-Brazilians in the minds of the nineteenth-century racist elites. In the midst of many compelling biracial female characters in *Tenda dos Milagres* such as Rosa de Oxalá, Dorotéia, Rosenda, Risoleta, Sabina dos Anjos, Dedé, and the Norwegian Kirsil, Pedro Archanjo stands out as the central figure of Amado's creation in this historical fiction. As João José Reis aptly notes, "the criticism of the repression of *Candomblé* and other manifestations of Negro culture comes to life on two historical fronts: the early twentieth century, during Pedro Archanjo's lifetime, and the historical context in which the book was published, during the military regime."[8] Pedro Archanjo thus represents both a fictional and historical figure, who incidentally also bears the burden of interpretation of the two decisive moments in Brazilian political formation: the repressive dictatorial moment that created the *malandro* (hustler) figure as well as the post-abolition period that captures the life and times of Manuel Querino, after whom Pedro Archanjo is modeled. Amado's creation is not only brilliant but magical; one cannot but admire the careful architecture of a unique character whose significance is not only rare, but essentially larger than life.

Parallels in Social History

While the connections between the historical figure of Manuel Querino and the fictional character of Pedro Archanjo have now been well established, a secondary character in the person of Inocêncio Sete Portas, who has received less critical attention to date, deserves to be highlighted. An assistant to the renowned Pedrito Gordo's ruthless and violent "civilizing" campaign against the adherents of Candomblé, Samba dancers, and Capoeira performers in Bahia, and a member of the Civil Defense (*Guarda Civil*), Sete Portas appears in archival records in the courts, feature articles, and editorials in local newspapers, which provide ample paratextual information in order to analyze the ambiguous frontiers between fiction and history in the specific instance of *Tenda dos Milagres*. In some sense, especially in the era of cultural studies, the borderlines between the fields of social history, literary criticism, ethnography, anthropology, and creative writing (among others) are now relatively porous due to the need for the social scientist *cum* critic to understand the contributions of the humanities to the social sciences and vice versa. Such interdisciplinary dialogues further lead both sides of intellectual inquiry to fortuitous discoveries as opposed to intradisciplinary research monologues that are often locked within a provincial and limiting terrain of self-deluding extrapolations, deductions, and conclusions.

Although some of Amado's fictional characters have their corresponding historical figures, it is presumptuous to suggest this is always the case. Yet Amado's characters often function in the shadows of their real characters even if the author has modified or altered pertinent episodes, time periods, or vital events in the lives of these characters. Pedro Archanjo not only transformed himself into a passionate self-taught intellectual, he also published books on cultural and religious syncretism of the Bahian people in which he openly challenged racism and Afro-Brazilian cultural repression—thus putting himself at a critical disadvantage to the whitened intellectual elites of the time, that is, the end of the nineteenth century and the early twentieth century. Persecuted and unemployed, he soon became neglected and unknown until a foreign scholar in the person of Dr. Levenson renewed interest in his significance—which was later celebrated in the novel as a theme in the Bahian Carnival of the Tororó School of Samba with which the novel ends as a triumphal moment of regeneration and resuscitation. Fighting against racist theories such as evolutionism and eugenics as propagated by real-life theorists such as Arthur de Gobineau and Nina Rodrigues in the quest for ideal national identity, Pedro Archanjo had to face the ire and persecutions of such fictional institutional figures as the Police Chief Pedrito Gordo and Professor Nilo Argolo, both of whom strategically sought to silence him as well as obliterate the Afro-Brazilian culture that he was ardently championing and defending. If Pedro Archanjo found a solution to Brazilian racial conflict in the biracial figure or the mestiço, Inocêncio Sete Portas, a collaborator of Pedrito Gordo, would rather exterminate Africa-derived manifestations such as Candomblé, Samba, and Capoeira, as well as their adherents and proponents.

In such a dialogue of social tensions and conflicts between miscegenation and racism, between erudite and popular culture, between political activism and mere chronicles of customs and traditions, lies the paradigmatic thesis of Jorge Amado—as well entrenched in *Tenda dos Milagres*. Published in 1969 at the peak of military dictatorship in Brazil, the novel refutes racist theories emanating from Europe at the beginning of the twentieth century while simultaneously celebrating the life, works, and times of Pedro Archanjo, whose epistemological position on miscegenation is unmistakable. Recalling the terrible era of persecution in which to go to a Candomblé worship was to risk one's freedom and life, he not only lamented the gradual erosion of all that blacks and mestizos had fought for in terms of Afro-Brazilian cultural heritage at the hands of police brutality that was persecuting devotees with cruelty, but he expressed a certain stoic optimism about the future when he asserted that the future of Brazil belongs in miscegenation:

> Everything in Bahia is a mixture, Professor. The Churchyard of Jesus Christ, the Terreiro of Oxalá, Terreiro de Jesus. I'm a mixture of men and races; I'm a mulatto, a Brazilian. Tomorrow things will be the way you say and hope they will, I'm sure of that; humanity is marching forward. When that day comes, everything will be a part of the total mixture, and what today is a mystery that poor folk have to fight for— meetings of Negroes and mestizos, forbidden music, illegal dances, *candomblé*, samba, *capoeira*—why all that will be the treasured joy of Brazilian people.[9]

Even when the forgoing idealistic statement is read as a romantic and uncritical summation of Pedro Archanjo's solution to Brazil's complex racial relations, in the racist context of post-abolition Brazil, his contribution, when considered from the viewpoint of the real Manuel Querino, must equally be understood as an effective strategy to force a dialogue with a society that was, in the words of Maria das Graças de Andrade Leal, "defined by racial discrimination and social exclusion."[10] While Pedro Archanjo's protagonism is well demarcated, the antagonistic posture of Inocêncio Sete Portas is yet to be highlighted in social-literary-critical historicism. As a biracial figure, Pedro Archanjo proposes a tolerant (syn)thesis on racial democracy in Brazil, while Inocêncio Sete Portas's intolerant (anti)thesis as a black man offers a counterpoint to understand why the racial controversy won't be settled until there is a constructive meeting of the minds, a less myopic perspective toward the causes and effects of racism in Brazilian society, and a proposal for constructive reparations to mitigate the mental scar on the Afro-Brazilian victims who, to this day, still need to seek some form of financial support from the government to sustain and promote their cultural and religious beliefs. The atrocities committed by Inocêncio Sete Portas and his like are a sampler of larger egregious criminal and prosecutable acts against humanity that time alone can begin to heal.

The spectacle of the government violating the civil rights of millions of Candomblé adherents, confiscating their sacred paraphernalia, and diminishing their sense of pride in their ancestry must be disturbing to all who do not support the gross miscarriage of justice in matters of racial equality. The solution at this juncture may not be to identify the likes of Pedrito Gordo or Inocêncio Sete Portas, but to send a message of hope to Candomblé devotees that such an occurrence will never be repeated in a democracy. Textual and archival evidence abounds about the shameful acts of Inocêncio Sete Portas; he even tried to justify his killing of a *babalorixá* (Candomblé priest) by accusing the victim of fetishism, to which the assistant chief of police agrees:

> Assistant Police Chief Pedrito Gordo had wanted to know exactly what had occurred.
> "A voodooist attacked me in the street. He called your mother names, Chief, and wanted to belt me one, so I shot him. I wasn't about to take any lip from a witch doctor."
> All's fair in war, said the auxiliary chief. The band of agents swaggered up and down the street and then went to roost in a nearby bar, where they drank and did not pay. All's fair in war, and soldiers in a holy war have their privileges.[11]

As with most oppressive colonial conquests, post-abolition era in Brazil did not guarantee that former slaves and African descendants would no longer suffer racial discrimination. The role played by the police in maintaining such a demeaning status quo calls for a critical examination especially of the violent character of Inocêncio Sete Portas. Ordinarily, Aimé Césaire's equational explication of the colonizer-colonized's permanent conflict would suffice,[12] but in this context, the oppressor acts with impunity, as if the value of the Afro-Brazilian life is almost nil since the post-abolition system can justify its actions as an act of a "holy war."

On numerous occasions in the novel, confrontations between the police and Candomblé devotees lead to violent beatings, disruptions of sacred ceremonies, arrests, and even summary clandestine executions. Culprits are often given a mild sentence, pardon, or complete immunity because the system cannot afford to be divided within itself. One such instance is the death of Manuel de Praxedes, who had resisted a police invasion of a Candomblé temple and ended up dead. Instead of remorse at the senseless killing, the members of the Secret Police gathered to celebrate while reassuring the people, futilely of course, that justice would be served:

> When the criminal and his weapon had been turned over to the proper authorities, the people dismissed.
> "He was caught in the act of murder."
> "Don't worry, leave him to us."
> The same afternoon at about six o'clock, Sam Coralsnake, secret agent of the auxiliary police chief, a murderer caught in *flagrante* and handed over to the police for justice to be done, was seen in the company of Bighearted Zé, Inocêncio Seven Deaths, Mirandolino, Zacarias da Goumeia, and Ricardo Cutlass in Baronesses' Alley, taunting and threatening the friends and neighbors who were holding a wake over the body of Manuel de Praxedes.[13]

Even in death, Manuel de Praxedes was not allowed a befitting burial without the supervision of the police who, probably, were fearful of possible bursts of rebellion and retaliation. Amado suggests, implicitly, that the culprit will go unpunished since the victim and his friends and sympathizers are still subjected to humiliation despite having lost a loved one to senseless police brutality and murder.

In the medical, legal, historical, and archival records consulted in Bahia, we were able to ascertain that on May 22, 1922, in the city of Salvador, the corpse of a certain strongly built biracial individual (1.79 meters tall and weighing about 91 kilos; black hair, yellow teeth, and wearing shiny dark trousers and a white cotton shirt) was found seemingly placed on the street corner. Finding bullet wounds to both the head and the back, the autopsy performed on the body identified the deceased as one Inocêncio Sete Portas. If we take this real-life individual as the same one who Jorge Amado fictionalized, his tragic end sounds more like poetic justice than a tragedy brought on by his atrocities against his own people or Afro-Brazilians in general since he represented the instrumentality of violence and repression at the hands of the Bahian post-abolition police. The police report documenting the criminal incident reveals the following details: "It has come to the notice of this Police Station that during the early hours of May 18, 1922, in the Alto Monte-Serrate neighborhood, the scribe observes that Inocêncio Firmino de Souza was assassinated and was examined by Drs. Álvaro

Borges dos Reis and Anthero Correia Cotias with the object of informing
the deceased's wife as well as interviewing all witnesses to the crime."[14]
These detailed factual records, while not invoked by Jorge Amado in
Tenda dos Milagres, are both forensic and ethnographic data that help
elucidate missing links as the reader seeks some form of justice for the
many Afro-Brazilian devotees brutally murdered by the real Inocêncio
Sete Portas. While literary criticism often prefers exclusive critical
analysis without resorting to the analysis of sources and influences, as is
the practice in the social sciences such as in anthropology, sociology or
even history, the interdisciplinary nature of cultural studies as we know
it today privileges such transgression of disciplinary borders in order to
allow the reader a more "scientific" approach to the deconstruction of
parallels in social and cultural history.

The violent death of Inocêncio Sete Portas sent ripples through
the Bahian governmental system, led by José Joaquim Seabra, especially
from the oppositional political group at the time. The oppositional press
had a field day on the matter as provocative editorials were written by
none other than Ernesto Simões Filho, the famous anti-Seabra journalist:

> Once I learnt of the murder of Sete Portas, I made a recom-
> mendation to the newspaper *A Tarde* to conduct an immediate
> investigation and report detailed information concerning the
> homage his contemporaries had planned on his behalf. Well,
> cognizant of the ingratitude of politicians, I realized that such
> a homage would be less pompous today than as required, say
> two years ago, when he dared to challenge Seabra, who was
> considered a sloppy dresser, to a fashion competition . . . Even
> when Counselor Rui Barbosa returned to the *Sertão* (back-
> lands) in peace as celebrated by the Our Lady of Good End
> procession, he had been sent as a security guard to accompany
> the Counselor and he was well received in his three-piece
> black velvet suit.[15]

Beyond the pedestrian attention paid by the feature writer to the professional demeanor and dress code of the deceased, it was as if the journalist
was trivializing the death of an oppositional figure. Ernesto Simões Filho
was indeed insinuating that Inocêncio Sete Portas was a member of
the anti-Seabra movement, particularly in the way he compared their
dressing styles as a strategy of differentiation between the two. In the

process of painting Sete Portas as a faithful anti-Seabrist, the journalist ended up diminishing Sete Portas's reputation by merely emphasizing his professional status as a security guard to attorney Rui Barbosa. Such are the complexities of details that cannot be uncovered in the Amado text but serve as paratextual ingredients for a better appreciation not only of the creative skills of the author, but also of the political and historical significance of Inocêncio Sete Portas.

Obviously, Simões Filho seized the opportunity of the death of Sete Portas to settle political scores. Indeed, a closer look at the journalist would reveal his intention as owner of A Tarde to dissociate himself from police violence, which had implicated the press for its lack of objectivity and corruption. Ironically, Simões Filho was one of the victims of such a police offensive, on March 25, 1919, during the visit of Rui Barbosa to Bahia. Inocêncio Sete Portas was identified as one of the police officers who had shot at Simões Filho and others; thus, by suggesting that the Seabra government had no better assignment to give to Sete Portas but to provide "state security," he was in fact mocking the inefficiency and corruption of the police by deploying Sete Portas as a quintessential representation of police brutality, hypocrisy, and double standards and an embodiment of the failure of the state. Simões Filho reports in a suggestive piece titled "O Fim de Um Facínora" (The End of a Fascination):

> Already a famed and feared criminal, often futilely brought to justice, because he was always protected by the top brass who needed his services for their own gainful ends, his greatest celebrity status dates back to the government of Antonio Moniz, whose objection got to the point of inviting to his clandestine group notorious professional criminals, whom he treated as precious and intimate death squad agents which he often deployed against the people such as in the daily assaults and public shootings that were highlighted by the opposition political group as exemplified in the occurrence of March 25, 1919.[16]

There can be no doubt about the duplicity of Simões Filho in portraying Sete Portas as both an instrument of state violence as well as a prosecutable criminal ironically protected by the same state.

In contrast to Inocêncio Sete Portas, who unlike Pedro Archanjo was not given sufficient consideration by Jorge Amado, Zé Alma Grande was given serious attention by Amado in the possible character mix-up of Sete Portas and Zé Alma Grande. We see this in the following excerpt of *Tenda dos Milagres*: "Zé Alma Grande did not contest the Chief's orders, did not hesitate in their execution. One needed not be a gangster to know the consequences of not heeding the orders of Pedrito. Beatings and killings were normal and simple acts for him [. . .]. Zé Alma Grande, strongly built black man, a devout trustee of Pedrito, never knew the color of fear."[17] With the close semblances between the two characters, it is arguable that Jorge Amado crafted similar qualities or characteristics in the creation of the two figures and provided ample evidence that the same may well be the case in many of his narratives. Whether we look at Pedro Archanjo, Inocêncio Sete Portas, or Zé Alma Grande, be they protagonists or antagonists, we see that Jorge Amado most definitely mastered the style of creative reconstitution of historical events, facts, and figures, thus rendering to his readers a generous sample of Bahian history and, by extension, Brazilian history with its creative twists, turns, textures, and contradictions. Through parody and history emerges a universal master story from a different perspective, but the authorial power of fictionalization also creates a new Afro-Brazilian cultural history: that which is, through its ironic twist, equal and opposite.

Challenges to Fictional Adaptation

The proverbial saying "old wine in a new skin" often translates the spirit of shifting tradition in modernity without minimizing the complexity of transformation, agency, and change. Jorge Amado's efforts in translating the political atmosphere of the post-abolition era in Brazil are marred by his own explicit "position" on race-mixture, religious intolerance, and racism—all of which are implied in the figure of Pedro Archanjo. Arthur de Gobineau, noted French author of the racist text *L'Essai sur l'Inégalité des Races Humaines* (Essay on the Inequality of Human Races), suggests that race-mixture erases that which is good in blacks and whites; this echoes social Darwinism or evolutionism, which also denigrate blacks and biracials. A more ferocious attack on the black race comes from the real-life Brazilian anthropologist and forensic medicine specialist Nina Rodrigues, who dared to argue in his books such as *A Degenerescência Psíquica e Mental dos Povos Mestiços: O Exemplo da Bahia* (1904) that race-mixture was the greatest danger Brazil had known, since (as he saw it) the black race was inferior and primitive, while the white race was superior to other races. Other racist theorists of the period included Sílvio Romero, who believed that nothing positive could come from race-mixture because the servility of blacks, the laziness of the Amerindian, and the authoritative genius of the Portuguese could produce only a sick nation. While sociologist Gilberto Freyre saw in miscegenation the greatest contribution to Brazilian racial relations, Florestan Fernandes criticized the "bias of not having a bias," and thus creating two types of racism: against the foundational races, and against the miscegenation thesis. In all of these theoretical and epistemological racial polarities, Jorge Amado's position is clearly the most progressive, as synthesized in *Tenda dos Milagres*. Pedro Archanjo may have argued with pride that "I am a hybrid of races and men; I am a biracial, a Brazilian"; yet this proud articulation is not without its challenges and contradictions, as manifested in the constant confrontation between Pedro Archanjo (representing persecuted Candomblé devotees) and Pedrito Gordo (representing the arrogant power of the racist state and the police). If Pedro Archanjo represents the hybrid Brazilian living in a "racial democracy," why is he persecuted in fact and fiction? Could the fictionalization of the Pedro Archanjo figure be a fictional reenactment of racial complexities still facing Brazil today? Through a careful examination of Amado's creative techniques and poetic license, we gather some conclusions on the challenges to fictionalization in *Tenda dos Milagres*.

Fully cognizant that tradition is not static and that what is considered modernity does indeed carry with it many shades of tradition, we are led by the notion of fiction and history, history and fictional adaptation, to the discussion of the complex relations between historicity (as a sum total of cultural reflections on the evidential past in which modernity is subsumed in helping to fully understand the present) and tradition (as temporal-spatial communal dynamics in which the past, present, and future are recurrent social practices). History, then, must not be equated with historicity in the same way that tradition cannot be completely divorced from modernity. What Amado has succeeded in doing in *Tenda dos Milagres* is to complicate the artificial borders between fiction and history in the same way that he has complexified the frontiers between historicity and meta-history. Karl Marx's historical materialism as well as the debate between Sartre and Lévi-Strauss[18] (on the use of history to make history) are quite rewarding here. Despite the heated debate, the existentialism of Jean-Paul Sartre does not necessarily negate the structuralism of Lévi-Strauss, or vice versa; indeed the two are complementary since the social theory of Jean-Paul Sartre dialectically produces the latter's structuralism. Dialectical thought is the terrain of generation of structural ideas; hence instead of seeing dialectics as a negation of structure, it is in fact an invitation to the formulation of dialectical social theory. In the context of Jorge Amado, the racist Brazilian structure invites a confrontation of that structure using dialectical thought, as in the example of miscegenation theory. While that theory is problematic, as seen in the contradictions of racial democracy, it is at least an instructive point of departure to the historicity of Brazilian racist tradition or racial relations. In this sense, Amado uses the dialectical *logos-tropos* of the city not only to fictionalize history, but also to deconstruct the historicity of the city.

In theorizing on the validity of cultural miscegenation, Amado recuperates historical tradition that distinguishes Brazil from other cultures while praising its uniqueness as a "hybrid" nation. The symbolic intervention of the "foreigner," or what may be called the Levensonian thesis (after Dr. Levenson in *Tenda dos Milagres* who represents Gilberto Freyre or even the alter ego of the colonial Portuguese adventurer), as the anthropophagic element attests to the "melting pot" hypothesis that the three races (Amerindian, European, and African) foundationally mixed in order to produce a miscegenated symbol of national identity—thus helping to forge a spirit of national unity in diversity. As Ana Rosa Ramos observes, "such is the case of the novel *Tenda dos Milagres* in which Jorge Amado seeks to show the emergence of a people as well as Brazilian culture through the recuperation of non-official history."[19] Amado is well aware that official history does not capture Brazilian reality, and through his socialist penchant and cultural orientation he chooses Bahia as a viable trope to speak for the silenced voices of Africans and their descendants who have not only been dislocated from their primordial roots, but have managed to resist the constraining forces of colonization and slavery, as well as adapt through subversion to the persecutions suffered at the hands of the police as they learn to negotiate through religious syncretism and cultural retentions in order to survive without abandoning their ancestral value system. The city in this instance is a dialectical amalgam of tradition, urbanity, and modernity—a combination for which Arjun Appadurai has appropriately coined the term "cityscape."[20] Appadurai deploys five global cultural flows (ethnoscapes, mediascapes, technoscapes, financescapes, and ideoscapes) as fluid overlapping categories to name the complexities of modernity. For him, "the central problem of today's global interactions is the tension between cultural homogenization and cultural heterogenization."[21] Of these five "scapes," the "cultural" best captures the crux of Amado's miscegenation thesis. Yet the remaining four cannot be divorced from interactions with the cultural. Taking Pelourinho as an example, or even Salvador, the first Brazilian capital that serves Amado as the ultimate setting in *Tenda dos Milagres*, the historical meshes with the cultural, thus making fictionalization problematic as even with the best creative defamiliarization, the aroma of the city of Salvador is found throughout Amado's creation. In terms of the creation of a singular national identity through race-mixture, Amado agrees with Gilberto Freyre that such an endeavor, even in theoretical sense, constitutes the symbolic essence of Brazilian originality. In so doing, Amado falls into the trappings of the fallacious racial democracy thesis.

Of the many fictional characters of Jorge Amado, Pedro Archanjo is perhaps the most closely modeled after a real or historical character. While other characters are equally Bahian and Brazilian, Amado seems to have been essentially influenced by his socialist and regionalist penchants to the extent of searching for representative characters in the everyday. By its very nature, intentionality is a zone of fluidity, as what an author intends may well be subverted by the critical extrapolations of others. As a result, it is one thing to uncover Amado's intentionalities (according to the author himself) and another thing to assert the provable semantical manipulations or interpretive deconstructions as suggested by many approaches to critical reception. In his study of Amado's intentions, Fábio Lucas sums up the Latin American writer's *oeuvre* by alluding to a moral indignation that is mediated by polarities and dualities: between nature and culture, men and women, city and country, the sea and the land, children and adults, labor versus capital, rich versus poor, and boss versus peasant. Lucas's central argument is anchored on the fact that Amado, for the first time in Brazilian literature, sought to prove the "superiority of [the] black race."[22] While such a statement may be termed "essentialist" in some critical quarters, it is a rewarding alternative critical assessment indeed to see Amado in a light sympathetic to the plight of blacks and their culture, beyond the narrow miscegenation theory. Lucas continues: "The humanist gaze of Jorge Amado revolves around the expansive excluded territory and is made up of multiple forms of racial composition with a special focus on the mestizo figure. The writer's sympathy is dedicated to the Afro-Brazilian sector of our racial formation, in opposition to the romantic fervor of the Amerindian" (163). In both rural and urban settings, Amado translates the aspirations and frustrations of the common people—reconciling his own creative genius with the ideological protestation of workers' conditions—as well as an overall angst for justice or lack of it.

The fictional adaptation of Pedro Archanjo is nothing short of masterful and uncontested. Despite the contradictions of the race-mixture thesis, Pedro Archanjo strove to prove his position by acting on his beliefs—having relations with whites, mestizas, and blacks—with many children to show for it. Although the society of the time was horrified at his belief that the way to solve racial relations in Brazil was for all races to intermarry and improve the lot of humanity, Pedro Archanjo practiced his beliefs to the extent that he could without resorting to violence. While racist attitudes that continue to this day were exposed and questioned, there were limits to the attainment of redress because the power of the police and other institutional instruments of racism were too overwhelming for him to effect any radical change. Albeit Pedro Archanjo, the pro-miscegenation hero, and the antithetical posture to Professor Nilo Argolo's racist theories, embodies all the qualities of social justice against all odds. Indeed, to prove his position, Amado, as author, seems to encourage his fictional character, Dr. Levenson, to emulate the miscegenation theories of Pedro Archanjo by applying such theories through having affair with a local mestizo woman by the name of Ana Mercedes. As much as Amado tried to fictionalize Manuel Querino, the verities of his life are betrayed in the subtleties of humor and irony with which the writer negotiates the creative process.

As a synthesis character, Pedro Archanjo represents both an archetype and contradiction of Brazilian racial relations. Despite the vehemently racist moment that he endured in the confrontation between two antagonistic forces (racist and anti-racist), Pedro Archanjo appears to have come out victorious from the embattled contestation in the metaphoric "university of Pelourinho" that defined the setting of this ideological struggle. The evidence of this "victory" is multiple, as in the voices of foreigners who have studied or come to live with Bahians and have learned their way of life, such as the Swedish woman, Kirsi, and Dr. Levenson from Columbia University in the United States. In the case of Kirsi, who at some point was bidding farewell to Pedro Archanjo and her other new friends in Bahia, she came to the conclusion that the "scientific" racism of Nilo Argolo was unfounded: "I won't tell you goodbye. A bronze child, a Bahia mestizo will run about in the snow [. . .] You are the best people in the world you Bahia mulattoes [. . .] why then, had Dr. Nilo Argolo [. . .] written those terrible pages, those scalding words, as hot as a branding iron about the mestizos of Bahia?"[23] What started as a casual encounter while having breakfast and meeting the blue-eyed blonde (Kirsi) turned into a romantic relationship that produced a mestizo child, who Pedro Archanjo predicted would be the smartest and bravest man ever, and who would live to become either the king of Scandinavia or the president of Brazil. And should the child turn out to be a girl, she would be extremely beautiful and gracious. Coincidentally, many years after the publication of *Tenda dos Milagres*, a queen of Sweden with a Brazilian background emerged. Regardless of the prophetic projections of Pedro Archanjo, the outcomes are problematic. On one hand, the fact that Kirsi left Brazil and returned to Sweden with the unborn mestizo child suggests that Kirsi did not love Pedro Archanjo sufficiently to marry him. On the other hand, even if Kirsi was pressured by family needs to return to Sweden, why would she not offer an invitation for Pedro Archanjo to join her in the remote or near future? Apparently Kirsi experimented with the miscegenation thesis but also took away the proceeds. The continuity is happening not in Brazil, where Pedro Archanjo could be a proud father, but in Sweden. Theoretically, then, the outcome of the union would be furthering the whitening ideal. As the *Ojuobá* and son of Exú, the deity of the crossroads, Pedro Archanjo subscribes to the limitless expansiveness of the world as a global traveler whose encounter with Kirsi is that of many races, cultures, and continents. Archanjo's victory over racism in Brazil comes as a desirable universal phenomenon in that he can extend his beliefs in miscegenation across continents, even if the phenomenon is problematic in Brazil.

Pedro Archanjo in Film and Fiction

Nelson Perreira's cinematic adaptation of *Tenda dos Milagres* closely follows the original text, while modifying details, such as in the warranted flashback techniques that synergize the "narration within a narration" mode with the multilayering and juxtapositional technique meant to elucidate contradictions and complementarities. The adaptation is similar to the Amado original in which two currents collide: the life history of Pedro Archanjo, and the academic search of Dr. Levenson into Archanjo's contributions to Afro-Brazilian culture through his seminal works. The "film within a film" mode is warranted by the contradictions of the external quest for Pedro Archanjo's life history (1869–1943) and the internal conflict of discovering a neglected intellectual who would have been forgotten if not for the research conducted by the North American scholar in 1969—the date of the publication of *Tenda dos Milagres*. The critical elements in both the film and book may be summed up as follows (although other details and dramatic instances may require close critical readings): (1) biographical discoveries by Fausto Pena, the local poet employed by Dr. Levenson as his research assistant; (2) a chance meeting between Kirsi (the Swedish lady) and Pedro Archanjo; (3) ideological and racial antagonisms between Dr. Argolo and Pedro Archanjo; (4) arrests, beatings, murders, and confrontation of Candomblé devotees with the police; (5) advice from Iyalorixá on invoking Ogun; (6) arrogance, racism, and repression of the police; and (7) the death and funeral of Pedro Archanjo. Humorous moments of passion between Dr. Levenson and Ana Mercedes as well as instances of tension between Pedro Archanjo and Dr. Argolo make for comic relief of rather serious racial and sexist matters that demand resolution and justice. For a book considered a masterpiece by critics, the challenge then remains the precise evaluative criteria for selection of the most pertinent episodes for critical analysis.

As a complex anti-racist narrative construction, *Tenda dos Milagres* alternates between past and present in the process of rediscovering the life and works of Pedro Archanjo in the first half of the twentieth century as well as of the recuperation of that past in 1969 when revisited by opportunistic media and Brazilian racist and elitist political institutions. The two antagonistic forces, Dr. Nilo Argolo and Pedro Archanjo, serve as an ideological terrain of struggle between social ideas. With four books on the subject of Afro-Bahian culture—*A Vida Popular na Bahia* (Popular Life in Bahia), *Influências Africanas nos Costumes da Bahia* (African Influences in Bahian Costumes), *Apontamentos sobre a Mestiçagem nas Famílias Baianas* (Notes on Miscegenation in Bahian Families), and *A Culinária Bahiana: Origens e Preceitos* (Bahian Cuisine: Origins and Recipes)—Archanjo became the object of racist attacks by Dr. Nilo Argolo, lost his job at the faculty of medicine, which embraced racist ideas at the time, was persecuted by the police, and ultimately was systematically subjected to public ridicule. One of the tense moments in the novel is the ideological confrontation captured by Amado in the following dialogue in which Argolo betrays his deep-seated racism when he concludes much earlier about Pedro Archango that "That fellow deserves to be white; his African blood is his misfortune."[24]

"Was it you who wrote a brochure called *Daily Life* . . ."

". . . *in Bahia*." Archanjo had recovered from his initial humiliation and was willing to strike up a conversation. "I left a copy for you in the office." [. . .]

"Call me professor," the illustrious lecturer corrected sharply [. . .]

"Yes, Professor," replied Pedro Archanjo in a frigid, distant tone. All he wanted now was to go his way.

"Tell me, those different notes about customs, traditional holidays, and the fetishist rites you call *cucumbís*, for example. Is all that really true?"

"Yes, Professor." [. . .]

"I read your brochure, and bearing in mind who wrote it [. . .] I won't deny it has merit, limited, of course. [. . .] It lacks any true scientific value, needless to say, and your conclusions about miscegenation are dangerous lunacy. [. . .] How dare you call our Latin culture mulatto? That is a subversive, monstrous statement [. . .]"

"It is based on fact, Professor." [. . .] He laughed again mockingly. "I advise you to read Gobineau [. . .] Listen to me: we must cleanse our country's life and culture of this mud of Africa which is befouling us. Even if it becomes necessary to resort to violence in order to do so."

"Violence has been used, Professor."

"Not enough, perhaps and perhaps not the right kind." [. . .]

"Well, Professor, maybe if you killed all of us, one by one [. . .]" [. . .] He decided to bring the conversation to a close with a command. "Go back to your work; you've wasted enough time already. I will say this: with all the absurdities in your book, there are a few things in it worth reading."[25]

While Argolo and Archanjo cannot ideologically agree on what is "scientific," "absurd," "lunacy," or "monstrous," each camp must deduce from its epistemological convictions, Argolo's being derived from the racist treatise on inequality of the races as propounded by Gobineau, and Archanjo's from ancestral power and equality based on spirituality and cultural/racial democracy.

The two oppositional characters not only help betray their thought systems via the foregoing dialogue, but their articulations also help to demarcate the different ideological penchants and contrastive tensions of each personality. In the general sense, the peculiarities and the particularities of each are exposed, while their specificities are cataloged by their own locutions. Nilo Argolo is portrayed as rigid, condescending, authoritarian, denigrating, inflexible, arrogant, and in sum, racist, while Pedro Archanjo is rendered as more "scientific," methodical, systematic, subtle, negotiating, humanistic, and visionary. Embodying and acting upon those characteristics of his, as the "eyes of Sango," that is, the vibrant preceptor of violence while constraining himself to act counter-violently, Archanjo deploys spirituality as a measure of balance and resistance. By describing himself as omnivisionary and omniscient, Archanjo, on the one hand, recognizes his African contributions to Brazilian society and culture, while ridiculing the racist ideas of his rival, Nilo Argolo. In order to challenge these racist theories, Archanjo had provocatively suggested to Argolo that perhaps it would be necessary to exterminate all blacks from Brazilian society in order to maintain the nation as racially pure. Dr. Argolo responds rather defensively: "Oh, I hardly think it will be necessary to go quite as far as that. It will be sufficient to pass laws prohibiting miscegenation and regulating marriages: white will marry white, black will mate with black or mulatto, and anyone else who does not obey the law will go to prison."[26] The threat of legislation or carting innocent victims of the unequal law to prison reeks of the hegemonic and arrogant racism engrained in Brazilian racial relations.

Facilely accepting the inequality of the races as propounded by Gobineau, the racist early-twentieth-century Brazilian elite society assumed that it could legislate racism via threats, beatings, humiliations, arrests, and even murders. It would be insufficient to imprison "troublemakers"; any attempt to celebrate heroes of the Afro-Brazilian cause of dignity and identarian affirmation would also need to be systematically eliminated. One such instance is the plan to celebrate the centenary of Pedro Archanjo by organizing a seminar, which was abruptly cancelled by the Executive Commission:

No one prohibited the Seminar, Dona Edelwiss, for crying out loud. We are in a democracy; no one can prohibit anything in Brazil, please! We are the ones, at this very moment, who are examining the subject matter, based on new data. We are the ones who decide—we, the Executive Commission and no one else—to suspend the Seminar. Notwithstanding this position, we cannot afford not to celebrate the centenary of Pedro Archanjo.[27]

Despite the hostility of the racist government with regard to the legacy of Pedro Archanjo, even the members of the commission agree that they could no longer make Archanjo invisible or continue to neglect his legacy. At the very minimum, his celebration must continue even if not everyone subscribes to his significance as a cultural activist and self-taught intellectual deserving of recognition and commendation. As a seasoned journalist, anthropologist, and novelist, Amado succeeds in blending the probing gaze of the anthropologist with the innovative mind of the creative writer, thus providing a lasting cultural masterpiece despite opposing perspectives on miscegenation and its problematic potential for resolving racial tensions in Brazil.

In print as in film, *Tenda dos Milagres* makes a bold statement about racial inequalities in Brazil, a subject matter as taboo as it is contested. In the film version of the Amado text, critiqued for being made by a "white outsider looking in"[28] (namely, Nelson Pereira, who has spent over twenty-five years striving to create a popular cinema in Brazil, and hence not as clearly critical of the myth of racial democracy) and praised for the director's efforts to confront the "difficulty of speaking honestly about a taboo subject,"[29] careful costuming and exterior sets make an authentic turn-of-the-century Afro-Brazilian setting in Pelourinho come alive, in two alternating time-frames: the early twentieth century and the present. In refuting the artificial division between religion and science, Archanjo painstakingly proves the complexity and resilience of African-derived Candomblé religion as a central locus for the development of resistance to white domination in Brazil.

On several occasions in the novel, as in the film, confrontation between Candomblé adherents and repressive police agents is highlighted, and we learn of the self-designated "holy war" that Pedrito Gordo claims as his mission as the assistant police chief. Joan Dassin rightly notes that Nelson Pereira's film version, in addition to respecting Afro-Brazilian religion, "makes it clear that Candomblé is not a mere psycho-religious release, but a vital source of cultural continuity, community solidarity, and political organization."[30] The direct assault on this sacred and cultural institution betrays the knowledge of its power by the racist Nilo Argolo and his cohorts. Otherwise, how can one explain the adamant and violent persecutions of Candomblé temples—a most dramatic one being that in which poetic justice was served when Inocêncio Sete Portas, the black police agent working for Pedrito Gordo, was possessed by Ogum, the Afro-Brazilian deity of justice, and ultimately turned his gun on his fellow police officers, shooting randomly in a frenzied, possessed, and confused state of madness. While the film is more dramatic in its depiction of the encounters, the novel synthesizes as if providing a critical commentary on a phenomenon so rampant and revolting that the police have become inured, and no longer see the violent acts as an anomaly:

> Even today in the *terreiros*, the docks, the markets, the byways
> and alleys of the city, you can hear many different versions,
> all heroic, of the clash between Pedrito and Archanjo, when
> that bilious representative of authority invaded Procópio's
> *terreiro*. They all tell how he stood up to the police bully
> whose look was enough to make hardened criminals shake
> in their shoes. The persecution of the *candomblé* celebrants
> was a natural corollary of the racist preaching that began in
> the School of Medicine [. . .] Pedro Gordo did nothing but
> put the theory into practice [. . .] Pedro Archanjo may not
> have finished off the racists—every era and every society will
> always have its fools and knaves—but he branded them with
> a red-hot iron and pointed them out in the streets: "There
> go the anti-Brazilians, folks," as he proclaimed the greatness
> of the mestizo race.[31]

While Amado and Pereira deserve our admiration for bringing to light (in a creative, bemusing, yet indignant fashion) a rather charged subject matter among Brazilians, white or black, we must step back to critique the simplification of the issues: miscegenation has not and will not resolve racial tensions in Brazil. Indeed, the intermarrying thesis has often been laden with contradictions. Kirsi, the Swedish lady, returned to Europe with the miscegenated baby. Where does that leave Brazilian miscegenation in terms of Brazilian national identity or continuity? Implicit imperialism looms large in the discourse on racial democracy, for as the literature shows, the biracial figure is often just that—a glorified figure head of racial mixture, who indeed is a victim of a fallacious treatise on wishful racial harmony. In order to harmonize or redress imbalances, both parties must be seen as equal partners, not one as "high" and the other "low" in terms of culture and intelligence. There cannot be harmony in such a blatantly disharmonious relationship.

In questioning the racial superiority of whites by presenting Pedro Archanjo as a credible Afro-Brazilian intellect who represents many Afro-Brazilian heroes refusing to be silenced or marginalized in any shape or form, Nelson Pereira, through *Tenda dos Milagres*, empowers the Afro-Brazilian communities by not treating Pedro Archanjo in a condescending or stereotypical manner. The cinematic gaze is clearly from the perspective of the oppressed, thus showcasing that the brutality experienced by many Brazilians under military dictatorship has always been the norm for Afro-Brazilians. Confirming what the passionate advocate of Afro-Brazilian dignity, Abdias do Nascimento, has articulated in many of his works, including the treatise on racial genocide in *"Racial Democracy"* *in Brazil: Myth or Reality?*, Nelson Pereira puts Candomblé side by side with the Christian religion, not as a substitute or alternative, but as a vital force in which is located the dynamics of Afro-Brazilian thought system, arts, and culture. Equally privileging Afro-Brazilian religion as demonstrated in the hypnotic possession of Inocêncio Sete Portas during a police raid and disruption of a Candomblé temple, Nelson Pereira not only popularized the Afro-Brazilian religion on screen (as intended by Amado), he has made it acceptable to many who used to be ashamed to participate in what was hitherto considered a heathen and barbaric practice. Both racial inferiority and racial superiority have thus been relatively eliminated in the careful rendition of a potentially racially egalitarian society. Whether Amado or Nelson Pereira succeeded in their fictional and cinematic endeavors remains to be seen in Brazilian society today, as most people are still judged not by the content of their character but by the color of their skin.

Far from being a thing of the past, the persecution of Candomblé devotees continues today, though it is not as rampant as in the nineteenth century and early twentieth century. Yet, in a recent study, Edmar Santos argues that despite the assumption that adherents are no longer subject to violent persecutions, mandatory registration, arrests, and overall repression, these worshippers are still being illegally victimized by being accused of frivolous acts of vandalism and arson that have nothing to do with the disruption of public peace or constituting public nuisance:

> Afro-Bahian cultural and religious practices remained within the melancholic decadence that the city found itself after abolition. A decree promulgated between 1972 and 1973 by the Foundation of Historical and Cultural Patrimony of Bahia fined nineteen *candomblé* temples and eleven live sessions in the city of Cachoeira. Meanwhile, in the years 1970 and 1971, the "pai-de-santo" (chief priest) José das Três Linhas, was processed and condemned to two months in jail. In the words of the prosecutor, as sanctioned by the Judge during sentencing, the chief priest was considered an "arsonist, trouble maker, unemployed wanderer, and exploiter of popular belief system."[32]

In this laconic evidential statement lie the contradictions not only of living in a racial democracy in Brazil, but those of enjoying all the benefits of citizenship and equality under the law. This fantasy cannot be further from the truth, as seen in the predicament of the chief priest. Since when is ritual burning within a religious ceremonial context a crime? Since when is being unemployed or being a wanderer a crime? Since when is having popular beliefs a crime? If this is the case, then all the musical mega-stars and their emerging protégés should be jailed for exploiting their flock and fomenting trouble. In sum, Amado and Pereira may have only scratched the surface of the entrenched political dilemma in *Tenda dos Milagres*. In so doing, they have opened a can of worms that cannot be covered until the debate is focused on the acknowledgment of racial inequalities and the redress of their disenfranchising consequences.

Racial Democracy as Historical Fiction

Pedro Archanjo, like the Exú and Xangô deities he is associated with spiritually, politically, and paradigmatically, embodies the characteristics of both duality and volatility. On one hand, as the manifestation of the contradictions of Exú, the agent of the crossroads, Archanjo manages to hold together the competing opposing poles of right and wrong while ensuring justice for the relative underdog. On the other hand, Archanjo translates the vengeful and temperamental attributes of Xangô in his daring posture and uncontrollable anger, which manifests as "fire" in his mouth. Both deities share a commonality of justice as they seek to restore a victim of injustice to a state of normalcy by revenging the wrong perpetrated against the innocent. In the context of racial democracy, *Tenda dos Milagres* indicts the concept by subjecting blacks and mestizos to unbearable stress that often obliges them to resist and on occasion even assault their oppressors in a strategic counter-offensive move toward equilibrium. The creative choice of Pedro Archanjo is instructive, since, based on the parallels between his life and that of Manuel Querino, he is considered a man of the people by virtue of his rapport with dwellers of Pelourinho. Based on his religious title, *Ojuobá*, the "eyes of Xangô," he is expected to protect the members of the community from the injustices to which they were subjected. Discursively, Archanjo confronts a racist white culture with popular culture steeped in African tradition and values. Beyond listening to ancestral stories and edifying one another, the community seeks counsel from the wise, such as Archanjo, who is grounded in traditional African religious values.

Given the foregoing spiritual responsibility, Archanjo resolves to confront the police chief with the power of Candomblé when the latter comes disruptively and arrogantly into the Candomblé temple uninvited. The episode confirms the linkage of Pedro Archanjo with the attributes of Exú:

> They say that just at that moment Exu returned from the edge of the earth and entered the room. Ojuobá said *Laroiê, Exu!* It all happened very quickly. As Bighearted Zé took the next step toward *Oxóssi*, he found Pedro Archanjo standing in his way. Pedro Archanjo, Ojuobá, or Exu himself, as many people had it. His voice soared imperiously in the terrible anathema, the fatal curse: *Ogun kapê dan meji, dan pelú oniban!*[33]

The consequence of the incantation is immediate, as Bighearted Zé loses his mind, turning against his own group as if possessed by Exu. His disorientation was not to improve as Ogun, deity of justice, comes to his assistance, compelling him to become even more aggressive toward his fellow officers: "Ogun's Zé gave a leap and a bellow, flung off his shoes, whirled around the room, and became an orixá. Possessed by the saint his strength doubled. Ogunhê! He cried, and all those present replied:

Ogunhê, my father Ogun! *Ogun kapê dan meji, dan pelú oniban!* Repeated Archanjo. 'Ogun called the two cobras, and they rose up against the soldiers.'"[34] While the Yoruba incantation has been somewhat adulterated in Brazil linguistically speaking (literal translation may be rendered as "Ogun, let us call on two mysteries (snakes) and perform a mystery (death, as in ordering a sentence) for the one with the gun (police), the essential meaning of protection against the intruders cannot be mistaken. In possessing Bighearted Zé, both Exu (now embodying Pedro Archanjo) and Ogun (now possessing Bighearted Zé) confront one another spiritually speaking, thus resolving the imbalance in nature by turning the aggressor into a weapon against aggression—in this instance, against the soldiers as well as against Pedrito Gordo, the police chief himself. All the chief can do is to wonder if Zé had completely lost his mind. At that very moment, he had—and that is the essence of spiritual vengeance and justice as creatively crafted by Amado in *Tenda dos Milagres*.

With this archetypal episode of confrontation between Candomblé devotees and the police, Amado is indeed questioning the validity of racial democracy, even if his thesis to propose miscegenation as the solution to Brazilian racial relations is complicated by that very case study. Amado's thesis, despite its lofty intentions, is nothing but historical fiction. As an ideological fiction, the official position on racial democracy has been maintained for too long by the elite hegemonic structure that such effort by Amado to expose the hypocrisy is now allowing militant blacks to speak against the implicit exclusion of Afro-Brazilians in the political, educational, and social sectors of the society. Successful Afro-Brazilians are seen as political exceptions to the rule of racial discrimination, and are often showcased as ample proof that Brazil is devoid of racism. Yet, a marginalized majority of Afro-Brazilian find themselves locked in their economically deprived status. Since the post-dictatorial re-democratization processes of 1978, and even in today's political agitation for reparations, white middle-class labor organizations have managed to achieve redress from the government, while the Brazilian Unified Black Movement, a militant group that represents over half of the population who can be considered black, is still struggling for cohesion, influence, and political mobility. One cannot expect that *Tenda dos Milagres* will radically solve the contradictions of miscegenation or racial democracy, but it is nonetheless a commendable effort in exposing the problem to necessary dialogue and perhaps problem-solving initiatives. Amado's effort in this regard is, however, stifled since his proposed solution is nothing but a rehash of the racial hypocrisy in the official position on racial democracy. Pedro Archanjo's son with the Swedish woman is a symbol of further whitening, since Archanjo, a mestizo, is lighter skinned. The child he fathers with Dorotea, a mestiza, produces Tadeu Canhoto, who is even lighter skinned than Archanjo. With the prospect of moving to Rio de Janeiro to take on an important position, it is implicit that the "whitening ideal" has given him the opportunity for social mobilization at the expense of the African element of his Brazilian identity. In sum, the implication in *Tenda dos Milagres* is that Amado has maintained the same perspective of whitening proposed by Gilberto Freyre in *Casa Grande e Senzala* (1933), while simplistically hoping that the problem will go away through theoretical wishful thinking. The reality of the life and times of Manuel Querino[35] as embodied in the character of Pedro Archanjo clearly proves that racism is very much alive in Brazil. Regardless of Amado's intentions, the limits of that goal reside in the contradictions and unintended consequences of historical fiction and miscegenation as a solution to Brazilian racial relations.

Chapter 6

Black Orpheus

Regeneration of Greco-Yoruba Mythologies

Myths and rituals do have their peculiar place in our understanding of the cosmos, whether classical or modern, ancestral or contemporary. The intersectionality of Yoruba myths and rituals when seen as analogous to those of the Greeks, especially, is not a recent development in human experience. Indeed, most societies seek cosmic explanations by resorting to myths of origin, celebrating heroes, venerating sacred places, or remembering cogent symbols that are often invoked in order to interpret that very world and the place of eternal reverence and belongingness associated with those iconoclastic symbologies, locations, and memories. The myth of Orpheus and Eurydice is one such famed Greek myth: a myth about love and passion, about weaknesses and excesses of the human spirit. Likewise, the myth of Obatala within the context of the creation of the Yoruba people and their world, while not exclusively about passionate love but of the ritual of sexuality, human frailty, and transcendence, does share what may be called a chthonic epiphany, for both myths transpire in the realm of the underworld as they make their way into the material world of the living through intense ritualistic drama of purgatorial proportions, dissolution, and reconstitution. Greek and Yoruba cultures in this regard are thus embodied in many deities, in their defining strengths and frailties, even as they help us decode complex mundane and supernatural phenomena.

Orpheus and Obatala naturally occupy such a complex web of antinomies, to the degree that they would not be who they are and remain

153

such legendary semi-deities and semi-heroes if not for those very peculiar complexities and contradictions. Obatala[1] is considered the father of all Yoruba divinities, so named as "Orisa-Nla or supreme divinity," and is said to be endowed with the function to make the inner and outer heads of all humans as he deems fit—a mission that predetermines the destiny of all humanity. Orpheus was a legendary musician, poet, and prophet in ancient Greek religion and myth. He had the special ability to charm both animate and inanimate objects with his music. These deified, heroic, fascinating, and humanized characters provide us with a window onto the dramas and tensions of the Yoruba Atlantic world as explored in this study.

This chapter investigates the emergence of Orpheus as an iconic Brazilian character by studying the historical, mythological, and cosmological contexts of the many ritualizations of Orpheus's classical narrative in select texts[2] and contexts. As a comparative mythological prism, Obatala, the Yoruba supreme deity endowed with creativity function in Yoruba creation myth, is interrogated analogically with Orpheus in order to assess the tragic flaw that both could not overcome. Jorge de Lima's epic poem *Invenção de Orfeu* (The Invention of Orpheus), partly inspired by the Orpheus myth, is examined; Vinícius de Moraes's *Orfeu da Conceição* (Orpheus of the Virgin Mary) and cinematic adaptations over the years are equally critiqued—from the Greek dramatic version, to the French classical cinematic adaption by Jean Cocteau in *Orpheus* (1950), to Brazilian dramatic pieces that led to two classic cinematic adaptations in *Orfeu Negro* (Black Orpheus; 1959) and *Orfeu* (1999). Studies on the Brazilian Orpheus to date have essentially compared him to Greek deities while neglecting potential parallels to African mythology. Yoruba mythology, however, provides us with Obatala,[3] who by virtue of his conscious descent into the underworld reveals peculiar characteristics of the conceptual duality of death and rebirth.

In Yoruba mythology, Obatala created human beings from clay but was not satisfied with his creations because, due to drunkenness, he created deformed beings such as hunchbacks, albinos, and cripples. Oduduwa, Obatala's rival as well as his younger brother, descended from heaven on a chain and created the earth in the sacred city of Ile-Ife (Nigeria), known by the Yoruba as the cradle of civilization. In some contexts, Oduduwa is considered the wife of Obatala, that is, the earth goddess, while in others, he is a male deity, a warrior king who defeated Obatala. In Ile-Ife, Obatala priests are driven out of town once a year and return from the forest after several weeks—a ritual performance reenacting the imprisonment and release of Obatala. The symbolic "three-day" descent of Obatala into the otherworld and his resurrection indicates the closeness of Obatala to the figure of Jesus. This chapter argues that while Orpheus the character acts out the global narrative of degeneration and regeneration, Yoruba and Greek mythologies help to provide illumination about the complexities of this larger-than-life figure who embodies all the contradictions of creation and destruction in the process of asserting his humanity, and about his ultimate tragic flaw that is present in every human being as aptly demonstrated by the metaphoric backward gaze that became his ultimate undoing.

Conceptualizing Orpheus or Obatala in Ifá Divination

In the Ifá divination system, Obatala's kaleidoscopic energies radiate clarity—the need to distinguish right from wrong, and consequently, the ability to make the right decisions. In this sense, Orpheus's need to look back and ensure that Eurydice was following him out of the underworld into the earth raises fundamental questions about human faith, lack of it, and subsequent tragedy: that ability to believe in abstraction with no concrete evidence of its actualization. These questions relate to the (im)possibility of restraining oneself in the face of danger and to trust supernatural powers in the face of uncertainty and frailty. The subject of the returning hero who remains alive after sojourning in the under-world or the "land of the dead" questing for a loved one and returning with this beloved figure has fascinated many societies and cultures, including the Greek and the Yoruba that are of concern to this chapter. Comparative mythology as well as world religions provide some clues to Orpheus's daring act. The dramatic heroic's descent is compounded by the intensified return in which the hero must submit to a challenge (usually of overcoming and overpowering death) that will determine life or death. The hero is also warned about deadly consequences such as the possibility of his own death as well as losing the loved one should he look back (quite tempting) to save the loved one. To overcome death is to become immortal, and to submit to death is to submit to human nature—that is, the impossibility of being superhuman despite beyond-mortal qualities and exceptionalities. Such is the puzzle that must be unraveled in order to better situate Orpheus and Obatala in comparative mythological perspectives.

In comparing Orpheus and Obatala as ritual archetypes in whose drama all humanity inadvertently is implicated, this comparative lens approximates Greco-Yoruba mythologies and their Afro-Brazilian connections. Beyond the two primary texts of analysis, namely, Obotunde Ijimere's *The Imprisonment of Obatala* and Vinícius de Moraes's *Orfeu da Conceição*, the study argues that divinities at large are in fact humanized and humanizable through their interactions with their supposedly human subjects and complementarities. Orpheus, for example, had the ultimate mission of his life to rescue his wife, Eurydice, from the underworld, a somewhat superhuman feat; while at the same time, he succumbed to death and loss of the same Eurydice by defying the warning against the backward gaze. Obatala's mission was to create human bodies, after which Olodumare, the Supreme Being, perfected them with the breath of life. Due to his drunkenness, this Bacchus-influenced tragic flaw, Obatala could not complete his divine destiny. So Olodumare sent Oduduwa to complete the mission of creation. In both instances, Orpheus and Obatala failed in their primordial missions and may well be said to be locked in perpetual chthonic epiphanies. In other words, they are victims of their inability to reenact control over disorder. Epiphanies are said to occur in conditions of ritual and crisis. While ritual epiphanies are conditioned by a predetermined schedule, epiphanic crises are normally unpredictable, for ritual has the power of coherence, inspiration, and allure, in order to compel the all-powerful deity or hero to activate and protect the center from inevitable disintegration. Similar to ritual epiphany, chthonic epiphany may thus be understood as the presence of a processional that leads to crisis and resolution, even when that "resolution" may be in the form of transformational death or "transitional gulf," as Wole Soyinka defines the liminal state between one stage of being and another.[4]

In revisiting the Yoruba creation myth we invoke the slave figure, or "Esu" (the trickster deity), who so hated his master, Orisa, that he rolled a huge boulder onto the top of the master's house and shattered it into many pieces. Orunmila or Obatala made abortive efforts to gather the pieces, but they had spread all over the world as rocks, rivers, and seas. This myth ascribes the inadvertent act of destruction as a regenerative possibility that makes the process of "putting the scattered Orisas together" all over the world an explanation for the naming of the "selected heads" or literally, "selected divinities." Femi Abodunrin notes in *Blackness: Culture, Ideology, and Discourse* that the trickster deity conspired with the oracle to effect the integration of the cosmic system despite what on the surface looks like a negative event. In his comparative analysis of Ijimere's *The Imprisonment of Obatala* and Wale Ogunyemi's *Obaluaye*, Abodunrin surmises that Esu has a mediating role in all of this in view of "his transgressive tendency and, above all, willingness to substitute grotesque realism for Obatala's plastic refinery."[5] Abodunrin's deconstructive reading of Esu is far removed from Tejumola Olaniyan's focus on the complementarity between Ogun and Obatala—an exegetic rendering that echoes that of Soyinka himself. Esu may have been the provocateur of disintegration of the original cosmic harmony, but it will take the interlocking productive relations between Ogun and Obatala to rectify the rebellious act of Esu. As Olaniyan aptly puts it: "Obatala's task is mainly formal and plastic—*creation* [. . .] comes only after the spark of creativity [. . .] is ignited. Obatala is the "aesthetic serenity" that comes after the hubristic, world-changing act."[6] This is where myth takes on a new meaning of multiple significance.

The mythic dimension of the intense dramas of Obatala and Orpheus is meant to provide a context for the resolution of ritualistic apprehensions that both entities embody as semi-deity and semi-human personalities. Richard Seaford suggests that without ritual it is almost impossible to generate resolution from disintegration, even if symbolic: "Ritual is the manifestation of traditional stereotypical action in the face of potential disorder or of (as in crisis) actual disorder. The absorbing manifestation of order in ritual may, even if only symbolic, be a model of and a focus for reversing the debilitating disintegration of the group or indeed of the individual."[7] In comparing the distinguishing qualities and characters of Ogun, the deity of creativity, and Obatala, the deity of fractured or arrested creation, Soyinka succeeds in contrasting the essential metaphysics of both deities—by ultimately recovering what he calls the "psychic abyss of the re-creative energies," which equally allows for the epiphanic process of disintegration and re-integration: "With creativity, however, went its complementary aspect, and Ogun came to symbolize the creative-destructive principle. This does not in any way usurp the province of Obatala whose task is to create the lifeless form of man. Nor is Obatala ever moved to destroy. Obatala is a functionalist of creation, not, like Ogun, the essence of creativity itself."[8] Not only does Soyinka appropriate the functionality of Obatala,[9] he identifies in Orpheus and other archetypal protagonsits such as Ulysees and Gilgamesh, what he calls "the gravity-bound apprehension of self," which is not only operational within "cosmic totality," but also only resolvable within the "chthonic realm" of human consciousness.[10]

Obatala's function within the realm of creation and mysteries of nature is to provide that magical spark of light that animates human consciousness. To call Obatala the "chief of the white cloth" (a literal translation of the name) is to align him with the material and symbolic substance that makes consciousness possible. However, the metonymic reference to "white cloth" is not a reference to the material used to make the cloth, but to a more profound metaphysical fabric that binds the universe together. The threads of this fabric are the layers of consciousness which, as the Ifá divination system teaches, exist in all living beings. Ifá teaches that it is the ability of the forces of nature to communicate with each other, and the ability of humans to communicate with these cosmic forces, that gives the world a sense of spiritual unity. It is the understanding of this ability that gives substance to the Ifá concept of good character, and it is Obatala who guides us toward developing this understanding.

In Ifá divination, Obatala is enjoined to make sacrificial appropriation as a measure to render as positive the creation of albinos, an element of anomaly as represented in the unusual melanin pigmentation that renders the skin of albinos extremely colorless. Yet, despite this human defect, albinos are naturally endowed with secrets of divination, especially the *erindinlogun* (sixteen cowries). Ifá stipulates that all albinos must practice a spiritual trade as their chosen profession and must study the art of divination according to the *odu ogbe irosun*,[11] which reveals that Obatala was enjoined to make a sacrifice: "Obatala heard and offered a sacrifice of long life, / because his male and female children, / that was how they got victory over death and sickness; / Hence, the heavenly children of Obatala were blessed / and so the chant goes / initiated ones have abundant oil / initiated ones have abundant oil / while uninitiated ones have abundant blood / while uninitiated ones have abundant blood."[12] Obatala, as fictionalized in Ijimere's *The Imprisonment of Obatala* (1966), offers a parallel between Yoruba myth and Yoruba religion as one and the same cosmological vehicle through which the world is explicated. Ulli Beier appropriately notes in his introduction to the play:

> *The Imprisonment of Obatala* is based on Yoruba myth. It seems likely that Ijimere was inspired to treat this theme by Susanne Wenger's repeated handling of the myth on her batiks and screen prints.[13] *The Imprisonment of Obatala* is an ambitious play, which explores the philosophy of Yoruba *orisha* worship and tries to show the interplay of cosmic forces that are personified in the Yoruba imagination as *orisha*—supernatural beings, half human and historical, half divine and eternal.[14]

The approximation of Obatala and Orpheus, while occupying the realm of the liminal by their far-flung African and Greek distant locations, provides a new universalizing vista for the theorization of the human condition and consciousness. The dividing line between myth and ritual, the chthonic and the earthly, tradition and transgression, the sacred and the profane, is all blurred and relativized in the context of a tragic vision. Both Obatala and Orpheus are indeed tragic protagonists: their descent into "hell" (material failure) offers no redemptive (symbolic victory in death) atonement but a sense of perpetual self-flagellation and punishment as they wander through existence paying for their primordial tragic flaws. Fyodor Dostoyevsky, in *Crime and Punishment*, introduces to the world a utopian and nihilistic vision that questions the chthonic predicament of both of our archetypal protagonists. Raskolnikov, the pro-tagonist in *Crime and Punishment*, a transgressor of the provincial norms, is caught up in the drama of crime, loss of innocence, and an ultimate resignation to the temptations of high society. As contradictory as he is alienated, he is unable to reconcile his contradictory principles: on the one hand, cold, apathetic, and antisocial, and on the other, surprisingly warm and compassionate. He commits murder in spite of himself. His chaotic interaction with the external world and his nihilistic worldview might be the central motivators of his social alienation and inevitable descent into the metaphorical hell from which he does not fully return or recover. When read against Bakhtin's polyphony, the only possible regeneration for Raskolnikov, as hinted by the epilogue, lies in "a new life [. . .] to be dearly bought [. . .] with a great future deed."[15] For both Obatala and Orpheus, the initial "crime" was the inability to complete their primordial missions, thus necessitating a supernatural intervention, for which they must now pay the ultimate capital price—whether as a romantic gesture or spiritual commitment—for which they are fatally bound and yet must transcend and regenerate symbolically.

Ritual, Myth, and Cosmic Forces:
The Imprisonment of Obatala

Invoking the myth of Obatala, and suggesting that "everyman's greatest punishment would be to be thrown on the heaven of potsherds," Ulli Beier, translator into English of the original in Yoruba by Obotunde Ijimere, sums up the essence of the play when he surmises rather passionately that *The Imprisonment of Obatala* examines how Yoruba divinities interact with human forces.[16] Though this dramatic text is "inextricable" from African literature despite the non-Africanness of the translator (Ulli Beier),[17] Nelson Fashina opines that such texts that were informed by African oral traditions but hybridized by the intervention of stylistic or linguistic mediators such as those of literary scholars like Ulli Beier and Karin Barber, must be considered a legitimate part of African literature and should not ironically become "its source of marginality in the jaundiced eye of both the Western hegemonic discourse and the radical 'nativist' Africana scholars."[18]

A similar self-apprehensive contestation guides Soyinka's questioning of Western theatrical practice in which the invoked Greek deities are considered imbued with "skygods" qualities as opposed to the African (Yoruba) theatrical principles in which the deities exist in close proximity with cosmic totality (the Earth). Soyinka may have been inadvertently anticolonial and anti-Western in his theorization of the African (Yoruba) world (in *Myth, Literature and the African World*) as more germane to the theater since it is more harmonious with Nature: more humane, and indeed more human; for short of his focus on differential racial identity and the privileging of the African world, no society is imaginatively flaccid, less "cosmic," or "human," simply because it is Christianity-influenced and detached from the complexity of terrestrialism. Ironically, Soyinka invokes *The Imprisonment of Obatala* as a model drama that is infused with the African worldview even if it has been co-authored by Ulli Beier, an Australian involved in Nigerian cultural life in the 1960s. *The Imprisonment of Obatala* is thus faced with speculative controversy on the basis of authorship and translation as well as its transnational significance since it has resonances in Yoruba diasporic space such as Brazil. Nonetheless, Soyinka's conceptual triad in *Myth, Literature and the African World* as formulated through the synergetic relationship of three deities (Sango, Ogun, and Obatala) suggests that in fulfilling their roles of hero-gods and their dramas of passage-rites, they inevitably become "a projection of man's conflict with forces which challenge his efforts to harmonise with his environment, physical, social and psychic."[19]

Sango, an exceptional being with superhuman qualities, is so powerful as king that he is uncontrollable and so conflictual that he ends up committing suicide in order to restore harmony to the communal will and cosmic continuity. Obatala, on the other hand, is a gentler soul endowed with such qualities as "patience, suffering, and peaceableness, all the imperatives of harmony in the universe, the essence of quietude and forbearance; in short, the aesthetics of the saint."[20] On the opposite spectrum is Ogun, who is both aggressive and assertive. Yet what the three deities have in common goes beyond essential purity and divinity, to a penchant for excess and propensity for frailty. Though Soyinka focuses on Ogun as the ultimate "ritual archetype," the contradictory and complementary principles of these cosmic forces are arguably shared by these deities. Soyinka himself surmises that ritual drama involves the process of dissolution and resolution of the protagonist's ritualized experience: "In the symbolic disintegration and retrieval of the protagonist ego is reflected the destiny of being. This is ritual's legacy to later tragic art; that the tragic hero stands to his contemporary reality as the ritual protagonist on the edge of transitional gulf."[21]

Regardless of Soyinka's focus on Ogun, the underlying thesis of challenging the European bias against African culture that leads to the representation that anything African can only be inferior explains why Yoruba metaphysics is placed side-by-side that of the European and the Western in general. Soyinka theorizes[22] on this disagreement with Western arrogation to itself the superiority of form and content of that which defines perfectly natural human performative experience in the African context. In establishing the African and Western worldviews, Soyinka vehemently posits that "the difference between European and African drama as one of man's formal representation of experience is not simply a difference of style or form, nor is it confined to drama alone. It is representative of the essential differences between two worldviews, a difference between one culture whose very artifacts are evidence of a cohesive understanding of irreducible truths and another, whose creative impulses are directed by period dialectics."[23] In associating the Yoruba worldview with "irreducible truths" and the European with "period dialectics," Soyinka articulates the defining characteristic of the African world in terms of the cycle of life or reincarnation that translates as the continuity of life even in death as opposed to the linear and temporal understanding of life in the European tradition. While Soyinka saves us specificities of all the deities that he considers theorizeable for the purpose of understanding human interactions with the very elements of nature as they are explicated through legends, festival, rituals, and ceremonies, three paradigmatic deities become complicit in the conceptualization of Obatala, even as exemplified in the story in *The Imprisonment of Obatala*.

In explicating Obatala's uniqueness as the deity of creation, Soyinka emphasizes his patient suffering and weakness in the drunkenness that made him produce hunchbacks and albinos. Obatala lacks the revolutionary spirit of Ogun, for he operates in the domain of harmonious resolution as opposed to the conflictual. Obatala's drama, for Soyinka, is a "play of form," a "Passion Play," all fused into the essences of captivity, suffering, and redemption: "Obatala is symbolically captured, confined and ransomed. At every stage he is the embodiment of the suffering spirit of man, uncomplaining. Agonized, full of redemptive qualities of endurance and martyrdom [. . .]. The sympathetic need to be redeemed by evidence of love and human contact [. . .] this is the province of Obatala, the delicate shell of the original fullness."[24] And this is where Ijimere's *The Imprisonment of Obatala* performs a ritual drama that best illustrates the defining archetype of the deity of creation. Through the ritual sequence of captivity, suffering, and redemption, Obatala will once again recuperate his "creative control" after overcoming the transitional gulf. Conceptually, Soyinka lays out the defining principle of the Yoruba worldview:

> For the Yoruba, the gods are the final measure of eternity, as humans are of earthly transience. Past, present and future being so pertinently conceived and woven into the Yoruba worldview, the element of eternity which is the gods' prerogative does not have the same quality of remoteness or exclusiveness which it has in Christian or Buddhist culture. If we may put the same thing in fleshed-out cognitions, life, present life, contains within it manifestations of the ancestral, the living and the unborn.[25]

It is against this cyclical background and the notion of perpetual regeneration that *The Imprisonment of Obatala* helps to exemplify such a Yoruba world as it differs, contrasts, and yet complicates the Western drama whose worldview is specifically temporal and linear.

One may be tempted indeed to question Soyinka's imposition of the Yoruba world on the entire African world,[26] but as of the time of its writing or publication in 1976, Yoruba culture was what Soyinka knew best. Even if for the sake of argument one opines that Aristotle and Augusto Boal have proposed the need for emotional impact and moral change on the audience, what matters to Soyinka is the process through which the tragic form serves only as a medium to bring into oneness and resolution the human paradox and temporary duplicity of being and non-being. Thus for Soyinka, the Yoruba ritual archetype (Ogun, deity of justice) differs from the Greek (Dionysus) by the ability of Yoruba tragedy to "plunge straight into the chthonic realm" as opposed to the Grecian "principle of illusion." Yet one remains at a loss for the limits of this ritual archetype, which is not applicable to all Yoruba theatrical performances, especially now that the stage has been traded for the screen, such as the explosive series of the Nollywood extraction.

In five scenes, *The Imprisonment of Obatala* unleashes a powerful statement on the defining characteristics of Sango, Obatala, and Ogun. In this ritual drama lies the reenactment of an entire Yoruba society, though its journey motif is limited to that embarked upon by Obatala (from Ibadan to Oyo) and his encounter with Esu (deity of fate) on the road, who complicated his fate, his suffering fortune, and need for perseverance based on the warning of the community diviner. But the society we are exposed to is more complex: that of annual yam festivals, the poetry of the female body, especially of the carnal and sexual extractions, and the manipulation of will by Esu. In his seminal comparative analysis of what distinguishes Obatala from Ogun, or the rest of the deities, Soyinka advances the argument that none of the deities is self-sufficient and each deity complements the others as they all traverse the mysteries of the universe on an individual epic journey of discovery: "With creativity, however, went its complementary aspect, and Ogun came to symbolize the creative-destructive principle. His does not in any way usurp the province of Obatala whose task is to create the lifeless form of man. Nor is Obatala ever moved to destroy. Obatala is a functionalist of creation, not, like Ogun, the essence of creativity itself."[27]

As *The Imprisonment of Obatala* aptly dramatizes, Ogun, like the women and Ifá oracle, urges Sango to heed the oracular voice of reason by setting Obatala free from captivity—given that Esu is the master of confusion who deliberately causes rifts among friends (Obatala and Sango) in order for both to fulfill their rites of passage. In this sense, Esu must trick in order for Obatala and Sango to be at odds with each other; likewise the negative consequences in the community (such as the hardship of childbirth, drought, and general mishaps) of transgressing the natural order of things requires sacrificial appropriation. The release of Obatala serves as that sacrifice, and ultimately restores harmony to the community. The ritual is completed. One can only speculate on the significance of the order that replaces the chaos, but the hint comes from the closure of the play where the women, serving as classical "chorus" of sorts, chant and dance to the music, ushering in the immortality of Obatala: "Young ones never hear the death of cloth / Cloth only wears to shreds. / Old ones never hear the death of Obatala / Cloth only wears to shreds."[28] In this poetic musical, the Yoruba worldview professes that when the innocent is punished, the consequent disintegration signals disorder for the entire community, while harmony can be restored only through sacrifice, thus ensuring the ritual and cyclical order of the cosmos. In other words, for Obata to regain his primordial virtue of creation, he must submit to a season of suffering and endurance in order to ultimately triumph and regenerate.

Yet *The Imprisonment of Obatala* is not only about the fate of Obatala. Rather it successfully brings together an entire community to perform a "ritual archetype" that binds the society together. The social themes evoked through the defining charactersitics of the deities range widely: the power of the deities to unleash significant havoc on the affairs of humans; the provision of counsel to resolve puzzles of life through consultation of the Ifá oracle as divined by the Babalawo (diviner); Obatala or Supreme Deity (Orisa-Nla), King of Ife, who is ordained to create human forms that are further given breath of life by the Olodumare (Supreme Divinity or God); Sango, the God of Thunder and King of Oyo; Yemanja, the Goddess of the Sea and wife of Obatala; Oya, Goddess of the River and wife of Sango; the fertility role of the Earth as well as women as harbingers of the seed, both earthly and human, and their symbolic interactions as demonstrated through rich and provocative poetic allusions and obscenities that evoke the creative force of human sexuality;[29] Esu, the deity of the crossroads, fate, and confusion; the concept of sacrifice and scapegoating (often through bloodletting rituals) as a form of expiation when societal harmony is transgressed; the ontological, reversible, and cyclical concept of time; the journey motif that intersects with the hunting tradition that may be associated with Ogun the deity of war and iron; and the agricultural occupation of the community as translated by the figure of the Farmer and the celebration of the annual yam festival—which also intersects with the natural seasons of rain and drought—ritualized phenomena that could upset societal harmony and must be guarded and celebrated.

From this forgoing catalog of themes, it is easily decipherable that the playwright intended this play to be about the Yoruba worldview. Even if the rituals of birth and death are not particularly focused upon, they are suggested through the cycle of life: drought and rain. The advent of rain after a decade of drought may be interpreted as indeed new birth after a season of barrenness. In sum, the Yoruba worldview as presented in Ijimere's *The Imprisonment of Obatala* has many resonances with Soyinka's *Death and the King's Horseman*. Both plays dramatize the Yoruba worldview as essential unity between the world of the living, the ancestral, and the unborn as well as the essential connections between human strength and frailty when confronted with Esu's power of confusion, fate, and the crossroads.

To invoke Soyinka's notion of the "transition gulf" in *Myth, Literature and the African World*, the drama of Obatala in *The Imprisonment of Obatala* reenacts the virtues of integrity as opposed to the frailties invoked in his creation myth. The play, indeed, inverts the inherent qualities usually associated with Obatala. According to the myth, as the deity ordained to create perfect human forms, his drunkenness however made him create those considered abnormal creations such as albinos and hunchbacks. Yet in Ijimere's version that operates as a reversal of the myth or its questioning, Obatala emerges as a more credible deity as he sets out from the very beginning on a ritual journey to see his friend Sango. Obatala is King of Ife while Sango is King of Oyo. While the usual controversy about whether the contemporary Ooni (king) of Ife is not invoked, it is suggested in the sense that it is Obatala, King of Ife, who is the one setting out on a journey to visit Sango, King of Oyo. The historical Alaafin of Oyo has always been deemed the most senior (symbolically or not) of Oduduwa's children. Yet the attitude of Obatala throughout the play, whether in obeisance to the directives of the Ifá oracle or his own natural qualities of functional creativity, peacefulness, forbearance, and reconciliatory principles as opposed to the confrontational and destructive ethos of Sango, cannot be mistaken for that of a peacemaker. In his urgency and thirst to see his friend Sango, even after the divination had warned and predicted death on this fateful journey, he was still determined to go on this journey, asking the diviner what sacrifices would avert this impeding evil, as he pleads with the Babalawo: "Father of secrets, your nuts portend evil, / Your prophecy is death. / [. . .] / Even if death is unavoidable / I am determined to behold the fire / That is sparkling in Shango's eyes. / Throw your nuts again and ask / What sacrifices may buy off / The greedy hands of death."[30]

Despite his good intentions, Esu proves a defiant deity of fate as he creates tension between Obatala and the Farmer, while still on this ritualistic quest to see Sango in Oyo, when as a premonition of death, Esu causes arguments and tensions between the two. Ultimately, he is also framed by Sango's soldiers upon his arrival in Oyo, when, on seeing one of Sango's horses he thought was astray and wanting to take it along with him to Sango's place, he is accused and humiliated by Sango's servants as a thief. Consequently, he is thrown into prison on the orders of Sango, thus beginning his period of deep suffering and transitional hibernation. Even after his release, overcoming the seemingly impeding death, and reconciliation with Sango, in which Sango pleads for forgiveness, Obatala speaks metaphorically and philosophically but ultimately blames his ordeal on Esu, the twister of fate and confuser of humans, as well as his need to pay for his transgression, his drunkenness, and for which Esu is only a tool in his process of regeneration and reconciliation with the heavens: "When death is not ready to receive somebody / He will send him a doctor at the right time. / So here I am at last / Beholding the fire in your eyes again. / [. . .] / The owner of heaven has not forgiven me / [. . .] / Friendship like lost virginity / Can never be undone."[31]

The spirit of atonement, reconciliation, and regeneration continues with Obatala even as the Babalawo also confirms a new season of creativity, as if suggesting that the era of drunkenness and weaknesses is over and "the time of creation has come,"[32] but not before the women have chanted the praise of Obatala to evoke his functional creative properties once again, as if invoking him into provocative action: "Obatala is patient—he is not angry. / He rests in the sky like a swarm of bees. / [. . .] / Obatala, the silent one: / [. . .] / Obatala who turns blood into children. / [. . .] / But I know you keep twenty, thirty children for me / Whom I shall bear."[33] Even as the play comes to an end, it is instructive to analyze the Epilogue in which Esu, the deity of fate, returns to praise Obatala as a counterbalance to his role of confusion. Instead of confusion and tension, Esu himself sings the praise of Obatala. Yet the spirit of celebration is short-lived, as Esu also predicts beyond the moment of merriment that he will surely return to confuse men—suggesting perhaps a sense of perpetuity in the cycle of life: "For years to come / The earth will never fail them; / The palm tree will not cease to bleed / For them with oil and wine. / [. . .] / Yet in serving Obatala, the father of laughter, / [. . .] / The time will come when the owner of Heaven / Will send me back to confuse the head of men."[34]

It is also remarkable that Esu not only warns of his imminent return, he catalogs through analogy with Ogun, as if to set the stage for a season when Obatala will be in conflict with Ogun, even if the current stalemate with Sango appears to be resolved. In Esu's logic, the devotees are actually serving two deities (Obatala and Ogun), for when they sacrifice to Obatala (in which there is bloodletting), the instrument used, the knife, resides in the domain of Ogun. Esu in this sense serves as an antagonist throughout the play: creating confusion, praising a temporary conquest, and predicting a return of his trickster games with passionate vengeance: "Yet in serving Obatala, the father of laughter, / In worshipping the father of peace / They still use iron. / Obatala's children must suffer the iron / [. . .] / The goat offered to the father of laughter / Suffer Ogun's iron on its throat. / The child that Obatala moulds in the womb / Is begot and born with blood."[35]

Esu's function is established from the beginning to the end of the play as agent of uncertainty and mischief. He announces himself as a shameless provocateur adept at twisting the fate of his victims at will— hence the constant reminder in Yoruba culture always to give to Esu, before anything else, what belongs to Esu. Sacrificing to Esu in order to maintain societal harmony is not optional, as Esu will always be waiting at the crossroads of transition where all human subjects, for good or for ill, must traverse. One could also advance the argument that in the ritual archetype, as well as in every stage of transition, Esu is constantly at the gates, earnestly expecting his ritual sacrifice in order to avert any mishap or potential twist of fate for his devotees who heed his instructions. In summation, regeneration may be impossible if Esu is not appeased. The questions remain: How much is Esu responsible for every human being's fortune or misfortune? Is the sacrifice to Esu not a sacrifice for the so-called everyman? In this sense, can we argue that in the Yoruba worldview, without appeasing Esu, there can be no regeneration, either symbolic or material? The moral for Obatala's predicament resides in the fact that before responding to his calling as the functional creator of human beings, he must have failed to sacrifice to Esu—hence his inadvertent drunkenness and the ensuing creation of deformed beings.

The versions of Yoruba creation myths are many, and each version seems to modify slightly the entire story without deviation from the main structure about the transgression of Obatala and the consequent punishment. In his own collection of nineteen "poetic chants" from Ifá verses, *The Adventures of Obatala: Ifá and Santería God of Creativity*, Ifayemi Eleburuibon names the first one as exactly the title of the play by Ijimere: "The Imprisonment of Obatala." In this poetic rendition,

Obatala is portrayed as failing to offer sacrifice before setting out on a journey in order to avoid embarrassment along the way. A probability equation can be drawn: if Obatala had sacrificed, the probability that he would have be mistaken for the mad man a community has been looking for and who must be arrested would have been next to nil. Yet, by disobeying the Ifá oracle, he was mistaken as the mad community harasser and was erroneously arrested. This is the divinational background to the "imprisonment of Obatala," which is not included in Ijimere's version. Perhaps this is a case of poetic license on the part of Ijimere, who invoked drunkenness as the tragic flaw of Obatala. Yet, even in that same version, Obatala was warned to persevere and not resist any attempt at humiliation by others since he would ultimately overcome the obstacles and adversaries. The mistaken identity and the consequent imprisonment serve as didactic experience in order for the community to learn from Obatala's tragic fate.

In three pages of chant-like Ifá verses on the incarceration of Obatala, Eleburuibon sums up many themes that can be structurally highlighted as follows: (1) journey motif; (2) divination, non-sacrifice, and transgression; (3) mistaken identity and imprisonment as punishment; (4) innocence and societal punishment; (5) release of Obatala, forgiveness of society, and restoration of order; (6) Constant veneration of Obatala with a white robe and snail stew.[36] Of these different moments of the plot structure, I find the first two the most compelling as they set Obatala up for his impeding success or failure. The following verses capture his tragic drama: "Before people undertake any important project / they must seek the advice of Ifá / Yoruba god of wisdom. / Obatala consults these priests [. . .] / and the priests advised him to sacrifice / to avoid embarrassment / Obatala did not make sacrifice [. . .] / The inhabitants of Isolu are aware of a mad man / who always comes to this river and molests the people. / [. . .] / This made people give warning to everyone / That whenever they come across him again / He must be arrested."[37] Though innocent of the "crime" he has been punished with by the society, the initial crime was not to have sacrificed as advised by the Ifá oracle.

In the Yoruba culture, justice is often tempered with mercy. A king who has transgressed in his hometown may decide to abdicate the throne and seek refuge elsewhere. Before his arrival, the new community in which he wants to sojourn anew may already be suffering from untold atrocities, and the oracle may have foretold the arrival of an itinerant who must be made king in order to restore order in the community. The logic of this tendency of integration after disintegration stems from the belief that such a transgressor must be given a second chance. The case of Obatala, whose devotees worship him today all over the world and is considered the "supreme divinity," also offers a didactic notion: even the most powerful is not immune from human frailty—and perhaps the morale is that even the deities are human and can make mistakes. And if the deities ae so frail and subject to error, human beings should take a cue from them that disintegration is but a stage in the journey of life and through a reverse sacrifice, even in the form of imprisonment or punishment, restorative justice and harmony can be regained. The entire journey of Obatala could be read as a series of restorative rites of passage, geared toward attaining cyclical or ritualistic regeneration.

Orphism, Ritual Vision, and the Carnivalesque: From Orpheus and *Orfeu da Conceição* to Cinematic Adaptations

Orphism,[38] as evoked in the Greek Orpheus, is the mix of the cult of Apollo (the purifier) on the one hand and Greek Dionysian (mystery) cult on the other. The reality of this religious movement, which dates to the sixth century BC, was revitalized due to the discovery in 1962 of the "Derveni Papyrus," a philosophical commentary on Orphic cosmogony. Orphism involves three relatively autonomous types of religious phenomena. First, there are traditions concerning the birth, life, and descent of Orpheus into the underworld, his singing among the Thracians, and his tragic death. Next we have a rule of conduct by Orphics, that is, those who believe in living in the "Orphic manner" regarding eternal salvation in the Hellenic world. Orphics believe that salvational aspiration stems from the ancestral soul being that of the fallen god, which may be restored to its original state through ritual purifications. The physical body is understood as a prison chamber for the fallen essence of a person. Orphics equally teach that individual souls are trapped in an endless cycle of reincarnations until purification is completed and the soul can be released from matter's deathly grip and return to the Eternity from which it fell. Experientially, evil is derived from the mixture of the material in the soul and the gradual dispersion of the soul into the material body because of prolonged contact with the latter in consequence of the necessary entropic increase. It is the mix of the material in the otherwise entirely immaterial soul that causes the latter's continuous return back to the material world subject to continuous entropic disintegration. The triumph of the divine over the bodily would be assured by following the Orphic rites of initiation, purification, and asceticism, which confirms the dwelling in the afterlife—that is, the blissful realm of infinitude with immortal beings or deities. Orpheus was the main representation of tragic arts and the significance of the lyre, with which he entranced deities, humans, and animals, along with his sonorous voice. He continues to be of high importance in the religious history of Greece. Religion and mystery surround the myth of Orpheus. Orpheus is said to be the keeper of rites and religions, one who founded or rendered accessible many important cults (such as those of Apollo and the Thracian god Dionysus) and prescribed initiatory and purificatory rituals.

Orphism thus suggests that the decisive disengagement of salvation within the milieu of the Dionysian cult in particular—and of the Hellenic mystery religions in general, leading the soul to Hades after death as in the case of Orpheus, the singer in search of Eurydice—justified all sorts of descriptions of the infernal world. This oracular ritual descent into the underworld, which is in order to know the future, may have been borrowed from the common religious cultural context of heaven and hell. Christian salvation seeks to withdraw from the karmic chain of cause and effect based on evil done (sin or moral fault), whereas Orphism as a mystery religion or cosmologic myth demands the recitation of the necessary knowledge learned in order to be saved during initiation. The death of Orpheus symbolically represents his self-sacrifice in order to redeem human suffering by way of sin. In the legends of Dionysus, Orpheus is represented as so devout in his love for Apollo (Sun, the greatest of the gods) that he scales the highest mountain in Thrace (Mount Pangaeus) in order to be the first to salute the Sun. Dionysus is subsequently so filled with jealous rage due to this daily ritual that he sends barbarian women to dismember Orpheus and tear him into pieces. Orpheus functions as the redemptive figure that saves mankind from their original sin by being killed in the same way in which mankind had killed the father-god. Consequently, Christianity appears to be influenced by the Dionysian-Orpheus mood in terms of sin and the redemption of sin through ritual sacrifice.

As a storehouse of mythological information, the myth of Orpheus contains a wide range of mythological thinking, as manifest in hymns and poems recited in mystery-rites and purification rituals. Though not much is known about the original Thracian Orphic Mysteries and rituals, through history Orpheus is known as a god of love and death whose adherents valued esoteric knowledge and an ascetic life as a prerequisite for their soul to achieve a higher level in the afterlife. The Greeks preferred Dionysian carnivals of rebirth and the consumption of wine to the stories of afterlife contained in Orphism. While the cult of Dionysus was simple, primitive, spontaneous, and emotional, that of Orpheus is elaborate, sophisticated, controlled, and intellectual. Yet both systems had much in common. Both centered in the same god, Dionysus. Both aimed at the same goal, immortality through divinity. Both sought to attain that goal through prescribed rites and ceremonies. Both made a strictly individualistic appeal and were highly developed along the lines of personal experience. But Orphism fostered an ascetic rule of life that was the exact opposite of Dionysian license, and developed an elaborate theology of a highly speculative character. In brief, Orphism represented a reformed Dionysianism. The interplay of rites, deities, and humans in Orpheus myth affords the reader a balanced perspective of Greek cosmology and mythology.

Features of the Grecian Orpheus

Celebrated as the mythic king of Thrace, Orpheus, the son of Apollo, the sun deity, evolved from the lineage of the Greek god of music— hence Orpheus's undeniable and intoxicating talent for song. He was not vulnerable to drunkenness as Obatala, the Yoruba deity, was, and he was able to play the lyre with little effort. Orpheus sang with such a sweet voice that he was able to soothe beasts, and caused trees to bend toward him in order to listen to his melodies. Orpheus was considered a hero not because he was a great soldier but because of his prodigious musical talents. A member of the exclusive group of Argonauts, Orpheus used his captivating voice to calm the seas and move the ocean rocks that would have destroyed other ships. It was also told that Orpheus's voice soothed the mythical dragon guarding the Golden Fleece into a slumber. The central defining character of Orpheus beyond his musical ingenuity was his deep love for Eurydice, whom he loved so much that he married her. They were passionately in love with each other, but an antagonist came along to separate them in the figure of Aristaeus.

Aristaeus, a deity of land and agriculture, was fond of Eurydice and pursued her. Devoted to Orpheus, Eurydice rejected Aristaeus's advances and one day, while running from Aristaeus, Eurydice ran into the path of a snake, the symbolic "death" figure in their relationship, was bitten, and died. Devastated, Orpheus vowed to make the heroic journey into the underworld to retrieve her from death.

Orpheus descended into the underworld, where he sang to Cerberus, the vicious three-headed guard dog, hypnotized him, and, using his musical talents, convinced Hades to let him take Eurydice back to their earthly home. Hades agreed but gave Orpheus one condition: if he wanted to take Eurydice home with him, under no circumstance could he look back. He must ascend with her following behind him, and without looking back, until they both reached the earth. Naturally in love, Orpheus could not stop himself. He desperately had to ensure that Eurydice was following closely behind him, and he tragically looked back, thus losing Eurydice forever. Orpheus became more agitated and devastated than ever. He self-secluded in his home in Thrace and was eventually torn apart by a group of women who were furious that he would no longer be able to participate in the Bacchanalian festival or carnival. Such was the legendary tragic end of love-deprived Orpheus. In Orphic mythology, it is strongly believed that Orpheus was reunited eternally with Eurydice since he did not make it out of the underworld. Perhaps his was a case of love lost and love regained, at least in Greek mythology.

The Grecian Orpheus has been portrayed exclusively as a hero. The need to see him as such has superseded that of seeing him as a potential villain. Yet, in order to have a balanced perspective, Orpheus must also be seen as fallible, as human, and as prone to flaws as anyone. Operating in a deified cosmological context of heroes and deities, it is odd that Orpheus should have doubted that Eurydice would be following right behind him. It appears that his "human" qualities overwhelmed his "divine" characteristics. Thus Orpheus's failure in his mission to bring back Eurydice to life is ample proof of his humanity. On one hand, he remains a hero because he did not require human intervention to overcome death since his metaphoric descent implies that he had to die in order to go to the underworld against all odds to retrieve Eurydice. On the other hand, his backward gaze raises issues of his insecurity that led him to momentary nervousness as he made the exit from the underworld. That sudden yet irreparable moment of confusion and vulnerability sealed his fate and rendered him quite human and less of a deity, even if he symbolically returned to the underworld to remain with Eurydice.

Dramaturgic Adaptations of Orpheus: Vinícius's *Orfeu da Conceição*

Many are the classical versions of the Orpheus myth, but varied are the strategies of adaptations. From the "master" narrative to the ambivalent versions, every adaptor has developed, expanded, modified, and radically reinvented the story to suit an interpretation. Though most of the inventions are focused on Orpheus through varied ancient Greco-Latin myths in poems, songs, plays, and paintings, Sarah Ruhl's *Eurydice*[39] is the most radical in that instead of portraying Orpheus as the legendary deity of music and reincarnation, it makes Eurydice call out to Orpheus and cause his backward gaze, thus complicating the prospect of her returning to the earthly world with Orpheus. In comparison to other versions, Eurydice has more political agency in Ruhl's work, especially regarding her relationship with her dead father. Virgil's *Georgics* and Ovid's *Metamorphoses* provide ample evidence of these significant structural modifications.[40] The myth of Orpheus is incomplete without understanding the story of Persephone, the goddess of the Underworld. In Greek mythology, Persephone was the enchanting daughter of Demeter and Zeus. While she was picking flowers as a young maiden with some Nymphs, Hades rose up from the earth and stole her away as his bride. Demeter, Persephone's father, searched everywhere for his lost daughter, and later, Helios, the sun deity, shared Persephone's ordeal with him. Consequently, Zeus obliged Hades to return Persephone to the earthly world. In the meantime, Hades fooled Persephone by making her eat forbidden pomegranate seeds, which obliged her to remain in the underworld permanently. As a result, Persephone was reunited with her mother, but was compelled to visit the underworld every year, thus explaining the tradition of seasons. Persephone's empathy with Orpheus for having lost a loved one inspired her to give him permission to regain his bride in the underworld.

On one hand, Virgil's *Georgics* narrates the plight of Eurydice as she was fleeing from Aristaeus, an immature demigod who often caused trouble. As she fled from him she did not see the poisonous snake lurking in the grass. She was bitten and later died. Orpheus, Apollo and

Calliope's son, famed for his beautiful music, was married to Eurydice. Following her death, Orpheus's mourning songs affected everyone, as if the entire world was mourning with Orpheus. Orpheus sang his way through the gates of hell. Persephone, the goddess of the underworld, instructed him to return with Eurydice following invisibly behind him. Unfortunately, Orpheus was overcome by love madness and turned to look back at Eurydice. For Virgil, those in hell would forgive Orpheus if only they knew the "madness of love." Eurydice cried "What is it, what madness, Orpheus, was it that has destroyed us, you and me, oh look!" Instantly, Eurydice went into a deep slumber as she slipped back into the depths of hell. Orpheus's fate was cemented as nocturnal women tore him to pieces. Though beheaded, he continued to sing his sad melodies.

On the other hand, Ovid's *Metamorphoses* narrates how Orpheus planned to marry Eurydice, but the wedding did not go as designed. Hymen did not bless the occasion with joyous fervor. Sadly, Eurydice was wandering through the fields with nymphs when she was bit by a poisonous snake. Orpheus played his sad song, and the whole world wept with him. Even the cursed Sisyphus stayed put on his rock instead of rolling it back. At the request of Persephone, Hades allowed Eurydice to return to the earthly world with the condition of not looking back. Due to his breaching the condition, Orpheus lost Eurydice forever. Orpheus withdrew to the banks of river Styx, fasted, and even castrated himself so as not to satisfy the burning desires of other women. Rather, he kept singing his sad songs, and after being beaten to death by the Thracian women whom he rejected and scorned, he was compelled to return to the underworld (through death) to be with Eurydice forever in the Elysian Fields.

Of the two classical versions, Ovid's interpretation of Orpheus is more sensitive than that of Virgil. Aristaeus, the mischievous antagonist or rival of Orpheus, portrayed in Ruhl's interpretation as the "nasty interesting man," is nonexistent. Hence, it is completely Orpheus's fault that he lost Eurydice; it was due to Orpheus's temporary confusion and madness that he lost Eurydice forever. Comparatively, in Ovid's inter-pretation, Orpheus was worried that his wife might be too tired and faint—hence the backward gaze. Above all, in Ovid's version Orpheus and Eurydice were reunited in the underworld, while in Virgil's version they were separated forever. Beyond these two classical versions, three others exist in which the myth varies from author to author. Euripides, for example, narrates the story of Admetus, King of Thessaly, who permitted the death of his wife instead of him. Admetus reasoned that if he had the powerful lyre of Orpheus, he could retrieve his wife from death and hell. Plato, in his own version, went against the musical musing thesis and argued that Orpheus preferred to die in the hands of other women than in the hands of Eurydice. Socrates, in *Busiris*,[41] equally postulated that Orpheus made it out of the underworld with Eurydice to create a cult that guaranteed reincarnation. In sum, Orpheus mythology in its variants suggests that the descent into the underworld was a rite of passage in order to discover the mysteries of the afterlife.

As Charles Perrone notes of the play and film,

> Black Orpheus and the predecessor play have similar multi-national connections and antecessors. The most fundamental of these is, of course, the Orpheus myth in Greek mythology, which since antiquity has been frequently represented in Western arts. The drama by Vinícius de Moraes, is part of a literary continuum that dates back to the classical period, and the film, a loose adaptation, adds itself to this tradition.[42]

The literary critic highlights the origins and new Brazil contexts of the Orpheus cultural production, especially regarding the increasingly problematic notion of racial democracy in Brazil. The Brazilianization of Orpheus is as appropriate as it is problematic for this political application of agency. Blending music and performance with local color, within a pre-military dictatorship milieu, *Orfeu da Conceição* re-imagines Brazilian identity in approximation with Greek mythology. Yet Orpheus is not the typical Brazilian *malandro*, for beyond his ability to soothe all animate and inanimate entities, his personal quest has an element of the supernatural, thus making him more of a semi-deity than a national hero. This mix of the hero and deity falls within an oxymoronic conceptualization since the two are not mutually exclusive. Deities by their very divinity have supernatural powers that qualify them as heroes and heroines.

Yet, as in many legends and myths, heroes and heroines become humanized, thus becoming susceptible to the foibles of all humanity. The naming of the original Brazilian Orpheus as "Orpheus, Child of the Virgin Mary" (referencing the Catholic notion of "Our Lady of Conception") evokes the Jesus–Mary dialectic: innocent, immaculate, flawless, pure, and yet human. If Orpheus's natural love for music, his passion for his Eurydice, and his struggle against antagonistic cosmic forces that sent him back to the primordial times are elements for the consideration of Brazilianness, such an idealized character seems quite a-Brazilian—for, as the saying goes, "no one is innocent in São Paulo," which may be extended to the entire Brazilian nation. In sum the Brazilian Orpheus is as human as he is divine, bridging all the elements of the sacred and the profane in order to represent a totality of the fallible Brazilian. After all, despite the complex issues of Brazilian racial relations, music, like the eternal voice of Orpheus that survives him, remains the unifying factor of Brazilian society.

From a Greco-Roman to a Brazilian tragedy of Orpheus, a number of dramatic changes are noteworthy: (1) a romanticized transformation of Orpheus from the quasi-divine Greek to the Brazilian *favela* dweller in Rio de Janeiro; (2) the Afro-Brazilian "Other" becomes the Orpheus "self" in an attempt to effect an egalitarian image of Brazilian society by adding the obvious African influence; (3) love between Orpheus and Eurydice remains a constant even if problematized by a human antagonist instead of a deity; (4) Orpheus's father, Apollo, is not quite developed as the one who passed on the knowledge of music to Orpheus; rather, Orpheus's love for music and the power thereof supersedes the source of the power; (5) all versions converge in Orpheus's search for deceased Eurydice in the underworld; (6) it was not apparent that it was through music that Orpheus gained access to the underworld in the Brazilian version, though music was part of his societal significance; (7) Orpheus loses Eurydice due to the forbidden backward gaze; (8) Orpheus was killed by resentful women he had scorned in favor of Eurydice; (9) the music of Orpheus transcends death and is eternal in the mouths of the people; and (10) *Orfeu da Conceição* takes place in the context of Brazilian Carnival. These changes are only noticeable when compared to the Greco-Roman versions that Vinícius de Moraes consulted in order to produce his Brazilian version.

The Orpheus myth was initially transcribed by Apollonius Rhodius, a Greek poet, in *The Voyage of the Argo*, in the thirteenth century BC while Virgil and Ovid, two Roman poets, interpreted the myth while preserving the essential characteristics of Orpheus as the enchanting musician who had inherited the qualities of his parents: Apollo, the father was considered "magical musician," while his mother, Calliope, was deemed the Muse of epic poetry.

Considered the most soothing mortal singer in all of Thrace, Orpheus was able to move rivers, rocks, and trees and attract birds, animals, and beautiful maidens alike to him. It is arguable that Orpheus used this musical art to attract Eurydice and marry her. But the joy was not to last: Eurydice is bitten by a snake, dies, and is sought after by grieving Orpheus. Orpheus fails to heed the warning of not looking back as he exits the underworld where he had gone to retrieve Eurydice, and loses her for a second time. Orpheus is thus condemned to sing sad songs under the trees and along the meadows and in the forests, and to be loved by many women whom he rejects. Ovid continues the narrative in *The Death of Orpheus*, where jealous Maenads in a frenzied rage destroy him, floating his head in the River Hebrus. Orpheus has since become the subject of many poets, playwrights, and cineasts focusing on ill-fated love, as in Shakespeare's *Romeo and Juliet*, for example.

From the viewpoint of the cinematic adaptation in *Black Orpheus* (1959), set in Rio de Janeiro during the colorful, musical, and vibrant celebration of Carnival, the Brazilian version of the Greek tale is enriched by the cultural diversity unique to Brazil where the indigenous mixes with the African, European, Jewish, and the Japanese to create a mesmerizing film version of the Orpheus myth as directed by Marcel Camus, along with the samba, bossa nova, and jazz of Antônio Carlos Jobim and Luís Bonfa. Comparative analogies between the Greek characters and the Brazilian are apparent, such as the personifications of Eurydice, Hermes, the Muses, Mira (the antagonistic Maenad), Death, Sarafina, and Orpheus, the ultimate tragic hero who succumbed to death in his quest for love. The cinematic adaptation is the celebration of life itself beyond spatial and national boundaries: the traditional Greco-Roman garb reminiscent of the Golden era meets with the music-infused, Africanized, sacred, popular, and flamboyantly colorful festival where the women remind one of Versailles and the children rekindle hope for a new beginning. Mira, the antagonistic Maenad, throws a deadly stone at Orpheus, who was carrying Eurydice in his hands, and both roll back to the underground, thus continuing the cyclical ritual of the Orpheus-Eurydice myth in a romantic and festive ambience suggestive of the triumph of the human spirit even in death.

The history of the production of *Orfeu da Conceição* dates back to 1942, when Vinícius de Moraes, a Brazilian career diplomat, met with Waldo Frank, an American writer who was researching Latin American cultures. This opportune meeting led to cultural research of Afro-Brazilian life in Rio de Janeiro. They toured many *favelas* or shantytowns, samba schools, and *terreiros* (ritual worship temples). While conducting these ethnographic visits, they noticed some approximation between Greek and Afro-Brazilian cultures. Such a discovery triggered an unconscious Atlantic crossing that ultimately produced a text that would radicalize Brazilian race relations globally, especially with the future adaptation of *Orfeu da Conceição* into a classic film, *Orfeu Negro*, in 1959. As Vinícius (as he is known) notes, following the reading of the classical Orpheus myth, he started thinking about "the life of blacks on the hillsides and how to Hellenicize their life,"[43] thus radicalizing and contextualizing a Greek myth into the reality of the *favela*. Vinícius wrote the play at different times: Act I was written in a single night, while the second and third acts were written while he was on diplomatic posting in Los Angeles in 1946, with a Carnival club serving as his inspiration for the underworld. Vinícius later lost the third act, but in 1953, João Cabral de Mello, a fellow diplomat, persuaded him to rewrite the lost act, and he eventually submitted the play to a competition, where it won first prize.

After almost ten years of fruitless seeking for funding for a cinematic adaptation, Vinícius received some help to stage the play. *Orfeu da Conceição* was performed on September 25, 1956, at the Teatro Municipal in Rio for an entire week. Under a new title, *Orfeu Negro* was staged by a small Rio theater company in 1974 to express the excluded life of the black population. In 1987, thirty-one years after the first staging, Haroldo Costa secured funding from the secretary of culture to stage another version of the play at the João Caetano Theater, but the plan proved abortive. In 1995, a full-fledged production of *Orfeu da Conceição* was directed by Haroldo Costa at the Rio Teatro Municipal. Reconstructing the three acts into two and using songs from the film version, the production of the play coincided with the tricentennial celebration of Zumbi dos Palmares, the leader of the Brazilian seventeenth-century maroon community. Critics questioned the timing of the state-sponsored production with Zumbi celebrations given the insignificance of race in the play.

Yet, in blending the African (Dionysian) with the European (Apollonian), Vinícius succeeded in drawing attention to the unequal lifestyles in the *favelas* or *morros* (slums) when compared to those of privileged whites in affluent communities, while at the same time drawing contrasts between Greek and Brazilian traditions as creatively meshed into the Carnival performance.

The story of love becomes a pretext to discuss racial relations even if Vinícius may not have consciously set out to do so. Perrone suggests that while the critical reception of the play has been "unenthusiastic," its "paratexts," including prefaces, afterwords, and notes, provide invaluable information about Afro-Brazilian culture. Perrone's claim that the play lacks "nuanced conflict" and that it "relies more on performance than on dialogue or the development of dramatic actions"[44] is a simplification of what indeed was a novelty on Brazilian stage at the time (despite the achievements of the *Teatro Experimental do Negro*, founded in 1944): the staging of an all-black cast on a national scale. Superimposed on the love conflict is the life–death conflict that Orpheus and Eurydice are faced with. Perhaps Perrone's remarks speak to the fact that the analogies between the legendary characters are rather too close to the Brazilian version for there to be an apparent contrast. I would argue that the fact that the setting is the Brazilian *favela* in itself changes all the dynamics and evokes both tension and agitation based on the stark reality of inequalities that the Carnival performance succeeds in masking.

Orfeu da Conceição enacts an overlapping story of love, conflict, and death, while the Carnival ambience soothes the tragedy by balancing sadness with ephemeral moments of joyful celebration of life. In Act I, Orpheus expresses his love for Eurydice against the objections of Clio, his mother. Following jealousies and rivalries that culminate in the death of Eurydice, Orpheus is grieved and determined to find Eurydice. Act II showcases a Carnival party during which Orpheus searches for Eurydice in vain. Since there was no indication of her retrieval from the underworld, the central conflict of her permanent loss to death, as in the Greek myth, is omitted—likewise the classical backward gaze that leads to her final loss. In Act III, Orpheus dejectedly returns to the *favela*, where he dies at the hands of angry Maenads while still reaching out to Eurydice even as he dies. In the concluding part, the Chorus sings the eternity of Orpheus's voice:

Juntaram-se a Mulher, a Morte a Lua	Women, Death, and Moon conspired
Para matar Orfeu, com tanta sorte	To kill Orpheus and with much luck
Que mataram Orfeu, a alma da rua	They killed Orpheus, the soul of the streets
Orfeu, o generoso, Orfeu, o forte.	Orpheus, the generous, Orpheus, the strong
Porém as três não sabem de uma coisa:	However the three missed something:

Para matar Orfeu não basta	In order to kill Orpheus
a Morte.	Death suffices not.
Tudo morre que nasce e	All that is born and lives
que viveu	must die
Só não morre no mundo	Only the voice of Orpheus is
a voz de Orfeu	immortal

In this philosophical ending lies the central conflict, even if it excludes Eurydice, since she had been lost to Death already, and that mysterious act engenders Orpheus's death. In Act I, Corifeu, who also represents the Chorus, had predicted that many are the dangers facing anyone madly in love, especially when "moon" appears suddenly, a metaphor for the loved woman (and the potential harm she can cause), who serves as the muse for the inspired lover. This cyclical framing indicates that, even from the very first act, the ambience of tragedy had been structurally set in motion.

Orfeu da Conceição made Brazilian theater history because it brought into motion subsequent protest theater of the 1960s and 1970s, as represented in such works as Arena Conta Zumbi and Gota d'Água, among others. Though subtle in its engagement with race relations, and accused of exoticization and objectification of Afro-Brazilian culture, Vinícius truly wished he could call attention to racial questions in Brazil. Though the Teatro Experimental do Negro (TEN) (Black Experimental Theater), founded by Abdias do Nascimento in 1944, has a more radical goal of black consciousness-raising, as well as promoting black theatrical organizations, Vinícius started writing Orfeu much earlier. Thus Vinícius may well have contributed to the emergence of black theater even if he was not as committed as Abdias do Nascimento was. Deploying theater as a means to an end, Nascimento sought to find solutions to racial discrimination, advocated negritude, subjected to critique the ideology of whiteness, and promoted African contributions to Brazilian culture. There was thus a conflict of interest for TEN actors, who felt that Afro-Brazilian experience was being presented by a white Brazilian from the viewpoint of a Greek myth that had minimal African influence. In his preface to Dramas para Negros e Prólogo para Brancos, Nascimento hoped to include Orfeu da Conceição in a second edition but also suggested that the play did not truly embrace black aesthetics. Vinícius seems ambivalent about racial tensions and falls in with the stereotypical view of blacks as contributing to Brazilian culture, not on an equal footing with European ideals but as an observer from a distance. What interested Vinícius may have been the mystifying nature of Afro-Brazilian culture through its music and dances, and less through its intelligence. The point of departure of the play was a Western myth imposed on an Afro-Brazilian experience and not vice versa. Implicitly, then, despite its pioneering accomplishments, the play remains an adaptation and not representative of germane Afro-Brazilian theatrical practices.

Jorge de Lima's *Invenção de Orfeu*

Though not dealing exclusively with the reality of Orpheus, the Orphic problematic resonates quite prominently in the epic poem *Invenção de Orfeu* (1952) by Jorge de Lima. The poet had also written on Afro-Brazilian issues, especially in his singular collection of poems *Poemas Negros* (1947). It was in the same context of Afro-Brazilian living conditions that Vinícius located *Orfeu da Conceição*, though he did not envisage the criticism the play would engender relative to the treatment of Afro-Brazilians as objects of exotica. Marcel Camus's cinematic adaptation of Vinícius's play evoked, among other issues, the racial complexities of living in the *favela*. Lima's epic treatment of Orpheus is as mythic as the Greek but with more universal incursions into Luso-Brazilian myths. Considered one of the most import works of Brazilian poetry, *Invenção de Orfeu* is an invaluable contribution to Brazilian cultural, poetic, and linguistic patrimony. It is a long subjective epic poem often compared to Camões's *Os Lusíadas*. The epic weaves together a number of notable classic epics within social reality, including the *Divine Comedy*, Aeneid, Camões, and the Bible. A mythic journey involving confrontation with Hell, Paradise, and some Muses (such as Inês de Castro and Mira), *Invenção de Orfeu* seeks to transgress tradition by fragmenting logical thought and replacing it with the senses, imagination, and fantasy. Granted that in comparison to the reality of inequalities, the theatrical portrayal of Rio's hillsides is nothing short of a superficial portrayal geared more toward exporting the "miscegenation" thesis about Brazil as a nation living in harmonious racial relations. The mythic element of the play must have overshadowed the social reality. What then is the contribution of *Invenção de Orfeu* to the reinvention of the Brazilian Orpheus?

Combining Catholicism with surrealism, Jorge de Lima in *Invenção de Orfeu* offers not a cohesive treatise on Brazilian identity but fragments of an Afro-European nation. Complex and erudite, the text navigates a number of genres and styles: metered verses, songs, ballads, lyrics—in sum, poetry in body and soul. From poems about childhood, to surrealist episodes steeped in the mortal search for meaning and plenitude, to the proposal for a sacred journey toward divinity and spirituality, the epic poem, structured as a unity of ten fragmented poems (cantos), creates a Brazilian version of a universal epic. In the introduction, Jorge de Lima states his intention:

> With this book, I intended to create a modern epic with a unique poem, divided into ten poems. A modern epic needs not have a novelistic content. It needs depend neither on a geographical history nor classical models of the epic. I realized once I had finished writing the poem that somehow unconsciously, due to my total submission to the poem, that not only Time and Space were absent in this my long poem, [but] that I had structured this my long poem against the grain of traditional Lusitanian and Camonian models, thus creating something uniquely Brazilian.[45]

In Poem III, verses 23 and 24, the analogy of the epic with the myth of Orpheus is apparent, especially the tale of Orpheus's descent as likened to that of Christ as He traverses the ritual of life, suffering, and death:

Orfeu e o estro mais forte	Orpheus, the strongest gadfly
Dentro da curta vida	Within a short-lived life
a teça toda fruída,	the all fruity capsule
frente que já não pensa	faced with the unthinkable
canção erma, suspensa,	song deserted, suspended
Orfeu diante da morte.[46]	Orpheus in the face of death.

In the same movement, the epic recaps the myth of Eurydice as Orpheus seeks to liberate her from the underworld. Jorge de Lima links this episode to that of the biblical Eva (Eve), who caused man to sin in the Garden of Eden and was consequently cursed, thus necessitating the death of Christ to redeem humanity. Through a mix of mythology, religiosity, and metaphysics, Jorge de Lima reinvents by approximating Eva's fall with that of Eurydice as well as all humanity through the prism of Muses:

Eurídice, Eva espessa,	Eurydice, voluptious Eve
musa de doces trevas,	muse of the sweet darkness,
mais do que todas as Evas	more than all the Eves
musa obscura, Eva obscura:	obscure muse, obscure Eve:
sextina que procura	the sextet that tries
acabar, e começa.[47]	to end, and starts all over.

These lines about Eurydice, like the ones about Orpheus, recognize the mortality and immortality of both heroic figures by situating them as demi-deities whose story is larger than life.

By creating a fragmented cosmology in which past mythologies interact with present and future truths or distortions, Jorge de Lima seeks a transgressive representation of reality while purifying poetic language to its esoteric limits. Through such a personal archeology of intertextuality, deliberate obscurity, and multiplicity of meanings, de Lima invents an Orpheus whose irrationality only begets rationality when all old logic is set aside for new possibilities of logical thinking. Orpheus is the coded image of Christ who must go through a series of temptations, suffering, anguish, and then expiation in which he sheds his blood for the transgressions of the world. The metaphorical descent is only a pretext for a necessary ritualistic sacrifice in order to return a chaotic world to its primordial harmony. Orpheus's music is the mediation of the dance of death and of life as Orpheus acquires a supernatural ability to bring all fragmented entities into a cosmic balance through the power of his lyre. Yet his songs, though they outlast him, cannot save him from making the ultimate sacrifice. Orpheus must pay the ultimate price for the transgressions of humanity as represented by Eva (Eurydice), whose error was to resign herself to the diabolic deception of the snake. The question is less about who is to blame for Orpheus's backward gaze than the acceptability of the logic of the inevitable. In order to save Orpheus from himself and from the agonies of the world, Eurydice must serve as the ultimate enigma—the enchanting embodiment of love, death, and rebirth.

Cinematic Adaptation of *Orfeu Negro*

Three years after the staging of *Orfeu da Conceição* in 1956, and amidst negative critical reception that contested the representation of Rio de

Janeiro as a metaphorical hell for the *favela* dwellers, Marcel Camus would in 1959 release a Franco-Brazilian film (now a classic), *Orfeu Negro*, which made an immediate national and international impact. *Orfeu Negro* not only broke box-office records, it went on to win the coveted Palme d'Or (Golden Palm) award at the Cannes Film Festival in France and an Oscar in 1960 for best foreign-language film in the United States. Using the festive context of Carnival as its setting, the film calls attention to the economic disparity between the haves and the have-nots, even if the majority of the actors were black. Through the overt celebration of African culture, the film covertly exposes the racial tensions in Brazil that have been denied or publicly downplayed by the myth of racial democracy. In suggesting that Brazil encourages multiracial relations with no racial or color bias, the theoretical supposition problematizes Brazilian identity and the complexity that such a masked form of discrimination engenders. In domesticating Greek Orpheus and making him Black in the Brazilian context, Camus may have succeeded where Vinícius de Moraes suffered a social stigma for trying to impose a European model on Brazil and thus perpetuate the implicit vitality but not equality of African culture with the European. Could Brazilian culture not have been evoked as a parallel of European culture? Granted, no culture can claim to be pure, but the appropriation of Greek mythology to Brazilian reality raises a question of whether the Greeks are closer to Brazilians in their origins than are Africans. Historically, the enslavement of Africans in Brazil has influenced Brazil more than any other traumatic phenomenon and should have been a matter of consideration beyond the simplification of classical drama as a Brazilian cultural continuum. Despite the substantial differences between *Orfeu da Conceição* and *Black Orpheus*, the central theme of death and symbolic rebirth persists. French film producer Sacha Gordine, Vinícius de Moraes, and Jacques Viot had worked on various versions, trying to adapt the play as much as possible to a Brazilian contextual reality. To this end, both Sacha Gordine and Vinícius de Moraes toured Rio de Janeiro and succeeded in filming some Carnival scenes in February 1957. In 1958, Camus finally filmed with an amateur cast of about 4,000, producing a riveting and award-winning film in 1959.

Black Orpheus concerns the life of a trolley-car conductor (Orpheus), his fiancée, Mira, and Eurydice, who shows up in town, fleeing from a death figure pursuing her. Similar to the musical drama, the movie's love story between Orpheus and Eurydice, while mythical, is reenacted through magical-realistic scenarios such as the love triangle between Orpheus, Mira, and Eurydice that will be resolved at the very end by Orpheus's dying at the hands of Mira, the jealous wife; the death of Eurydice herself at the hands of Orpheus, who was trying to save her from death; as well as the mythical descent of Orpheus to search for Eurydice in the Umbanda temple, only to be warned not to look back, as in the Greek myth. Sensing a truce at the warning, he of course looked back as he heard the voice of Eurydice and could not help himself. The ending where Orpheus suffers a fatal descent with Eurydice in his hands signals a rupture with life, while at the same time the dancing children reference a reunion with life in spite of death as the symbolic young Eurydice offers a flower to a young Orpheus, thus confirming the continuity of the myth. Though the critical reception of the film has been mixed, without the film, the drama may have been long forgotten as an effort that did not surpass national boundaries. *Black Orpheus* globalized Brazil in a way that *Orfeu da Conceição* could only have hoped for, thus leaving Moraes with a feeling of disappointment that all the credit given to the film is associated with France and minimally with Brazil, the country that nourished the idea in the first place. The accusation of exoticism notwithstanding, *Black Orpheus* contributed to the inclusion of blacks in Brazilian cinema and a timely emergence of Brazilian cinematic production.

In retrospect, the limited negative reception of the film, for the most part, stems from the suggestion that it represents a "Brazil for tourists" image, given its focus on touristic images of the city and Carnival-related allegories as well as folklorization of Afro-Brazilian experience through such images as samba, Macumba, and sensuous and euphoric wild dance.

Marcel Camus, erroneously assuming that Afro-Brazilians had fled to the favela to avoid modern civilization, was accused of ignoring "the dynamics of national formation and the extreme socioeconomic disadvantages that drive the dispossessed to shantytowns."[48] While on one hand Camus sought a nostalgic rendering of a utopian European civilization in Africa as expressed by Afro-Brazilian culture, Moraes, on the other hand, sought to balance the Greek myth with the verity of African influence on Brazil by emphasizing the miscegenation prism that portrays Brazil as a nation devoid of racial tensions. Brazilian cultural critics suggest that *Black Orpheus* suffers mainly from stereotypical representation where samba, soccer, Carnival, semi-naked women, and wild partying sum up the image created not by Brazil but for Brazil by

outsiders. This "imported" view of what Brazil looks like has many implications for the romanticized image of Brazil, as pointed out by Glauber
Rocha, who criticized Marcel Camus for his mystification of the favela.[49]
Abdias do Nascimento would also connect the French exoticization of
Black Orpheus with Brazil's emergent Cinema Novo and the black poetry
of resistance emanating from the Francophone African and Caribbean
world in form of Negritude consciousness. For Nascimento, the appropriation and beautification of Rio de Janeiro as a newly found "paradise"
contradicts the reality of dispossession in the favelas while at the same
time exploiting the natural ambience of merrymaking implicit in the
lives of the *favelado*. Orpheus, in this sense, ceases to be the messianic
figure, one who rises from humble beginnings to represent symbolic sacrifice for humanity. Rather, Orpheus, in Camus's film, is the archetypal
Afro-Brazilian at once rooted within his community and yet isolated and
marginalized outside of it during Carnival, where he is nothing but local
window-dressing as well as a transcendental figure destined for symbolic
erasure and insignificance after the ephemeral festivity. Within the
reconciliation of the contradictions lies the vitality of Carnival culture
and the misplacement of the politics of representation, since race and
its discontents are inadvertently subsumed under the uncritical prism of
celebration and national pride.

That *Orfeu Negro* played a vital role in internationalizing Brazil's
image as a problematic racial democracy is not in question. What remains
debatable is the acceptability of this representation given that the pre-
ponderant representation of blacks in a supposedly "multiracial" society
sends a contradictory message viewers that blacks are both happy in their
marginalized condition and accepted by all in the society beyond the
limited cordial atmosphere in which they have been represented in the
film. The contradiction is better reflected in the original title of *Orfeu
Negro* than in the actual release title of *Orfeu da Conceição*, which seems
to mask the blackness that qualifies Orpheus in the reversed ideological
context of Brazil as opposed to the Greek, where color was not an issue
but faith and myth. Yet the overzealous representation of Rio as almost
exclusively black, where Carnival is the enchanting locale of vitality
for blacks with instinctive African-derived spectacle and dance, further
simplifies a rather complex phenomenon. Part of that simplification lies
at the heart of what can be called the musical material of the film,
since most of the film's success is predicated on the percussive drive that
enriches it. Lyrical theme songs such as Vinícius's "A Felicidade" (Hap-

piness) and Luiz Bonfa's "Manhã do Carnaval" (Morning of Carnival) both gave a necessary push to the emerging bossa nova movement at the time. As Chris McGowan and Ricardo Pessanha suggest, the success of the film was equally instrumental in putting "bossa nova on the world map."[50] Yet a contradiction persists: samba is curiously Afro-Brazilian and communal, while bossa nova is white and elitist, reserved for the elites of the southern part of Rio de Janeiro.

The backward gaze of Orpheus has often been interpreted as a decisive symbolic moment in the tragedy of the mythic hero as well as in the broader significance of the black social movements in Brazil by those who insist on reviving Africa as a measure of connecting with their own historical past.[51] *Orfeu Negro* mirrors this closure: at the end of the film, Orpheus looks back at Mira's call, while carrying Eurydice from the morgue to the favela, and is ultimately struck with a stone from Mira that sends him rolling downward to a symbolic hell or to his death. Simultaneously, the dancing of three youngsters, at least two of whom mirror new Orpheus and Eurydice, brings a comic relief to the ending of the film. This mixed (tragicomic) ending idealizes Afro-Brazilian life as an illusory setting of happiness and cordiality in spite of the socioeconomic odds against Afro-Brazilians even as depicted in the film. Both the drama and the film raise issues of ambiguity about racial identity in view of the preponderance of European values (Greek) imposed on the Brazilian and African ethos, thus creating an implicit embrace of idealized Brazilian life. Often regarded as a Brazilian film, *Orfeu Negro* is the most successful Latin American film of all time, despite reservations in Brazil about its Brazilianness. As a transnational piece, the film bridges the limited knowledge of Europeans of Brazil with the rich cultural tapestry of Rio de Janeiro during a Carnival parade, which also integrates the life of Afro-Brazilians, even if that representation is at the expense of the full import of their marginalized experience. When considered as both an imaginative and sociological study, *Orfeu Negro* at once fulfills the aesthetics of an artistic revival of Greek legend, while at the same time problematizing the contradictions of Brazil as a racial democracy. The music of Orpheus will continue in the mouths of Brazilian revelers past and present, while the essential ambiguity of Orpheus's blackness persists for critics who may or may not accept his representation as a necessary illusion for the larger population craving a racially egalitarian Brazilian society.

If racial equality is the central concern in *Orfeu Negro*, Jean Cocteau's 1950 *Orpheus* offers a more evocative social reality that may be more surrealistic than realistic since the tragedy of Orpheus is neither socially engendered nor individually caused but a mix of sacred and tragic impulses. Instead, one observes death as enacted in a public space, only to be relocated to a private space for the possibilities of regeneration. As if in a mysterious nightmare, Orpheus is resuscitated by a woman who may well have been complicit in the orchestration of his death. Even Orpheus seems to be living in a trance-like mode, as he is commanded to arise by this strange woman only for him to accept that "you are my death" upon being asked if he knew who she was. Death in *Orpheus* is female, an antagonist reminiscent of Mira in *Orfeu Negro*, who may well want to be with Orpheus but must ensure his death first since she herself is no simple living figure but a mysterious divinity. The many journeys back and forth to the otherworld makes the film somewhat dreamlike; it uses the mediation of mirrors as the strategic "gulf of transition," to invoke Wole Soyinka's term from *Myth, Literature and the African World*.

Yet *Orpheus* is not the first time Cocteau will deploy the Orpheus myth in his films. He first used the myth in *Le Sang d'un Poète* (The Blood of a Poet; 1930), and then, after *Orpheus*, he returns to it in 1955's *Le Testament d'Orphée* (The Testament of Orpheus), thus creating a trilogy of Orpheus mythology. All three films are lyrical, dreamlike, and surrealistic. Orpheus is considered the most compelling, in which a successful poet is hated by his contemporaries. The plot is similar to the Greek original, but before that similarity may be deciphered, Cocteau craftily invents two major characters: Death and Heurtebise. Death is a cold and calculating woman, while Heurtebise, who has just committed suicide by jumping in front of a motorcycle, suddenly rises up to become Death's driver. The plot becomes complicated when Orpheus falls in love with Death, and Eurydice falls in love with Heurtebise, as Orpheus begins his journey to the underworld in the quest for Eurydice. Cocteau's Orpheus differs from the subsequent Carlos Diegues adaptations in his focus not on what Lúcia Nagib calls "black paradise,"[52] hence the artificial rendition and implicit critique of Rio de Janeiro as a paradise for Afro-Brazilians, but as a compelling setting for the exploration of creative ingenuity, ritual sacrifice, and sexual perversion.

Even as a black-and-white film, the visuals of Orpheus are strikingly vibrant, especially with the mediation of mirrors, which in Hollywood's terms are a traditional "gateway" to the wonderland of fantasy, the unknown, and unsolved mysteries. Using what is neither flashback nor futuristic techniques, Cocteau makes the characters travel forward and backward, as if deluding the viewer of their very existence in past, present, or future, fluidities where they fade in and out of consciousness and visibility to the extent that magical realism emerges in a deliberate intertextual relationship between reality and fantasy. Visually engaging and imaginatively provocative, Cocteau's Orpheus effectively translates an avant-garde cinema that challenges the standard conventions of the classical Hollywood cinematic model by exploring the poet's concerns with the power of poetry as intersecting human preoccupations with the cycle of life and re-imagined through Orpheus's myth of regeneration. By turning seemingly simple acts of fantasy into surrealistic enactments of conflicting reality, Cocteau seems to align with surrealistic imagination, while at the same time defamiliarizing the familiar by inserting the poet as the agent of magical production and medium who navigates between the world of the living, the dead, and the afterlife. In going against Hollywood's conventional style of filmmaking in the late 1910s through the mid-1950s, in which the illusion of reality is the norm, *Orpheus* deviates by characterizing Orpheus as a transcendental figure who reacts not humanly through his passionate advances, but divinely and heroically when he pursues Eurydice to the underworld and looks back against the warning of the deities. His tragic flaw is also his essence of regenerative possibility as he remains in the underworld to sing to his beloved Eurydice. This classical plot in the Greek mythology finds creative echoes not only in Cocteau's *Orpheus* but also in the many South American adaptations.

Black Orpheus evokes the contradictions of racial democracy in Brazil by questioning why Carnival, in this specific movie, beyond its luxurious manifestation of beauty and Afro-Brazilian community, fails to redress the social inequalities perpetuated by racial discrimination. The gap between the rich and the poor is skillfully depicted at the very beginning of the movie when the landscape below (a high-rise metropolis) contrasts with the squalor and poverty above in the hilly slums. Orpheus, himself a trolley driver, is not the influential intellect as in the Greek myth; he is barely making ends meet, as evidenced by the fact that he has had to put his guitar on layaway and also depends on his fiancée, Mira, to buy their wedding rings. Serafina is also depicted as constantly buying on credit at the local supermarket; she cannot even afford to buy bread, having spent all her savings on Carnival. Moreover, the living conditions in Serafina's shack (we never get to see Orpheus's home at all, as if he is a loafing womanizer without a stable home), with hens, cocks, goats, cats, and birds commingling in an idyllic ambience of harmonious relations with nature, are suggestive of economic deprivation, to say the least. It is curious whether the realism of poverty somewhat overshadows the pretext of racial harmony in the Brazilian state that the playwright, Vinícius de Moraes, sets out to showcase. If the Moraes project fails at the level of exoticism for which it has been accused, it nonetheless succeeds at the level of global propaganda of black presence in Brazil, which took the world by surprise, at least in the context of the late 1950s when the movie was released. With the exception of the little girl signifying the new Eurydice at the end of the movie, the children look very deprived, in their tattered clothes; and if the movie indeed wants to portray the lives of Afro-Brazilians in the best documentary light, it succeeds on the realism side but fails at the level of their humanity. The street, as opposed to the home, is where most of the actions take place, as if the Afro-Brazilian life is indeed subject to the wiles of the *malandro*—the typical Brazilian survivalist who must make ends meet by always trying to outsmart others.

Robert Stam's critique of the limitless possibilities of Orpheus as a transformative agent not fully explored in *Orfeu Negro* is worth examining in the context of the contradictions of racial democracy:

> The possible resonances between Orpheus as shaman and Exu as a figure of mediation and metamorphosis are never explored. Nor is the film ultimately "carnivalesque." The film registers the phenomenal surface of carnival, but Brazilian charac-ters play out the archetypal patterns provided by European myth against a photogenic tropical backdrop. Whereas the carnivalesque proposes a dialectical critique of everyday life, *Black Orpheus* hints at a metaphysical transcendence within an idealized décor.[53]

The critique of idealized realism as evoked by Stam complicates the prism through which *Orfeu Negro* has hitherto been perceived. Orpheus, in this regard, could well function as the Exú-esque figure who mediates between the contradictions of racial democracy and the resolution of the same limitations. In order for redress or reconciliation to happen, Orpheus must be privileged, not disadvantaged; he must transcend the ephemeral power of song and dance and be a political voice of mobilization beyond the popular culturalism. Though he visits the Umbanda ceremony in his quest for Eurydice, the limited moment of transcendence is further diminished in his disappointment with Afro-Brazilian rites, from which he feels estranged and consults only in necessity.

Alienated, idealistic and idealized, exotic and exoticized, European-ized (by virtue of his Greco-Brazilian representation or adaptation), yet humane and humanized, not only is Orpheus an embodiment of racial democracy, since the lighter-skinned Mira ends up being his killer, but his relationship with Eurydice, though mythological and desirable in some respects, has been cursed from the very beginning. Eurydice is unable to reconcile her own triangulation of Death pursuing her to Rio de Janeiro with the (im)possibility of a new beginning with Orpheus (at whose hands she fatally dies), nor with the antagonistic exigency of Mira. As rivals, neither Eurydice nor Mira is a redemptive agent for Orpheus; rather, they are facilitative agents for the fulfillment of his own tragic destiny as manifested in their varying moments of intervention. Mira is emblematic of irredeemable destruction, while Eurydice signals metaphorically at the possibilities of renewal even in codified afterlife terms. Indeed, Orpheus himself embodies the redemptive possibilities equally verifiable in Exú, the crossroads agent of resolution and interpretation. Framed as Exú, Orpheus must be seen as his own undoing. As the divinity who counsels others on the appropriate path to take to resolve the complexity of life, he is, sadly, unable to counsel himself. It is arguable that the process of self-discovery of his human frailty is as important as his inescapable fatal destiny. Should he have been able to counsel himself, control his insatiable thirst for his loved, lost, and regained, he probably would have resisted the temptation of looking backward to see Eurydice. The tragic flaw is by nature inevitable in the Janus-faced divinity. In the place of Exú, Obatala emanates as the purifying agent of the human blemish, which varies in gravity according to the transgression, and which ulti-mately led Orpheus back to hell. His songs, though melancholic and nostalgic, remain therapeutic in the twilight gates of life and death. Carnival and Samba alike fill those voids of socioeconomic equality that torment many marginalized Afro-Brazilians in the midst of plenty. Thus the "metaphysical transcendence" that *Orfeu Negro* proposes can only be, at best, escapist, wishful, and illusory, as captured in the ephemeral performance that is Carnival.

Cinematic Adaptation of *Orfeu* (1999)

In responding to the criticisms of lack of authenticity leveled against both Vinícius de Moraes and Carlos Diegues based on their variations and adaptations of the Orpheus myth in the Brazilian context, the celebrated cineaste, Diegues, proposes in *Orfeu* a new way of reading Rio de Janeiro with a dire call for political intervention. The Rio de Janeiro in *Orfeu* is less romantic, less exotic, yet even more problematic due to the problem of drug trafficking that Diegues privileges well beyond the Carnival-Passion motif. As the complex realities of contemporary Brazil are foregrounded, the narration of love and that of Carnival are compelled to occupy a secondary plane, while not completely expunged from the dramas of violence and police brutality that are assaulting, for the most part, on the psychological well-being of the Afro-Brazilian *favela* communities. Released in 1999, it is strikingly different in the cover, where Eurydice appears lighter skinned than the 1959 Eurydice, and with the title devoid of the adjectival "black" of *Orfeu Negro*. Instead of the folklorization of Rio de Janeiro as a location of exotic exuberance soothed in jubilant Samba echoing in the songs and dances of enchanting and humble people in Camus's *Orfeu Negro*, *Orfeu's* Rio de Janeiro is a tapestry of hip-hop community as reflected in graffiti-inscribed walls and floors, recollecting a new era and generation that visually and vocally expresses itself against the grain and in spite of the odds of daily living. Representing the voice of the people, Orfeu, played by pop star Toni Garrido,[54] is no longer the struggling trolley driver but the seemingly self-sufficient community pop-hero and business tycoon, a successful composer, and an accomplished musician who uses a state-of-the-art laptop to produce his samba lyrics. Entrusted with organizing the annual Carnival in his Samba school, Garrido's life revolves around preparing for that unique annual performance as well as mediating the often tense atmosphere of drug-related gang wars and the brutality of the police when they strike the *favela* communities with the vengeance of an angered lion.

The *malandro* figure, as delineated by Roberto DaMatta's *Carnival, Rogues, and Heroes* (1979), ceases to be a unilateral character but is a fragmented individual who can negotiate the multiplicity of identities that Exú, the deity of the crossroads, evokes. Even if Orfeu is clearly that heroic figure (since he dies at the end of the movie still in close proximity to Eurydice, whose dead body he was carrying to Rio's "hellish" *favela* community), his fragmented soul is simultaneously in conflict with that of the drug leader and in synchronicity with that gangsta posture that terrifies the community. Yet Orfeu can only empathize with, cajole, and negotiate with this debilitating force—the same way that he is the one asking the police not to hurt some of the gang members for his own sake. The gang leader is a different *malandro*—not just the hustler and rogue but one who is both the enemy of the state as well as the enemy within the *favela* space: two antagonistic forces that can be resolved only through mutual ritual sacrifice. One must be eliminated in order to have peace, while the other must willingly self-sacrifice as a price for eternal love. Ironically, the social web that links both Orfeu and the drug leader dates back a long way: the drug leader (Lucinho) is Orfeu's childhood friend. As much as he wants to continue being his friend, Orfeu must choose between the peace the community will ultimately gain and the price of losing a friend, who has actually become a social enemy. The Death figure persecuting Eurydice in *Orfeu Negro* is here embodied by the drug dealer. Drugs signify the epidemic that devastates the *favela* community through their inherently unhealthful qualities as well as the violence they engender. One can only speculate on the high level of violence in *Orfeu* and the realism or naturalism of it. Perhaps it should be expected in a Hollywood-style movie reminiscent of the hyped necessity of violence and horror, or a recasting of the gangster movies of the 1930s, meshed with the hip-hop ambience of the 1990s that echoes the urgency of intervention evoked by Grandmaster Flash in his "The Message"? The realities of the *favela* in Rio may not be far removed from those reenacted in his call for intervention: "Don't push me cause I'm close to the edge / I'm trying not to lose my head, ah huh-huh-huh / [. . .] / It's like a jungle sometimes / it makes me wonder / How I keep from going under." Orfeu, in this sense, succumbs to Death, a mix of an antagonist and a childhood friend—as if Death has been pursuing him since the foundation of his destiny.

Orfeu's attempt to rid the *favela* of Lucinho's drug dealing is faced by a social explanation for his choice, however destructive. Abortively, Orfeu persuades Lucinho to leave the *favela* before it is too late, or rather before Lucinho meets his death. Paradoxically, it is Orfeu who self-sacrifices in death. Lucinho, whose father was a street sweeper—a reality that caused him much anguish—refused to follow in his footsteps. As a white character living in the *favela*, it is remarkable that unlike the message of Diegues in *Orfeu*, blacks and whites suffer the same fate, and the issue of race need not be so overstated. Yet the reality is that race often does play a factor in marginality. Lúcia Nagib argues that "social exclusion is unrelated to racial issues, as opposed to Paulo Lins's *City of God*, in which similar exchanges cannot be separated from the colour factor" (*Brazil on Screen* 76). Nagib, however, is not justifying the lack of racial tension in Orfeu, but rather explaining the perspective of Diegues in *Orfeu* as opposed to what obtains in *Orfeu Negro*, where race is indeed a factor of disenfranchisement. Realities are indeed quite different in *Orfeu*: Eurydice is lighter skinned, a quintessential embodiment of the three races (Indian, African, and European); she arrives by plane to Rio as opposed to *Orfeu*'s Eurydice, who arrives by boat; Lucinho, the Death figure and drug dealer, is white. The black–white and good–evil polarities are thus complicated to suggest that class is often a contributing factor to social marginality and exclusion. Women are not left out of this new societal configuration; they are more empowered and seemingly more independent than the men. Exploitation of the poor indeed can be at the hands of both blacks and whites. Orfeu and Lucinho are clear examples of this contradiction, due to their childhood relationship. Lucinho even suggests that Orfeu leave the community before it is too late for him. Of course, Orfeu, as the death-bound hero, must stay on in the *favela* to fulfill his destiny even as he also loses Eurydice to Death. A fundamental question remains: considering Diegues's many movies on black slavery and its resistance in Brazil, why would he represent a Brazil that is more racially harmonized rather than a more realistic Brazil where racial tensions are still the order of the day? The answer lies partly in the company that produced the film (New York Films), as well as Diegues's intention to correct or rebrand the 1959 version, *Orfeu Negro*, with an all-black cast that would make Brazil more exotic than realistic. Whatever the justification, *Orfeu* fails to be the "correct" representation of Brazil: the mix of myth and realism, while echoing the contradictions of culture, brutality, and violence in the *favela*, also confirms that there are limits to representational accuracy. The cinematic balance of *Orfeu* remains anchored between the allegories of the past and the efforts to better understand the realities of the present.

Beyond the triangulation of Eurydice, Orpheus, and Luciano, where a charismatic lover such as Toni Garrido meets an enchanting diva in Patrícia Franca in a Romeo-and-Juliet type romance, and a childhood friend turned Death as played by Murilo Benício, Orfeu's family represents a microcosm of a society divided within itself, as his father, Inácio, played by Milton Gonçalves, struggles with his newly found religious faith (having abandoned his musical career) when contrasted with his wife, Conceição, a devotee of Candomblé, and played by Zézé Mota. The entire film is an effort to document the historical event in the present while deviating from the anteriority, yet without escaping the persistence of Greek mythology and melodramatization of archetypal tragedy. In a lengthy film (almost two hours), the many contradictory enactments are soothed by the many songs written by Caetano Veloso as well as the Carnival sambas and bossa nova infusions, giving the performance a dose of agitating suspense coupled with a feeling of living the experience as it unfolds in fast-paced, riveting, colorful shots of Rio de Janeiro in its most realistic and most fantastical modes, especially as the city sprawls with joy unperturbed during the Carnival parades in the closing scenes. One feels the pain of Inácio at the end, as he fails to wake his son up using the whistle of the musical regent that Orfeu used to be, and emotionally dramatizing his invocations, as if expecting him to rise from the dead. With tears rolling down their eyes, the community gathers to mourn, to remember, and also to be in solidarity with a hero it once had and now has lost to the fatally violent nature of life in the Rio *favela*. Through the microcosm of *Orfeu*'s Rio de Janeiro, the viewer is exposed primarily to a conflicted setting between sanity and insanity, normalcy and abnormality, violence and fleeting peace, drugs as a source of wealth and power on one hand, and on the other the impoverishment of the larger community living in constant fear of being caught in the crossfire of rival gangs. Diegues may not have set out to produce a violent film, but in an effort to portray a "realistic" Rio de Janeiro, he inadvertently called attention to a state of emergency in the reality of increasing urban warfare caused by drug trafficking.

The overexploited theme of romantic love between Orpheus and Eurydice resonates in the Greek creation myth itself, in which Orpheus invents the lyre, the instrument through which he enchants all creatures. While Lúcia Nagib sees Orpheus as embodying the characteristics of the one who "breathes life into things" (*Brazil on Screen* 87), she equally evokes the consequences of such power amongst mere mortals, who are now jealous of his divine qualities, leading to enmity between Orpheus and Aristaeus, the rival lover, from whom Eurydice tries to flee, only to encounter her own fate in the bite of a serpent that sends her to the otherworld.

Music was Orpheus's obsession, while drunkenness was Obatala's tragic flaw. As a creative divinity by nature, Orpheus cannot deal with the death of Eurydice and must recover her from the dead by journeying to the land of the dead, using his creative and musical energies. The rivalry of Orpheus and Aristaeus echoes in the rivalry between Obatala and Oduduwa. When Obatala failed to create perfect humans, Oduduwa was charged to complete the task. In this Yoruba worldview's concept of substitution, the principle of complementarity is evoked without any contradiction, whereas in Greek mythology, rivalry brings about death in a frame of double jeopardy—the fall of both Eurydice and Orpheus. Even if Obatala had not been overtaken by drunkenness, his having created perfect humans would have meant that Oduduwa, who becomes the progenitor of the Yoruba race, would not have been able to fulfill his destiny to be the patrimonial agent of the Yoruba. The love between Obatala and Oduduwa is pure and divine, not romantic or earthly. In this comparative analysis, Eurydice would not have needed to flee from Aristaeus as a potential antagonist but could have be the reason for Orpheus to appreciate Eurydice even more. Greek mythology suggests that pure love free of self-interest is quite impossible. Carnival as ritual performance also gives an opportunity to both Orpheus and Eurydice to consummate their love publicly at the instance of the entire reveling community. Whereas in the Greek mythology, Orpheus and Eurydice are bound by romantic interlocking principles, in Yoruba mythology, the interlocking principles are both divinely inspired and complementary, not antagonistic.

Far beyond the forgoing Greco-Yoruba contradictions and comparisons, death and regeneration walk hand-in-hand in *Orfeu* since the love triangle between Orfeu, Eurydice, and Lucinho (symbolizing community death) is complicated by the homosexual crush Lucinho has for Orfeu. The idealized vision of the *favela* in *Orfeu Negro* falls apart even if the new hip-hop *favela*, while more inclusive in terms of the invocation of the possibilities of homosexual orientation, is also threatened by the very figure who would have been integrated and no longer marginalized. Orfeu kisses Lucinho even as he kills him, as if showing compassion to him in his journey of transition, but not before Lucinho accidentally kills Eurydice. Interestingly, the film had opened aesthetically with another possible triangle between Mira (with whom Orfeu makes passionate love and then kicks her out), Eurydice (whose love scene was not "televised" due to the sacred bonds between them), and Orfeu himself. The regeneration of the community depended on getting rid of Death (Lucinho), but the death of Eurydice and Orfeu remains more than a mystery and takes on a mythological dimension. Societal purification is usually justified by the error of transgression in order to bring about preexisting harmony that has been disrupted. It is not very clear or explicable why Orfeu and Eurydice became ritual sacrifices. Lúcia Nagib captures this paradox when she sums up the ending of the film as "trance-like,"[55] as the samba frenzy sets the tone for a set of ritualizations: Eurydice is accidentally shot by Lucinho, Orfeu kills Lucinho, Orfeu is killed by the jealous Maenads. The ultimate ritualization is actualized with Carnival performance where, in a flashback of sorts, Orfeu and Eurydice dance during a Carnival parade in the Sambadrome, during which the illusion of Carnival is contradicted by the return to the daily routine of violence and counterviolence that constitutes the cycle of life in the Rio *favela*. Drug trafficking, while an integral yet covert part of community operational reality, is further complicated by the complicity of the police, who often supply arms to these drug dealers, only to return with an air of violent and hypocritical sanitization in order to "cleanse" the community of urban violence and its hardened perpetrators. One can argue that the entire movie is nothing short of a ritual performance from beginning 'til end.

Comparative Analysis and Conclusion

Brazil's cultural landscape in the last fifty years has been marked by the transition from military dictatorship (1964–1975) to a moment of reflection about what could have been in terms of the integration of blacks in the Brazilian "paradise" since the abolition of slavery. In the same vein, Obatala remains a revered deity among his devotees despite the ambiguities of his tragic flaw and ultimate redemption in form of an outlet of creativity found in Oduduwa. In this sense, both deified personalities symbolize a complex cultural heritage that has survived the passage of time. The many versions of both myths are enduring legacies of the triumph of the human spirit in the midst of a tragic fate. The analogy with Obatala that this chapter has invoked with respect to Orpheus as an embodiment of the creation myth seeks to broaden the possibilities of its interpretation cross-culturally. As the mediator of human consciousness, Obatala possesses the power to generate human consciousness and thereby provide the pathway to be one with nature.

Despite the hype about Carlos Diegues's *Orfeu* (1999) in terms of its "authenticity," Marcel Camus's *Orfeu Negro* (1959) remains a closer reflection of Rio de Janeiro. While both versions, as well as those by Jean Cocteau (1950) and Vinícius de Moraes (1956), evoke the plight of Orpheus as a victim of the divine, in the final analysis, the reconstruction of the Orpheus myth in Brazil has not negated the reality of racism and the theories propagated through the enslavement of Africans in the Americas. By subjecting each adaptation to critique, the richness of a society torn between itself and the claim of fictitious racial democracy offers an opportunity to redress the myopia toward improved racial relations through dialogue. It is only through such openness that a lasting solution can emerge. Paradoxically, the Brazilian audience seems even more enamored by Marcel Camus's stereotypical version than by that of Carlos Diegues, which seeks to deconstruct the ambience of "black paradise" that Rio de Janeiro has been associated with while providing a more balanced perspective about the reality of violence, drug trafficking, and police brutality. Conceptually and performatively, each Orphic version succumbs to the primacy of Orpheus's human frailty as he criss-crosses heaven and hell in search of the elusive Eurydice. Obatala and Orpheus are icons of humanity and divinity at their very best manifestation of regenerative possibilities that only their weaknesses made possible.

Chapter 7

City of God

The Ghettoization of Violence

Throughout history, conventional wisdom placed favelas as a symbol of social and economic segregation, the main locus of poverty, a place where moral degradation mixes with poor sanitary conditions, a dark dystopia [. . .]. "Negative" motifs associated with a supposed "favela lifestyle," such as narcoculture and violence, also started to be aestheticized and exploited in ways which further add to the allure of "Brazil" with significant impact in the construction of the favela as a tourist destination.[1]

Introduction

Although postmodernist society naively pronounced the end of the densely populated urban peripheral communities such as the *favelas* or slums in terms of their relevance or contribution to the fast-growing global, virtual, and digitized society, these marginalized communities continue to re-insert themselves into mainstream discourses, especially since the early 1990s, when the hip-hop phenomenon and generation took Brazilian society by surprise in such states as São Paulo and Rio de Janeiro. These restless young urban minds not only refute the label of "marginality" that the society has imposed on them, they instead re-inscribe themselves in the public discourses of violence as a legitimate response to police brutality, drug trafficking, and overall transgressive acts of survival on a daily basis.

199

The so-called "marginal literature" indeed questions its own marginality while explicating its relevance within Brazilian mainstream discourse.

This chapter focuses on three main novels by two established Afro-Brazilian writers of the "margin" that are indeed now part of mainstream contemporary Brazilian culture by default. In analyzing the ghettoization of violence and the deployment of transgressions as coping strategies in marginalized black communities of *Cidade de Deus* in Rio de Janeiro, the cultural melting pot of the world of Samba in Rio de Janeiro in *Desde que o Samba é Samba*, and the fictionalized world of São Paulo's Capão Redondo in *Capão Pecado*, this study seeks to exemplify the recurrent landscapes of globalized ghettoization of violence, particularly since the 1990s, while arguing for its inclusion in what may be called a Brazilian cultural archetype—not as a marginal entity but as a centrifugal force demanding recognition and visibility. Through a careful delineation of representative discursive strategies of this emergent literature, this chapter redefines marginal literature as a cultural phenomenon that has indeed come to stay and must be recognized as one of the landmarks of the Brazilian postmodernist cultural landscape and heritage.

Novelist, scriptwriter, and poet Paulo Cesar de Souza Lins was born in Rio de Janeiro in 1958. Having grown up in the celebrated Rio slum that gave name to his first novel, *Cidade de Deus* (City of God; 1997), Lins was strongly influenced by music, especially samba, which also gave title to his second novel, *Desde que o Samba é Samba* (As Long as Samba is Samba, 2012). Lins studied Brazilian Literature in the 1980s at the Federal University of Rio de Janeiro (UFRJ), during which time he joined the "Cooperativa de Poetas" collective and published his collected poetry, *Sobre o Sol* (Regarding the Sun) in 1986, which was said to have been infleunced by the critical movement known as *Concretismo*. Inspired by the sociological work he did as an assistant to Alba Zaluar, an anthropologist of criminality, Lins embarked on a ficional portrayal of life in Cidade de Deus, his own very intimately known social environment. Published in 1997, it took only five years for the narrative to hit the screen in 2002, as cinematographically adapted by Fernando Meirelles and Kátia Lund, with many awards following, including the "Globo de Ouro" and an Oscar. Seeking to capture the cultural and social apprehensions of the dwellers of the Cidade de Deus slum, Lins paints an expansive image of social and individual criminality that is multidimensional in its critique of social decadence and persistent violence that often leads to social death. Between the sociological research, the fictionalized experience, and the cinematographic adaptation, a blurry line is created given the success of these creative transformations. Part of the success may well be attributed to Paulo Lins, whose original narrative is characterized by a detective penchant, a thriller sensibility, and a sensationalist curiosity that betrays both the original search of objectivity and wholeness. Through economic use of language, poetic sensibility, and a consciousness of an anti-heroic ideology, *Cidade de Deus* goes against the grain of the traditional elite novel, often focusing on a protagonist whose life attracts our empathy or indifference until his or her destiny is defined as failure, survival, or death. In the case of *Cidade de Deus*, the community itself becomes a character—incisively analyzed through the prism of multivalent characters whose fragmentation is a strategy at unity in diversity since the common denominator among the many protagonists is the *favela* as location of social conditioning and violence.

Representing the São Paulo side of social violence is Ferréz, the pseudonym of Reginaldo Ferreira da Silva, a hybrid combination of Virgulino Ferreira, otherwise known as Lampião (Ferre) and Zumbi dos Palmares (Z), a personal effort to pay homage to major Brazilian folk heroes. The street was Ferréz's school, a territory he knew well since he plied practically all the possible professions on the street, including kiosque seller, broom seller, general worker, and hustler (*malandro*). He started writing at the age of seven, when he tried his hand at poetry, short stories, and musical lyricism. His self-published first book, *Fortaleza da Desilusão* (Fortress of Disillusionment, 1997), did not attract serious critical attention but signalled what was to follow. In 2000, when Ferréz published *Capão Pecado* (Capão as Sin), it was an instant success. Like Paulo Lins's Cidade de Deus in Rio de Janeiro, *Capão Pecado* paints a picture of the violent *favela* neighbourhood of Capão Redondo, a periphery in São Paulo, which is the author's own native social environment. A founding member of IDASUL, a hip-hop movement responsible for promoting cultural activities in peripheral neighborhoods, Ferréz is a contributor to *Caros Amigos*, a monthly Brazilian magazine. His mature *Capão Pecado* chronicles in agile and dry rhetorical style the voices of revolt and perplexity, coupled with compelling quests for hope and dignity for the battered and violated people of Brazilian urban peripheries. The fictional world portrayed by Ferréz offers readers the opportunity to access and examine how the marginalized respond to urban operational dynamics in which the mainstream is the center of the city, while marginals are relegated to the outskirts, thereby coping with an exclusive language of violence, survival, and, in many instances, the constant reality of death. Ferréz's other works include *Manual Prático do Ódio* (The Practical Manual

of Hate, 2003), *Amanhecer Esmeralda* (Emerald Dawn, 2005), and *Nin-
guém é Inocente em São Paulo* (No One Is Innocent in São Paulo, 2006).
The literary corpus of Lins and Ferréz provides a forceful context for a
constructive discussion of the globalization of violence and marginality
through veiled manipulation of political economy.

Theorizing Social Marginality

It is imperative to understand the relationship of place with social marginality. Marginality itself describes the sociocultural, political, and economic
conditions that deny people from resources and social participation. In
other words, marginalized individuals or communities will usually be
neglected through lack of social amenities or inferior standards of living
that make them vulnerable to social victimization and stagnation. For
Sommers and colleagues "Socio-economic marginality is a condition of
socio-spatial structure and process in which components of society and
space in a territorial unit are observed to lag behind an expected level of
performance in economic, political and social well-being compared with
the average condition in the territory as a whole."[2] Social marginality is
indeed a global phenomenon despite variations in social contexts and
specificities. Marginalized communities, by their very nature, have poor
access to basic human infrastructures, including social amenities, health
care, technology, and information—all the pertinent services that could
empower them and make them competitive. Resultantly, these communities become vulnerable, in contrast to the mainstream communities
where power is entrenched in the hands of the influential few. In this
sense, locus becomes a vital factor in the determination of extent and
limits of participation and inclusion. Only by reversing or mediating
those factors that have marginalized such communities can they begin to
transform their lives, living conditions, options for change, negotiation of
power, cooperation, and recognition of diversity as a positive measure to
eradicate the stagnancy of poverty and deprivation in their lives. This is
in addition to identifying root causes that many would rather not know,
since the chances of change are quite remote within the context of the
limited resources available to them.

   First conditioned by their locus, marginalized urban communities
of Rio de Janeiro and São Paulo, who historically migrated from the
northeast's drought of the early 1900s, find themselves as the "wretched
of the earth"[3] in new industrial locations where they were not origi-

nally equipped to survive. The menial jobs they were able to secure as domestics, cleaners, cobblers, shoe shiners, and (with some education, skills, workshops, and luck), bus drivers, the reality of poverty correlates quickly with marginality to the extent that their earning power becomes a measure of where they can afford to live or call home. Most adjusted and devised a cultural mode of survival through cultural production, such as music, especially through schools of samba, through which they were able to place themselves in the center during Carnival. Yet marginality evokes a mix of economic, social, spatial, and political implications for social injustice that remain largely unredressed. In formulating a theoretical framework for the understanding of the textualization of marginality in such works as *Cidade de Deus* and *Capão Pecado*, it is imperative to understand the multidimensionality of the concept as a complex social process that is not locked into a uniformed theorization. Marginality is such a dynamic state and process that despite its negative characteristics it often invites critical analyses in order to tease out the relativity of the contexts and social conditions that can determine when and why a community is labeled "marginal" while others are "affluent" or mainstream. Yet the commonality of defining factors shaping marginality lies in a sense of exclusion from the mainstream society, inclusion in the impoverishment process, and powerlessness to change the status quo without radical social mediations.

The consequences of exclusion or social marginality are primarily threefold: (1) socioeconomic and political disparities (such as equitable access to resources and decision making affecting competing interests of both) between the marginalized and the mainstream; (2) underlying conditions of societal marginality that result in lack of ability to participate in the political process; and (3) reduced sense of community and resultant low self-esteem. These factors ultimately lead to a social conditioning in which the marginalized are discriminated against based on race, gender, age, class, culture, ethnicity, religion, education, employment, and the social status they occupy. On the global stage, marginality will also lead to vulnerabilities that are affected by political instability and level of national industrialization. In a democracy, for example, a marginalized population would suffer from lack of educational preparation to participate in the democratic process through informed political consciousness, especially if they are immigrants, whether legalized or illegal. However, a non-democratic society is also problematic in its marginalized populations due to political and economic corruption, ethnic rivalries, tribalism, and religious fanaticism. Social marginality logically creates spatial marginality, such as when comparing capital or urban areas of development with opposite rural settings. Even within the urban space, living standards can differ between the metropolis and suburbia. Mainstream or higher-earning households naturally share the same neighborhoods in the same way that marginalized people also find themselves sharing the same neighborhoods based on occupational classification as "low income" or wage laborers.

Disadvantaged or marginalized communities naturally develop internal coping mechanisms through resistance and resilience by which they overcome societal risks and vulnerabilities that include violence, violation, self-destruction through drugs and alcohol, and ultimately a total disregard for human life in the face of survival and struggle for self-preservation. Such communities excluded from the mainstream find themselves victimized by virtue of their locus, which equally influences their minority status due to profiling and stereotyping by the forces of the mainstream. Social marginality translates into extreme poverty by the very nature of lacking access to basic social resources and services such as shelter, food, health care, and political representation, and from a sense of worthlessness that may then trigger a feeling of not having future material or financial security. While marginality deals with the process, poverty embodies the measurement of social inequity. To be marginalized, then, is by default to be impoverished, living on the margins, and unable to overcome poverty due to lack of the new industrial values that compel individuals to have technological sophistication in order to access information and process the same for personal survival and even informal networking. The specificity of poverty contrasts with the flexibility of marginality, which may be associated with even bourgeois communities when compared with upscale social communities. The relativizing of marginality complicates the conceptualization theory, since such communities of gays, drug dealers, and gangsters are not poor but are stigmatized and marginalized as social misfits or "outsiders." In the final analysis, social marginalization is determined by the location of the individual or community in question, to which the cases of marginalized communities of Rio de Janeiro and São Paulo attest in this chapter.

Globalizing the "Ghetto" through Cultural Dynamics

As a sociological term, the urban "ghetto" has been used by scholars to signify "the result of society's explicit interests in segregating ethnic or racial groups who, as a consequence of deprivation, experienced the welling-up of internal forces of resistance and of the creation of specific subcultures."[4] In the Brazilian context, the surge of various terminologies to refer to marginalized communities—"Morro," "Favela," "Condomínio," "Engenho Velho" (old plantation), "Cidade de Deus," "Casa Verde Alta," "Jardim Periperi," and "Rocinha," among others—signals a shift in the definition and configuration of what constitutes a "ghetto," since some of these communities, while located on the outskirts of the city, are also beginning to attract the middle class based on declining living standards and the need to stay on top of a stagnant economy. The contradiction emerges in the fact that, when convenient to entrepreneurs who have found a new market in selling "favela tours" to naïve visitors to Brazil, the ghetto becomes both an alluring and a marketable site despite its marginal status. In the United States, the notion of the ghetto evokes squalor and overcrowded living conditions where blacks and minority groups such as Latinos and Caribbean folk congregate in an oppressive and deprived setting in which violence, drugs, gangs, and a high mortality rate compete for audience in the "hell on earth" that the ghetto is often associated with.

Though Wacquant has identified four interrelated elements of the ghetto—stigma, boundary, spatial enclosure, and institutional encapsulation—the critic of the ghetto (Wacquant) further contends that although "all ghettos are segregated areas not all segregated areas are ghettos,"[5] implying that gated communities on the periphery of Latin American cities, especially in Brazil, should not be referenced as ghettos. Rather than a generic term that does not capture all the contradictions of emerging globalized cultural capital within the ghettos, the shifts within which not even the notion of "hyperghetto" begins to address, Monteiro suggests not only setting aside the term but also taking seriously a new term such as "neo-favela," which captures these contradictions:

> The favelas of Rio de Janeiro were formerly known for their culture, such as being the cradle of samba and important cultural manifestations which defined the identity of Brazil as a whole. The occupation of the hillsides promoted at one and the same time the advantages of segregation and the advantages of being close to the city [. . .] Under organized crime [. . .] the favela now imposes fear and controls the outside city [. . .] In an extreme demonstration of control,

during a recent war between favelas, they ordered people to stay at home, kept the police under siege, and dictated rules for their co-presence with "the ghetto" [. . .] Far from being a place of poverty, the favela now has local branches of major banks, post offices, language schools, and all kinds of services. Their inhabitants are classified under all ranges of income and there are already companies promoting internationalism tourism in the area.[6]

This ability for the ghetto to be on the one hand a weak social force and yet a threat through its cultural capital on the other, which then places it alongside major players in the economy, calls for closer analysis. Since Brazilian society refuses to accept the fact it is racist, the coinage of *favela* to refer to mostly Afro-Brazilian and indigenous communities reeks of an a priori assumption that these ethnic groups belong to the lower class by virtue of race and social exclusion. However, if we conjecture that the ghetto could be a metaphor for disadvantaged social representation that can easily be modified with the presence of affluence in the mix, then the term takes on a new positive meaning, as if influential people could meet exclusively in a metaphorical "ghetto" setting. This complexified idea can only be for the sake of argument, as such scenarios are limited and uncommon, though the thesis is that rich people will be accepted into the mainstream without regard to race, gender, or religious background. Being classified as "ghetto," then, is a matter of social belonging and not a racialized classification—an argument that I find not quite plausible.

In collapsing all marginalized communities together under the unitary umbrella term of the "ghetto," the consequent analysis of urban spatial segregation ultimately leads to biased generalizations based on similarity in social patterns of such communities, even when dealing with poor or rich neighborhoods and the relative elements of their differentiations. Valadares argues, for example, that "urban segregation" is driven by the forces of exploitation, economic imbalances, and the faulty results of urban policies.[7] These capitalist forces are, however, alarmed that the segregated communities are balancing their deprivation with some hope and sense of resistance as they reverse their marginality and turn it into a weapon of intimidation and fear for the mainstream society. In sum, a neo-favela movement is emerging under the guise of coerced segregation, where advantages are supposed to be derived from belonging to such communities where organized crime and drug trafficking become an informal structure for the provision of security for members who adhere to their rules of engagement and belonging. It goes without saying that such an arrangement questions the "ghetto" label of such a dominant community, where poverty is no longer the mode but affluence, although through illegitimate business. In the case of government-built peripheral neighborhoods, their living conditions are quite similar to those of the ghetto, even when conditioned by poverty and government's response to segregation by relocation in the outskirts—that is, outside of the urban space. The result is a direct relationship among poverty, segregation, and urban periphery.

Beyond the ghetto question lies the fast-growing number of gated condominiums that are now surfacing along the highways of São Paulo, for example. These condos are being built to replace the city and have their own social services, such as malls, schools, medical facilities, and cinemas. These settlements create a certain sense of dislocation from the city, as they are located far from the metropole. Through valued individuality and distance from each other despite physical proximity, the dwellers are living in a whole world of their own, where even the police are afraid to come near. The line between crime and legal authority is blurred since law, crime, and neighbors keep to themselves, or simply assume other inhabitants are not even there. Monteiro refers to such a setting as a "cluster" and not a ghetto. If considered a ghetto, it will be called a "Golden Ghetto"[8] or, rather, a place that is so "self-sufficient" that the rules of engagement are unique and peculiar. Regardless of the naming of disadvantaged communities and the appropriateness or political correctness of such names to represent marginalized and segregated residential neighborhoods such as gated condominiums, walled residential communities in Rio or São Paulo, the historical *quilombos* (runaway slave settlements), and the Landless Workers Movement residential camps, ghettos within and without the urban spatial limits are calling for political intervention, dignity, and respect—despite a sense of frustration for being socially stigmatized, marginalized, and considered inferior by mainstream society. It is this feeling of frustration that will be redressed through violence in the texts that concern this chapter.

Freire-Medeiros provides a touristic and problematic aspect of the culturalization and commercialization of marginalized communities. For her, study of the favela is a polemic proposition, since she must balance voyeurism with a sense of humanity for the dwellers whose environment is being subjected to an outsider's lens. She discusses the development of the favela into a tourist attraction and examines how promoters in four different favelas attempted to place them in the tourist market. The development of the favela into a tourist destination is seen as part of the so-called reality tours phenomenon and of the global circulation of the favela as a trademark. After long interviews with qualified informants, field observation, and participant observation in different tours, Freire-Medeiros concludes:

> I have attempted to demonstrate that favelas are tourist destinations that can be advertised, sold and consumed in many ways: as a social and/or physical landscape, an ecological site, or an extreme tourist experience. More often than not, such tourist practices have at least two arguments in their favor: their potential to enhance the local economy and the inhabitants' self-esteem; the opportunity they provide to the tourist to combine solidarity and leisure in one package [. . .] On the other, human misery and suffering are not straightforwardly associated with recreation. It does not come as a surprise that turning poverty into a commodity, a tourist attraction with an established market price, would provoke moral anxiety. Tourism in favelas is part of a global phenomenon which has been reaching unexpected proportions, and which can be used as the basis for wider discussions, such as the politics of commodification of places, cultures, and people in a context of globalization and inequality.[9]

Indeed, the publication of *Cidade de Deus* in 1997 and the release of the film in 2002 has been the cause for this neighborhood's remarkable increase in popularity as a tourist destination in recent years. Fernando Meirelles's film was promoted worldwide as a localized memory of life in Rio's ghettos. Since it is based on Paulo Lins's epic narrative and the author himself is a native of that famed "City of God," the film became an instant success based on a sense of legitimacy and realism it brings to every household about life in Brazilian urban peripheries. As we turn our attention to the complexities of the text of *Cidade de Deus*, we must be reminded that the colorful film that boasts of a mix of funk, samba, and rock, is not always the reality; and the favela is not always that sexy, romantic, and normalized environment of daily living but a dungeon of violence where survival means "kill or be killed" in the game of outsmarting each other to stay alive.

Cidade de Deus and Desde Que o Samba é Samba: Between Exu and Xangô in the Neo-Favela World

When disparate manifestations of violence, racial marginalization, residential overcrowding, hellish living style, and exotic representation fuse into a singular drama of contentions between the art of aesthetic pleasure and that of anguish, between an oppressive class and a segregated other, the outcome can only be transcendental between the chaotic interpretive energies of Exu and the violent temperament of Xangô as both unleash their creative and destructive energies into a problem that has no solution but is resolved only through artistic venting, such as in the masterpieces that Paulo Lins has given us in the sociological drama of Cidade de Deus (1997) and the recourse to Carioca and national history in Desde Que o Samba é Samba (2012). Much has been written about "productive prison" (da Matta et al., 2009), "racial and class difference" (Lorenz, 2010), "racial resentment" (Fitzgibbon, 2009), "ImagiNation" (Amparo-Alves, 2009), "cosmetics of hunger" (Chan and Vitali, 2010), "multitude literature" (Justino, 2012), and "marginal literature" (Silva, 2012), yet these readings are guided more by the academic discursive necessity to prove right from wrong than by the quest for the holistic reward of understanding the totality of the burden of being marginalized due to historical factors of slavery, industrialization, racial discrimination, and the aftermath of globalization that craftily returns to the marketplace in order to "recolonize" rather than to decolonize. Against this background awareness of inadvertent dislocation in academic discourse, I approach Lins's works from a cultural-political perspective, drawing from Afro-Brazilian religious and mythological paradigms of Exu and Xangô to interpret artistic productions rooted in history and the search for cultural revival.

Cidade de Deus, as the title suggests, acknowledges a curious divine intervention in the struggle for survival that characterizes its modus operandi even as it seeks to make sense of life itself. In this seemingly epic narrative saga, Paulo Lins familiarizes us with a bizarre community where society is constantly on edge, along with its marginalized counterpoint—the favela community of Cidade de Deus. When a society is defined by violence and criminality typical of the 1960s that has now graduated into gang and interrelated drug-trafficking rivalry, we are indeed dealing with what Lins refers to as "New-Favela," as if there is a new social order that privileges drug trafficking and social death as the order of the day. Jaime do Amparo-Alves, however, challenges this perspective, suggesting contrastively that the vision of Lins corresponds to the official Brazilian racist reality where young blacks are set up for failure and are represented as if deserving of death and with no possible positive contribution to the larger society. For Amparo-Alves, "the dual bind through which the nation is ambiguously imagined is made explicit also in the consumption of Blackness as exotic at the same time that it represents a threat to the national harmony. The nation is then written and re-imagined as a racial paradise even/and mostly by inscribing death to the black body."[10] This critique challenges the popular view of the original text and film as masterpieces based on the larger implication of the ideology that informs their anthropological perspectives. The notion of a "new favela" thus falls apart if there is an inherent negative portrayal of that disadvantaged community, and an attempt to make it more alluring to outsiders does more disservice than good if blacks are ultimately the perpetrators of violence, while whites are the innocent victims. The "old favela" implicitly references that self-imposed *malandragem* (survivalist behavior that subverts the official norm through creative deviation to achieve personal gains) as a cultural performance and the *escolas de samba* as a "melting pot" of cultural renewal in Rio de Janeiro.

Based primarily on an anthropological study of criminality among the masses of Rio de Janeiro between 1986 and 1993, Lins invites his readers to a world of devotees of Candomblé, lovers of samba, Pagode, and Carnival, constant attendees of bars and clubs during weekends, and lovers of life in general. Divided into three fast-paced parts reminiscent of cinematographic scenes in which detailed descriptions of characters are mixed with occasional flashbacks and new characters coming into the picture, as if the writer seeks to ensure that the reader has all the information necessary to make sense of the plot structure, even as fiction seems to mirror the reality of the quest for power by the powerless as sought by all means necessary, including violence and violation. In the end, marginal elements of the society seize artificial power by evading the authorities, taunting their neighbors, and disempowering those who seem to be making progress in the community. Everything signals the inevitability of degeneration in the midst of the marginalizing power of urbanization and increased social mobility for the powerful.

Evoking a Naturalist novel of the Balzac (France) and Azevedo (Brazil) extraction, *Cidade de Deus* follows the lives of young gangsters from adolescence to adulthood, their petty thieving, love stories, moments at the beach in harmony with nature, playing soccer, using drugs, evading the police constantly, deploying multiple strategies of survival in a cruel and violent setting that is not too far from a jungle and the laws of which they have well mastered, settling for the law of survival, ready to eliminate each other as necessary. Loyalty is earned, not assumed, and cannot be taken for granted, as at a moment's notice the reality of survival might change, altering all the rules. The novel consciously deploys lots of slang and curse words intended to aggravate the situation of the characters and bring realism into focus, with no sense of sentimentality or attempt to temper with compassion the horrific, grotesque, and explosive dramas of life and death. Lins gives it to us as it is in the real world of Cidade de Deus.

In three carefully crafted biographical narratives, accounts in fact based on real-life stories, namely "A história de inferninho" (Story of Little Hell), "A história de Pardalzinho" (Story of the Dark One), and "A história do Zé Miúdo" (Story of Little Zé), Lins dissects detailed activities of these juvenile delinquents as they strive to take control of their neighborhood, initially as mischief makers, then pranksters, gangsters, and later drug dealers. Whether the narrative is focused on the community itself or on the three gangsters that will be the focus of the novel in addition to the community itself, Lins ensures that there is no boring moment, given the extensive nature of the details he provides on the characters and their troubling activities. As the omniscient narrator informs the reader, invoking the old nostalgic times as opposed to the current reality of violence: "ANTIGAMENTE a vida era outra neste lugar onde o rio, dando areia, cobra-d'água inocente e indo ao mar, dividia o campo em que os filhos de portugueses e da escravatura pisaram" (15) (IN LIFE PAST, living was different in this place where the river, releasing its sand, an innocent stream that leads to the sea, used to separate the countryside in which descendants of the Portuguese and enslavement settled). This poetic invocation of nature signals a time when life was tranquil, unpolluted, and devoid of the "little hell" that the environment has now become. Only poetry can capture the premonition of violence and death, as Lins captures the inability for words to capture a situation in which words have now become bullets, spoken with fewer words and with devastating consequences: "POESIA minha tia illumine as certezas dos homens e os tons de minhas palavras. É o verbo, aquele que é maior que o seu tamanho, que diz e acontece. Aqui ele cambaleia baleado [. . .] Massacrada no estômago com arroz e feijão a quase-palavra é defecada ao invés de falada. Falha a fala. Fala a bala" (21) [POETRY, my Auntie, illuminates uncertainties of men and the sounds of my words. It is the verb, that which is bigger than its size, which speaks and comes to life. Here it falters through bullets . . . Massacred in the stomach with rice and beans, the broken speech is defecated instead of being spoken. Real speech is missing. Bullets speak instead.] It is hard to talk about "Cidade Maravilhosa / cheia de encantos mil" (Marvelous City / full of a thousand enchantments) (17), especially when the enchantment referenced in the new dispensation of favela-life is all about violence and death.

Despite the many characters populating the grotesque world of City of God, a few who are in close proximity to each other are worth analyzing, namely, Cabeleira, Bené, and Little Zé. The first part focuses on Cabeleira, an anti-hero of sorts, but whose mission overlaps with that of the community only in terms of his surreal dreams of living a life of the affluent or the bourgeois. Appropriately named "Story of Little Hell," this biographical account of the life of Cabeleira details the occupation of Cidade de Deus by the dwellers and the subsequent emergence of gangs. The gangsters modeled themselves on Italian and Chicago Mafiosi, but focused on the consumption and sale of narcotics. Once addicted to drugs and fearless, there was no stopping them, they thought. Yet the local police were effective in at least curbing the criminality of the gangsters. It was a war game of survival. The police eliminated some of the kingpins, but the operation persisted. The causes of Cabeleira's fortunes are traceable to his family backgrounds through details provided by the writer. As a black youngster from a modest family, he had to deal with the pain of his father being a drunkard and his mother a prostitute. The most important people in his life partly sealed his fate. He had no real positive role models to look up to, and the street became for him an alluring attraction since he spent most of his time there anyway. Quite surreal in his aspirations in life, he did not join others to rape women, and respected the community and his gang. Despite his good intentions, such as insisting that his gang must not rob their community as a basic law of self-respect, he was, however, cruel with his enemies, killing them without pity and believing in Exu, the Yoruba divinity of the crossroads, to protect him.

As a "walled-in" community, Cidade de Deus does not depend on the social benefits from the municipality, such as providing sanitation or making basic amenities available. These must be provided by the collective efforts of the inhabitants. As a result, Lins reminds us, the community was responsible even for its own Carnival preparations and implied financial costs:

> Cidade de Deus não contava com os incetivos da prefeitura, por isso não tinha coreto na praça. Curvadinho, um dos comerciantes do conjunto, encarragava-se de fazer o coreto e encontrara os músicos para fazer o Carnaval. No último dia da festa, a escola de samba desfilava na rua Principal, assim como os blocos Os Garimpeiros e Os Anjinhos da Cidade de Deus. (81)

> [City of God did not have the support of the city hall, thus did not have any bandstand at the townsquare. Curvadinho, one of the sellers in the compound took upon himself to build a bandstand and found some musicians to organize Carnival. On the last day of the festival, the samba school, as well as the Carnival groups, "Garimpeiros" (Rubber tappers) and "Anjinhos da Cidade de Deus" (Angels of the City of God), were parading on Main street.]

As we follow the life of Cabeleira, we are reminded of the rest of the gang since the protagonists seem to die one after the other; hence, the community itself becomes the longest-lasting character. After all, the story of Cidade de Deus is all about war. Not just the war in the ghetto, but a constant struggle for power, social mobility, and money. Through the eye of an insider / nonparticipant, we appreciate the close contact we have with the characters, even as they each fulfill their bleak destiny with death. But who is to blame? Lins deploys Cidade de Deus as a metaphor for Rio de Janeiro and the rest of Brazilian society in terms of exclusion, abandonment, and decadence. In order to protect itself, the community has come to terms that they need the gangsters; as a result, and to secure their protection, they often must silence themselves in the face of their atrocities, and it is through this silencing that peace is possible in a condition of wild violence, brutality, and complete disregard for life.

When an episode starts with a couple of characters getting high on drugs, as in the case of Busca-Pé and Barbantino, it signals a serious social problem of addiction and a premonition of ultimate destruction and social death. Lins characterizes them as homeless groups of people striving for any place to rest their heads. The author observes the activities of the bandits who have invaded communities and have gradually set up their robbery operations in a sophisticated manner, as they imagine that through these deviant behaviors they can possibly escape poverty and social dislocation:

> A maioria dos bandidos raramente circula de dia, preferia a noite para jogar ronda, fumar baseado, jogar sinuca, cantar samba sincopado acompanhando do som de uma caixa de fósforos e, até mesmo, para bater um papo com amigos. Somente Tutuca, Inferninho, Martelo, Pelé e Pará eram vistos de dia. Assaltando os caminhões de gás, fumando maconhanas esquinas, soltando pipa com a molecada, jogando bola com rapaziada do conceito. Os outros assaltantes preferiam agir na Zona Sul, "local de bacana." Assaltavam turistas, lojas comerciais, pedestres com pinta de grã-finos. (31)

> [Most of the criminals were invisible during the day, they preferred the night time in order to mess around, smoke hemp, play snooker, sing syncopated samba, accompanied by the lighter box, as well as chat with friends. Only Tutuca, Inferninho, Martelo, Pelé, and Para were seen during the day. Robbing the gas trucks, smoking hemp on the corners, playing kites with other kids, and playing soccer with the neighborhood's children. The other robbers preferred to operate in the Southern Zone, "a great location." They robbed tourists, commercial stores, and pedestrians with style.]

In the social hierarchy and power structure created by the bandits themselves, we find on the top, Cabeleira, Marreco, and Alicate, while at the bottom are situated Salgueirinho, Pelé, and Pará. Military police officer Cabeção and the detective Touro lead the counter-offensive against these criminal activities; they know exactly where these criminal elements live, know they are armed and dangerous, and often pursue them with vigor to arrest or to eliminate outright people they consider as "enemies of the state."

The gravity of the vicious crimes increases exponentially since these are not limited to the main protagonists but also concern the secondary characters. Such is the absurd case of a husband who suspects his wife of having had extramarital affairs and reacts by cutting their child into pieces and delivering it to the wife in a shoe box. In addition, the husband cuts off the head of the rival lover and delivers it to the unfaithful wife in a plastic bag. Violence is the order of the day as the bandits divide their time between watching their TV heroes, having fun their own way, swimming, and getting introduced to drug use. Some memorable moments of descriptions include the death and burial of Salgueirinho, a "ladies' man" run over by a car; it is rumored that his death is part of divine justice since he is known for jilting women after exploiting them sexually, and one such woman put *macumba* (black magic) on him. Not only do we get to know the lives of the bandits, such as Touro, Pelé, and Pará, we also witness through detailed description how the police execute these marginals as if they are at war with each other. Violence creates tension, as in the killing of a cat to make a barbecue, in a descriptive passage filled with impressive narrative suspense. The catalog of criminality and punishment is strikingly endless: Jorge Nesfalto is condemned for thirteen crimes he did not commit; Damião eliminates his partner, Cunha, in order to take control of the drug-trafficking business and also be with Cunha's wife, Fernanda; Marreco loses his mind, claiming to be a child of the Devil, then rapes the Paraiba woman, whose husband later kills him; Alicate becomes an evangelist for the Baptist Church and, in what appears to be a dream, sees all his friends (Marreco, Salgueirinho, Haroldo, Pelé, and Pará) drenched in blood. This may well be a premonition of death for these peripheral individuals.

As much as the bandits evade police detection via various machinations, wiles, and deceits, in the end, they always fall into the hands of the law. Cabeção eventually catches up with Wilson Diabo, kills him, and makes Cabeleira his next target for elimination and community sanitation. When he finally finds Cabeleira, they exchange gunfire, but both are so skilled they do not hit each other. Marimbondo even offers a .45 pistol to Cabeleira to even up with Marimbondo. But to no avail. Ultimately, the narrative seems to return to the beginning, offering the reader intimate insights into the lives of Busca-Pé and Barbantino. We follow their aspirations and dreams, the life of the *cocotas* and playboys from suburbia and the favelas. All the bandits want is community respect, "matare ser respeitado!," that is, kill and be respected. In vain, detective Touro pursues Marimbondo to eliminate him. Cabeleira, on the other hand, is tired of being with the group and sets out to rob on his own. It was as if something subconscious was pushing him to his fatal end at the hands of Touro, which ends the first part of the narrative:

Cabeleira se cansa de ficar entocado com os colegas e resolve sair sozinho. Queria ver os amigos de Cidade de Deus. A narrativa descreve uma manhã calma e silenciosa. [. . .] então por que aquela aflição? Por que aquela vontade de voltar para perto dos amigos? Aquela sensação de vazio lhe trazia sobressaltos, frios na espinha. [. . .] A qualidade da paz era superlativa também na Rua do Meio e fazia crescer aquele temor, temor do nada. [. . .] Não sabia o porquê, mas pequenos pedaços de sua vida vinham-lhe repentinamente de modo sucessivo. As mais vivas cores do dia tornaram-se significantes de significados muito mais intensos, confundindo a sua visão. O vento mais nervoso, o sol mais quente, o passo mais forte, os pardais tão longe dos homens, o silêncio inoperante, os piões rodando, os girassóis vergando-se, os carros mais rápidos e a voz de Touro agitando tudo: —Deita no chão, vagabundo! Cabeleira não esboçou reação. Ao contrário do que se esperava Touro [. . .] Talvez nunca tenha buscado nada, nem nunca pensara em buscar, tinha só de viver aquela vida sem nenhum motivo que o levasse a uma atitude parnasiana naquele universo escrito por linhas tão marginais. [. . .] Aquela mudez diante das perguntas de Touro e a expressão de alegria melancólica que se manteve dentro do caixão. (170–171)

[Cabeleira is tired of being bothered by his mates and decides to set out on his own. He wants to see friends in the City of God. The narrative describes a calm and silent morning. . . . so why such an affliction? Why that will to return to be close to friends? That feeling of emptiness that brought him trepidation, chills in the bones. . . . The quality of peace was also rising on the Middle street and developed within him a certain temerity, the fear of nothingness. . . . He could not understand it but bits and pieces of his life flashed through suddenly in a successive manner. Most vivid colors of the day became pregnant with more intense meanings, confounding his vision. Most nervous wind, hottest sun, fastest steppings, sparrows so far away from men, inoperative silence, spinners circulating, sunflowers bending, the fastest cars and the voice of Touro agitating everything: —On the floor vagabond! Cabeleira did not react. Contrary to what Touro expected . . . Perhaps he never sought nothing, not even thought of searchcing for anything, he only wanted to lead such a lackluster life that led him to a Parnasian attitude in that universe created by groups of marginal . . . That strange silence faced with Touro's questions and the expression of melancholic happiness that he maintained within the coffin].

Such were the last moments of Cabeleira, as he makes his appointment with death, with which that segment of the narrative ends.

Beyond the life of Cabeleira, which ends as it starts, the stories of Bené and Little Zé share a commonality in that they will both die by the bullet. From the very beginning, Bené focuses on finding the commandant of the favela, and through negotiating additional drug territories, he plans to head a new generation of bandits who will provide protection for their community. Alongside the issue of drug trafficking lies the corruption of the penal system, as well as the homosexual lifestyle. By demonstrating his cruel and fearless nature alongside Little Zé, Bené is able to take over the drug-trafficking business in the community. So daring is Bené that he joins the *cocotas*, who are seen to have higher mobility status in the community. He starts wearing their coded outfit with dragon tattoos on his arm. After suffering a number of failed romantic relationships, he resolves to make a lot of money, enough to start a new and alternative community of his own. The third part is the all-out war among rival gangs, as a series of suceeding drug lords take over the drug traffic business within the community. Manoel Galinha emerges as a man of faith, hope, and justice, but is not able to change the status quo of marginality. The more central figure of this part, Little Zé, is the most cruel of the gangsters in Cidade de Deus. An irony of sorts, for a "City of God" should be devoid of hellish living, yet the reality is that there is no mercy in the eyes of these gangsters. Little Zé's trademark is to be decisive, brutal, and deadly as he unleashes terror on his community and rivals. Since he is unhappy in his love life, he chooses to rape Manoel Galinha's girlfriend, which causes ripples of tension within the community, of which Zé is the embodiment. While Vanessa Fitzgibbon has argued that "Inferninho's violence is triggered by the discrimination and prejudice he experienced throughout his youth,"[11] the propensity for violence is also stimulated by unabated frustrations, thus forming a bottled-up anguish ultimately released through the barrel of the gun.

The tradition of drug trafficking in Cidade de Deus sets the tone of the beginning of chapter 2, the second part of Lins's narrative, which also focuses on the life and times of Bené, as well as on the initiation of Dadinho into the world of crime. As the world of crime, gang violence, and drug trafficking become even more alluring, the struggle for power increases. Dadinho seeks spiritual guidance through Umbanda, and soon reaps the benefit, as the drug kingpin dies and Dadinho takes over at the helm of affairs. The crimes do not stop, as Bené and Zé Pequeno emerge as the most feared criminals in the pack. As complicated and intrigued as the adventures, struggles, and parties get, the group never forgets its primary mission of solidifying the drug trade even as internal power struggles lead to inadvertent brutal killings. Little Zé kills off Sandro Cenoura and all competing drug lords, dividing his loot with his new partner, Bené. As the saying goes among them, "Trafficking drugs has become the fashionable thing; this is what brought in the money." Following Cabeleira's death, Ari, his brother, returns to the vicinity of Cidade de Deus, but has always had conflict with Pouca Sombra, who has left his wife to be with another man. The homosexual underworld is exposed in terms of how they live, love, and relate to each other. Cabelo Calmo was imprisoned when he turned eighteen, and was named the sheriff's "woman" within the prison. The sheriff was also running a drug operation within the prison, kept secret from everyone. Once Cabelo Calmo left prison, he joined Bené and Little Zé but kept them ignorant of his homosexual lifestyle in prison. The narrator seizes the opportunity to inform the reader of the underworld of corruption within the Ilha Grande Penitentiary. Marimbondo, unaware of the dangers, tries to be the same maverick in prison that he was in the ghetto and is horribly stabbed to death.

As the gang becomes more powerful, they commit more atrocious acts of violence, such as eliminating potential rivals. For example, Ari do Rafa and his gang are murdered and buried in a mass grave. The Carlinhos Nervo Duro group tries to challenge the leadership of Bené and Little Zé, and find themselves dead, with the exception of the leader, who barely escapes. After a series of power struggles that ultimately lead to the death of many rivals, Bené and Little Zé solidify their leadership over Cidade de Deus. Drug trafficking soon requires a high level of arms dealing with the police to sustain their business, while robberies and death squads continue. Eventually, Bené and Little Zé become local pop stars as they are invited to the local School of Samba by the Portela composer, Voz Poderosa, in the process of selection of the next Carnival samba. Though it feels for a while that the gangsters are untouchable, Touro, the detective, is on an intensive manhunt for them. Their luck soon runs out as police officers Lincoln and Monstrinho arrest Bené, while Touro is released from his duties for stabbing a prison guard. In the midst of the succession of deaths and betrayals, Bené's mother dies while he is still in prison. Once he is released, he vows to share his loot with the police. He also decides to spare the life of Butucatu, who had had an affair with his ex-wife and was to be killed by Little Zé. Bené himself is betrayed by Mosca, who had an affair and became pregnant. In the process of aborting the baby, she dies. In the unforeseen gunfight between Butucatu, Bené, and Little Zé, all the rivals and friends are hit; Bené dies from gunshot wounds to the abdomen, but Butucatu survives. The series of violent death and burials turns *Cidade de Deus* into a hellish cyclical narrative of life and death in an enclosed entrapment of violent gang life.

The last major player in the drama of gang leadership lies in no other than Zé Pequeno or Little Zé. Occupying the center of attraction of the third chapter, Little Zé has been hunting down Pança and Butucatu for a while. The two bandits have promised to wipe everyone out in Cidade de Deus. While Zé Pequeno falls in love with a blonde woman, it is not always a romantic relationship. When he felt jilted by her, he decided to rape her in front of her boyfriend as a form of revenge. That not being enough, he seeks the blonde's boyfriend, Mané Galinha, in order to further vent his rage; when he does not find him at home, he decides to kill his grandfather. Mané Galinha resolves to have his own poetic justice as well by eliminating two gangs led by Little Zé swiftly and violently. Galinha had earlier served in the Leftist Army Brigade, and had a reputation not only for his intimidating athletic build but for using different types of military weapons. The conflict between Little Zé and Galinha later intensifies and degenerates into a gang war. When they finally face each other, Little Zé's gunshots hit Galinha, but he manages to escape, while the struggle for leadership continues. Sandro Cenoura even tries to team up with Mané Galinha to form another gang, but to no avail. Galinha finally succumbs to his wounds, and his funeral rites last three days. Despite efforts of the police to rid the community of gang violence and drug trafficking, the pervasive police corruption gets in the way. Once again arrested and caught with money, drugs, and weapons, Little Zé is sentenced to the famous Milton Dias Moreira penitentiary, where he continues his illegal operations behind bars. He later bribes someone to get out of prison and goes underground outside of Cidade de Deus.

Even when horrific cases appear to turn hopeful, they turn out tragic in the end. Otávio, for example, commits attrocious crimes, killing nearly thirty people and burying them in a mass grave, but later, after his prison term of two years, he becomes an envagelist pastor, gets married, and has children. His conversion does not last, however: he later tears pages of the Bible and claims to have been possessed by evil spirits, turning his anguish on police officers, whom he kills mercilessly.

Partly a twist of fate or a spiritual renewal of sorts, partly a necessary turning point that has been wanting in the lives of many in Cidade de Deus, Messias, the last drug trafficker of Lá de Cima, makes peace with rival gang leaders, including Borboletão and Tigrinho, thus bringing peace to the community. Some abandon the lifestyle, others continue the business, while Busca-Pé fulfills his dream of becoming a photographer. Little Zé returns from prison with the dream of taking over the drug business one more time, but he is killed during the New Year festivities. Thus ends the cycle of death and violence.

Despite the controversies surrounding the success of Lins's work, in text and film, it is remarkable that such a work of intense urban anthropology was ever written, given its high risk of failure. Accused of a stereotypical portrayal of the Brazilian favela, especially in Rio de Janeiro, a place where youngsters are condemned to a life of crimes, drugs, and violence, Lins in is later work, appears to find within himself a peaceful location through recourse to researching samba, a national music and dance, and rendering it in an accessible manner as a historical document. Contrary to the popular belief that a people's history can be told only through writing, Lins approaches music as a form of historical memory by tapping into the contextual emergence of an expressive cultural phenomenon that has not always been accepted, embraced, and celebrated. Yet, even as part of "national culture" and heritage, samba is still considered by some to have its origins in the lower class, and thus not a part of high culture such as bossa nova. It is remarkable that *Desde que o Samba é Samba* (2012) may well have been a sequel to *Cidade de Deus* (1997) in this sense. Lins may have felt the need to respond to his critics and detractors by giving the explosive gang violence in *Cidade de Deus* a historical context. On the one hand, 125 years after the abolition of slavery (1888), descendants of African slaves are still marginalized in the slums, where they produce their samba and sing of their frustrations and aspirations. From the viewpoint of social commentary, *Cidade de Deus* is based on an intimate relationship with the community and the real context of war and revenge among rivalring gangs, whereas the plot of *Desde que o Samba é Samba* is based on a love triangle between pimp Brancura, prostitute Valdirene, and underworld entrepreneur Sodré. This story, however, is told against the background of the emergence of Samba do Estácio, the first school of samba (Deixa Falar [Let me speak]), and the popularization of Umbanda as Rio's Afro-Brazilian religion.

Beyond the stereotypical image of the slums, where the only freedom allowed blacks and marginals is to become a hussler (*malandro*) and learn survival tactics (*gingas*), Lins portrays Rio de Janeiro as a cohesive blend of historical pioneers of the 1920s' climate of samba and fictional characters such as Ismael Silva Alcebíades Barcellos (Bide), Armando Marçal, Edgar Marcelino dos Passos, and Rubem Barcellos, among others. These musical maestros suggest that music can also be a legitimate form of cultural preservation and artistic expression. Lins portrays Rio de Janeiro in its formative years, when samba was indeed part of the cultural space to assert one's subjectivity. Samba then was equivalent to cultural capital, a priceless vehicle for the articulation and preservation of black culture. The ex-slaves expelled from Bahia during the Malê rebellion found refuge as exiles in Rio de Janeiro or chose to return to Africa. In the early twentieth century, samba was illegal and listed under article 399 of the Brazilian Penal Code, meaning whoever played samba professionally was subject to imprisonment since samba was considered an "offensive manifestation against moral and good social conduct."[12] Setting the story in Estácio in central Rio, the core of samba gyrations, Lins invites readers to witness the Rio of the 1920s, when slums were practically inaccessible and meant for those who knew the codes of survival. Lins return to his Naturalist mode reminiscent of *Cidade de Deus* while replacing the degenerate lives of Cabeleira, Bené, and Zé Pequeno with that of Ismael Silva, a character who synthesizes all the melancholic dramas and intrigues that beset samba in its formative years of police persecutions. Like *Cidade de Deus*, *Desde que o Samba é Samba* is highly cinematographic and fast paced; the reader follows the protagonist Ismael along the inner streets of Rio and through the house of Tia Almeida, sees the new inventions in samba instruments, visits the Umbanda temples, which are adjacent to schools of samba, and understands the overall sense of living in harmony with nature and music. Lins observes that the cultural industry that samba is today was not always the case, and sees samba as a vanguardist art: "Samba is a genre that emerged with the objective to differentiate, to provoke change. The musical genre emerged in the 1920s and led to the creation of the Samba schools. These schools were created in order to avoid police persecution. Samba was born running from the Police."[13]

Combining the best samba composer in the person of Ismael Silva with the greatest hustler of the Estácio Samba group, Brancura, Lins was able to re-create, with some poetic license, the ambience of the 1920s. Lins privileges artistic invention over facts, such as in the claim that Brancura slept with close to a hundred prostitutes or that Ismael Silva went to the Estácio Samba school and asked that he be registered. Who can refute these claims since the history of samba itself is yet to be reconstructed faithfully, as many of the pioneers have passed on, taking archival memories along with them. Lins's attempt here is something between fact and fiction, hence a first attempt to fictionalize history in order to be able to return to verifying that history exactly as it was. Lins, for example, ends his narrative by evoking poetically what it was like to be persecuted by police simply for wanting to express what should be unconstrained:

> Até o vento fazia a curva em causa própria, assim como as pessoas que sentiam aquela energia vinda da criação artística para superar a vida em que o povo negro da pós-escravidão colocou a cultura como arma para conquistar dignidade com duas batidas fortes no surdo feito deixa para o solista sair improvisando [. . .]. Tiveram a ideia de fazer parte da sociedade em forma de canto, mas mesmo assim foram espancados pela polícia, sofreram desdém, foram presos, tiveram a dor do preconceito, mas saíram sambando em busca de uma avenida para fazer dela uma passarela com o reforço do tamborim, do reco-reco, da cuíca e do surdo.[14]

> [Even the wind made the curve for its own sake, as well as people who felt that energy coming from artistic creation to overcome life in which the black people in the post-slavery era deployed culture as a weapon to conquer their dignity with two strong beats on the *surdo* (large bass drum) leaves the soloist no other alternative than to improvise. . . . They

had the idea of being part of society through their singing;
yet, they were beaten by the Police; they suffered from hatred;
they were arrested; they felt the pain of prejudice; but they
came out of it all looking for where to sing their samba while
searching for an avenue to turn into a walkway with the reinforcement of the tambourine, the scraped bamboo percussion
instrument, the friction drum, and the large bass drum.]

The question of faithful rendition of historical facts is less relevant than
the ultimate goal of reconstructing history fictionally. Lins may not satisfy
every critic or taste, but his narrative is not outlandishly far from the
truth. Starting with some musical historical premises about the Estácio
group, Lins identifies the main players in the history of samba, such
as Sinhô, Donga, and João da Baiana, while adding the asides of the
place of batucada (percussion), Candomblé (Afro-Brazilian religion), and
Umbanda (spiritism mixed with Indian and Afro-Brazilian religion), thus
explicating how samba came to be what it is today in terms of influences
and polyrhythms. In recognizing the influence of Afro-Brazilian religions
on samba, as on Carnival in Bahia, for example, Lins confirms that
samba is not fully immune from its African origins for which it recalls
today as a symbol of resistance and as a model of how to integrate the
sacred within the popular. Whether it is Samba-Reggae, Samba-Canção,
Samba-Duro, Pagode, or Pagodão, the basic elements of dance, spirituality, and self-exaltation in the midst of melancholy remain a constant.

Capão Pecado: Bound to Social Violence

Ferréz, author of Capão Pecado, is also the author of Literatura Marginal,
a rather manifesto-styled work in which the essentials of such a literature are laid as a counter-measure to canonical literature. The term
"marginal" references life on the edge, as far as society is concerned,
thus representing delinquency in the midst of violence, criminality, and
unemployment. Marginal literature is produced primarily by marginalized
subjects, who often live on the periphery of society and deploy their texts
to bring awareness to issues of daily social injustices. Such a literature
is also referred to as "literature of violence," especially since it sets out
to show what is real. The attitude of the self-denominated writers of
marginal literature is based on their lived experience and background,

which they have transduced into a positive instrument of legitimation of the truth. The writers also feel as though they are marginal because they are neither recognized by mainstream publishers nor by the media or academic circles. When a certain segment of the population lacks access to material and cultural goods, such a group is considered marginalized and often is located on the peripheries of society. *Capão Pecado* faithfully represents such a group. Most of these works have been written since the 1990s. *Capão Pecado* was published in 2000. It seeks to denounce the deprivation of people of basic human amenities that most privileged people in society enjoy. These marginal communities lack basic infrastructure, and this lack is consequently addressed by marginal literature. In the case of *Capão Pecado*, there is a sense that the characters are exploited and betrayed by their bosses and the system in which they are conditioned to work.

Since criminality is often associated with marginality, Ferréz takes it upon himself to emphasize the violence that is also a form of revenge for the marginalized, since the oppression results in bottled-up anger that must be released. As the author puts it in his blurb, violence is a constant that is real and inevitable: "Capão é um livro de mano pra mano. É ácido e violento. É um grito." Violence becomes manifest at many levels—as police violence, gang-on-gang violence to avenge honor, or even violence engendered by being in prison. The language deployed, often mixed with slang and adulterated Portuguese, serves as a form of identity affirmation that must not be subjected to the same expectations of standard Portuguese, as its first preoccupation is to function as an instrument of contesting the mainstream paradigm, which is not how marginalized communities express themselves based on duration of exposition to formal instruction. For dwellers of Capão Redondo, the conflicting notion of center and periphery comes into reality as marginal characters resist the social expectations of canonical literature. Deploying orality through informal use of language, the characters of the Paulistan periphery of Capão Redondo seek to speak "in the natural" without regard for linguistic normativity or objectivity. As a result, the narrator often shifts between the norm and the deviation by virtue of the street language that marginals use to codify and to differentiate themselves from the mainstream.

Rael, the eighteen-year-old protagonist, often represents the voice of the group as he deploys the language of the collective, especially when he is with friends, while varying his language when a more cultured register is expected during a serious conversation. This ability to oscillate and mediate between two worlds (cultured and noncultured) comes from his being an avid reader. Throughout the text, Rael expresses concern for education and reading, qualities that distinguish him from other youngsters.

Contesting the dominant ideology of privilege and that of living in a faulty "racial democracy," Ferréz deploys a ferocious critique of this state of affairs, in which one class dominates the other, by placing Rael in a conflicting situation that will make him rebel and seek resolution of his inner and external conflicts. Rael represents the marginal and excluded youngsters who must fight for survival daily and must assert their identity through resistance against domination.

Even as he aspires to change his condition, Rael dreams of having a better future and decent employment that offers him better social benefits. But as he negotiates this transformation through hard work, education, reading, good core values, and staying away from crime, he realizes that social mobility will not come without sacrifice. He is faced with a dilemma: he is different from his friends, who often end up in prison, and for whom crime and violence go hand-in-hand as a way of life. By virtue of his increasingly privileged position, Rael seems to be becoming part of the dominant ideology that preaches the falsehood (as does his wife Paula) that anyone who works hard will not only get ahead but will be able to have a happy family, as he does. His happiness is short-lived, as his boss becomes a threat to his overall dignity: his wife trades him for his boss, he loses his job, and he plans violent revenge. He ends up in prison, and while paying his dues to society, dreams of reconstructing his life—but he gets murdered in prison. With this tragic resolution, it stands to reason that Ferréz questions whether it is ever possible for the oppressed class to attain social mobility without violence, or whether a decent and ethical social life is meant only for the privileged few.

The likes of Rael are bound to violence because society gives them no other viable recourse. In the end, Rael feels a sense of social injustice, and all his reading and education do not help when he resorts to violence to settle the score between him and the boss, who stole his wife and disintegrated his family. If Rael's search for happiness is met with social corruption and death, his logical transgressive acts ultimately lead to violence and death—a vicious cycle consistent with what the entire marginalized community appears to be condemned to. Despite his efforts to do the right thing, efforts to overcome social obstacles to his dream, he transgresses as a classic tragic hero and finds solace in death. Rael represents the social figure with lofty ideals to change the world who ends up being a victim of that same world. Ferréz may well be proposing the need to be more active in the discursive engagement of the periphery and to come to terms with violence as a social phenomenon that erupts when nothing is done to avert it. *Capão Pecado*, in this sense, is an invitation to the world of Rael, while a society is bound to violence regardless of efforts to redress the situation. If *Capão Pecado* is an urgent cry for intervention, it is because there are so many communities that do not have a voice to make their aspirations known to the public, or who may have the words, but not the enterprise, such as a believing and beneficient publisher to get the word out to the larger public. Ferréz concludes his narrative on a somber note. In his postface, he theorizes on the exclusive poverty and deprivation of the favela dweller, predicting they will not be part of any relief or group of privileged members of the community appreciating nature and dreaming of a better life:

> É muito raro um favelado parar para ver as estrelas numa grande e farta cidade que só lhe entrega cada dia mais a miséria, mas que é sua cidade. Uma metrópole definidora de destinos cruzados, inutilmente ligados pela humildade e pelo carinho que os cercam. Família é sintonia, dizem os poetas urbanos sobreviventes do inferno para aqueles de mentes tristes, porém fascinadas em igual proporção com as ilusões carnavalescas de um país que luta por seus times de futebol, mas não luta pela sua dignidade.[15]

[It is very rare for a slum dweller to stop to see the stars in a large and abundant city that only gives him or her more misery every day, but that is still his or her city. A metropolis that defines interwoven destinies, futilely linked by the humility and affection that surround them. The family is symptomatic of the reality faced by those who urban poets, survivors of hell, see as melancholic, but who are equally fascinated by the illusions of carnival held by a people who would rather fight over their soccer teams than fight for their own dignity.]Sadly, it is not just the future dream that is deferred; the present, according to Ferréz, is locked in a cycle of misery and depressing reality of poverty.

The sociological approach adopted by Ferréz calls for a comparative analysis, even if cursory. But the conclusion also invokes poverty as a permanent cause of violence. In deploying the image of the "locked door into the future," the author comes to terms with his frustration that articulates that the situation may never be better. Of course, there is some hope in the urgent call for intervention, but that is all a frustrated writer can do:

> A pobreza aqui é passada de pai para filho, assim como a necessidade de se trabalhar dia e noite para comprar um pão, um saco de arroz, um saco de feijão. Mas é com amor e carinho que criamos nossos filhos, sem nos damos conta do local, dos amigos incertos e das coisas que injetam aqui—armas e drogas. Embriagados contiaremos assim, andando no chão frio com os pés descalçados, um sorriso na boca ainda seca da corrida contra a lei. Toda uma nação está olhando para uma janela eletrônica; através dela está o passado manipulado, o que ninguém vê é a porta que fica ao lado, a porta do futuro, que está trancada pela mediocridade dos nossos governantes.[16]

> [Poverty here is passed on from father to son, as well as in the need to work day and night to buy bread, a bag of rice, a bag of beans. But it is with love and affection that we raise our children, without paying attention to our environment, to the dubious friends and things they inject here—weapons and drugs. Being drunk, we are able to cope; we walk barefooted on the cold ground, with our mouth still dry from running from the Police. An entire nation is looking at a virtual window; it is through her that the past is manipulated; but what no one sees is the door on the side, the door of the future, which is locked by the mediocrity of our rulers.]

In addition to analyzing the forces of the powerful over the powerless, the author suggests that it is hard to see the cataclysmic effect of how the rich have impoverished the people. As a result, it behooves the marginalized to make a clarion call of urgency to wake up leaders who are obsessed with their own welfare and oblivious to the people they represent. In sum, *Capão Pecado* indicts while facing the prospect that it may take a while before a solution is reached between the powerful and the downtrodden, who for the time being are basically condemned to a life of violence as a legitimate response to deprivation and nothingness.

Conclusion

Both Lins and Ferréz propose a re-reading of contemporary Brazilian literature and culture by privileging what is called "marginal literature," which speaks directly through the very voices of the people themselves, that is, the marginal. Deploying testimonial and sociological approaches, both writers are able to introduce the reader to a world otherwise unfamiliar because of its marginal location and the socioeconomic structures that perpetuate its marginality. The search of the quotidian in the lives of oppressed people in the urban periphery of Rio de Janeiro and São Paulo moves both writers to document, while simultaneously indicting, the violent lives of protagonists such as Cabeleira, Bené, and Little Zé in *Cidade de Deus*, and Rael in *Capão Pecado*. Much discussion about realism in Brazilian literature has focused on the Naturalism of Adolfo Caminha and Aluízio Azevedo and less on the postmodernist reality of the favela. Subconsciously, the literary production recently denominated "literatura marginal" has signaled the need to recuperate other excluded voices of Brazilian literature and make them part of the Brazilian literary canon. If the contexts and experiences described by these writers are marginalizing and violent, such a state of affairs did not happen overnight or in a vacuum.

The political system and its allied machinery must examine the causes of such a situation in which the urban periphery finds itself in a virtual state of war due to violence perpetrated by guns, drugs, and trivial competition for leadership—a reality that suggests low self-esteem and need to use machismo to establish much-needed power and control. If these communities come to feel they are part of the mainstream through political participation, there will be less allure to create their own world where they can feel like being "somebody."

The temperaments of Exu and Xangô invoked at the beginning are meant to bring spiritual harmony to the apparently chaotic lives of these marginalized populations and to see in their response to a debilitating situation a search for a solution that may well lie in the multiplicity of Exu in the interpretation of the crossroads as well as the channeled violent energies of Xangô, which when properly coordinated could be directed not to violence but to creative reinvention and reconstruction. The reconstructive possibilities within the texts of Lins and Ferréz are limitless. Though the images are filled with hopelessness, violence, and death, they also serve as a call for intervention. By taking the remedial measures along the lines of educational access; scholarships for the needy and struggling within such communities, who are in the majority; better social amenities; medical and psychological treatment for those who have reached a boiling point and are on the verge of lunacy; and empowerment workshops that will help with boosting self-esteem, the change and amelioration required in the lives of these neglected populations will occur sooner rather than later.

Beyond the efforts of redressing social inequalities, editorial imbalance and access must also be addressed. Great presses worthy of the name must take responsibility by ensuring these "marginal" voices are heard through publication of their work. Brazilian cultural discourse must not be limited to the canonical alone. Cultural phenomena, after all, are matters of national patrimony that should endure well beyond commercial interests. Marginal communities are waiting to receive all interested in the joint effort to reconcile the center with the periphery, and vice versa. The neglected must be reabsorbed within the center, not as a gesture of sympathy or out of fear, but as a collective responsibility to remind ourselves that the urban periphery is part and parcel of Brazilian popular discourse and reality.

Conclusion

Despite the official claims of racial equality in Brazil, the reality of identity fragmentation and attendant racial ambiguity presents a conflictual ideology that contends that racial harmony remains an illusion. Over the years, Afro-Brazilian history has documented adaptations of African culture into such cultural expressions as Candomblé, Capoeira, Samba, Maculélé, Maracatú, Congados, Bumba-Meu-Boi, and Afro-Bahian Carnivals, among many others. Yet these hybridized zones of identity for all races have become rather folklorized in that though their politics remain veiled, these annual rituals and performances offer only temporary escapes from a more sophisticated hegemony that maintains an engrained white supremacy in Brazil. The solution, of course, is not to radically create an African state outside of Brazil, as has been euphemistically proposed about the possibility of the state of Bahia potentially breaking off from Brazil and joining the African continent, but to mount a constructive and legitimate political offensive against exclusionary racial democracy without which the rights and responsibilities of full citizenship will never be granted to Afro-Brazilians.

Against this background, and coupled with the need to broaden my own scope of understanding of Brazil within the rest of the Lusophone world, I opted for what I consider migrating identities in Brazil. In this even more complex and complicating geographical scope, I was able to tease out commonalities within the realities of Africans and Afro-Brazilians in relation to their common albatross: slavery and colonialism. The outcome is a colorful, dispassionate, yet dissonant tapestry of iconic characters and images that define the experiences of dislocation from Africa and relocation within Brazil—coupled with their attendant traumas, tensions, pleasures, and negotiations, as the migrating subjects traverse not just the Atlantic but also the Brazilian historical, cultural, religious, economic, and political landscapes in the quest for their own humanity, spiritual survival, and ultimate political triumph. In the broader sense, the Brazilian migrating subject is thus a cumulative and yet distinctive character that encompasses the native, the settler, the enslaved, the refugee, the labor migrant, the corporate player, the mixed race, the social mobilizer, the cultural producer, and the anti-racist protagonist, among others.

In terms of specificities and limits, the paradigmatic migrating identities that I have proposed and analyzed in this book are primarily Afro-Brazilians who have made significant impact on Brazilian society, even if they may not have been given their due recognition or been fairly represented in Brazilian intellectual, cultural, and social history. These "archetypal" identities include those of Manuel Querino, Zumbi dos Palmares, Xica da Silva, Pedro Archanjo, Black Orpheus, and Cidade de Deus. While these cultural icons dialogue and contest with Brazilian hegemony as a zone of struggle where myths are equally competing for hegemony in terms of discourses of identity and, to a certain degree, of superiority or of counter-ideological self-affirmation, they offer an outlet for a better understanding of their plights but are far from presenting a definitive solution to the crisis of consciousness and of identity that continues to betide Afro-Brazilian quest for social equality. The Aryan myths of superiority, which became even more pronounced and appropriated in the nineteenth century, gained further currency with Gilberto Freyre's social theory of miscegenation in the twentieth century, in which white supremacy remains intact and undisturbed despite the theoretical claim of racial harmony. Regardless of the thoroughness of critical analysis, no one school of thought will win the argument of being oppressed by an oppressor that feigns ignorance of the basic motives of that oppression: economic exploitation and social control. Even the middle ground of negotiation and accommodation is laden with tensions, as the struggle for hegemony that Brazilian racial relations embody must now move to the political domain beyond the cultural symbologies that often mask the inherent contradictions of living in a mythical racial paradise. Only through pragmatic education can the masses of Afro-Brazilians make sense of the extent to which the proverbial racial rain continues to beat down on them as they succumb to negotiations that often cosmetically and temporarily solve a structural problem without getting to the roots of inequalities and the attendant long-term consequences of inaction.

In my discussion of Manuel Querino, the very first Afro-Brazilian historian, artist, and archivist, which qualifies him for a befitting place among African American intellectual counterparts such as Booker T. Washington, W.E.B. Du Bois, and Carter G. Woodson, I find in his mix of trailblazing cultural research on Afro-Brazilians and his defiant politics a rather courageous soul, especially given the hostile period in which he lived (1851–1923). In challenging the Eurocentric perspectives of Brazilian history, he focused on African contributions in their minutest details, about their skills in arts, culinary, crafts, and literary production. His controversial argument that sent waves throughout the Brazilian establishment of the nineteenth and early twentieth century was that Africans provided both skilled and unskilled labor for Brazil as well as defended its national identity by virtue of the inalienable African contribution to that national character. He challenged the negligence of previous European scholars who had given no recognition to Africa in terms of Brazilian history. By calling attention to African contributions, he edified the significance of a continent that has always been misrepresented as "barbaric," especially when it comes to the justification of police brutality and violence against the Afro-Brazilian temples whose structures were destroyed and their religious artefacts carted away. The *pais-de-santo* or *mães-de-santo* (spiritual leaders in Candomblé) were often beaten and arrested for practicing "pagan" religions. Not only did Manuel Querino intervene through the legal system, he also challenged the pseudo-scientific racism prevalent at the time. His carefully researched and seminal works, such as "Contribuição para a História das Artes na Bahia" (1911), *As Artes da Bahia* (1913), "O Colono Prêto como Fator da Civilização Brasileira" (1918), and *A Arte Culinária na Bahia* (1928) seek to put Afro-Brazilians on the map of recognition and visibility as co-partners in the building of Brazilian history, culture, and identity. Despite his late acknowledgment as a vital Afro-Brazilian intellectual, Querino's works bridge class, race, and religion to assert him as a migrating identity between Africa and the Afro-Brazilian diaspora toward recuperating Africa in Brazilian culture, and thus redressing its dislocation in the annals of Brazilian intellectual history.

Following a chronological order, my focus on Zumbi dos Palmares, known as the leader of the seventeenth-century Quilombo dos Palmares, who resisted colonial invasion against the settlements of slaves who ran away from slavery to be independent, pays homage to this Brazilian icon whose death is now commemorated as a Day of National Consciousness on November 20 throughout Brazil. In addition, through the analysis of dramatic adaptations about his life story, such as *Arena Conta Zumbi* and the classic film *Quilombo*, I seek to elucidate the historical facts, adaptations, and contradictions from competing perspectives that tend to portray Zumbi as hero and villain. Regardless of the divergence of the schools of thought, it is a fact that Zumbi has become a national hero to all Brazilians, even if only symbolically or reluctantly acknowledged. The irony of the controversy is even further illuminated by the proponents of cultural hybridity when Brazil is appropriated as a "Zumbi Nation" by Chico Science and Nação Zumbi (Zumbi Nation) in the song "Etnia." In this nationalistic song, the poetic voice makes a bold statement in considering all Brazilian races as one "ethnicity," as if arguing for one nation and one destiny: "Somos todos juntos uma miscigenação / E não podemos fugir da nossa etnia / Índios, brancos, negros e mestiços / Nada de errado em seus princípios / O seu e o meu são iguais"[1] (We are all united as a miscegenated people / And we cannot escape our ethnicity / Amerindians, whites, blacks, and mixed race / Nothing is wrong with our origins / Yours and mine, all the same). This notion of a "Zumbi Nation," draws from the ideals preached by the veteran leader who wanted a settlement where all races were equal.

While the song "Etnia" reads like an interpretation of Gilberto Freyre, it makes Zumbi look even more like a racially inclusive icon, as Freyre's miscegenation thesis proposes. Such a migrating identity for Zumbi, from a radical Afro-Brazilian revolutionary to a symbol of national unity, calls for a new reading of this warrior at heart. Through this chapter, the lessons of Zumbi as a "rainbow politician" constitute a radical shift in the interpretation of this historical figure to date. A character who appeals to all races to come together, to abandon hate and oppression, cannot be perceived as a threat to the Brazilian state, which ultimately eliminated him through repeated military invasions of the Palmares maroon settlement. The insinuations that he was also betrayed by his own people, and thus was a victim of internal strife, do not undo his legacy as a model of racial unity, equality, and harmony—in a way that predates Gilberto Freyre, who minimized the violence and brutality inherent in the facile theorization of racial miscegenation. Race mixture, as Zumbi perceived it, could only be a natural process, not a convenient political experimentation to maintain the myth of nondiscrimination. The freedom for all races to coexist as equal partners is the ultimate migrating flexibility, as each race could move freely in and out of and from one settlement to the other without fear of persecution from any hegemonic power structure in which one race is ruling over the other.

Xica da Silva (Francisca da Silva de Oliveira, 1732–1796) injects a troubling but savvy dimension to the discussion on racial democracy and migrating identities. In her subversive sexualized strategy, she gains her freedom from slavery and manipulates an oppressive situation into an empowering one for herself; though that "power" may be cosmetic and ephemeral, it is above all dynamic and transformative. Through the multiple versions of her representation (historical, dramatic, and cinematic), I reach the conclusion that Xica da Silva represents different and shifting identities to many people. As a female offspring (daughter) of an illegitimate relationship herself, between a Portuguese man, Antônio Caetano e Sá, and a slave, Maria da Costa, she carried the burden of extramarital legacy that may have normalized for her the sexual relationship with the Portuguese diamond contractor João Fernandes de Oliveira, with whom she lived for fifteen years and had thirteen children. Through sexual exploits and seductions, she rose to prominence among the high society of Diamantina. Her success has led to a number of myths surrounding her character, accomplishments, idiosyncrasies, and personality. Before becoming Oliveira's mistress, she "belonged" to Sergeant Manuel Pires Sardinha, owner of mines in Arraial do Tijuco. When Oliveira arrived in Arraial de Tijuco in 1754, Xica da Silva made herself visible to him, and he fell in love with her, causing a love triangle among Xica, her former owner, and the diamond contractor. The same year, Xica da Silva gained her independence from slavery and became Oliveira's lover, though they never officially married. In the colonial context, this "scandalous" affair between a rich Portuguese aristocrat and a slave created its own sensation since the love affair was often openly acknowledged.

Despite the romantic or sexual escapades that lasted fifteen years, by 1770, when Oliveira had to return to Portugal, Xica da Silva was anguished, as separation became inevitable. Xica da Silva died in 1796, twenty-six years after Oliveira's departure, having had ample years to live and enjoy the properties left by Oliveira. As a hypersexualized and hybridized character, Xica da Silva embodies the problematic migrating identity, as she must successfully play the roles of a black female slave, a sexual object, and a pragmatic woman who used her body and acute intelligence to secure her freedom, while at the same time liberating her miscegenated children from the burden of slavery by the illegitimate "union" with the Portuguese contractor. The extent to which Xica da Silva is permanently registered in national consciousness is debatable. Yet the fact that the character has led to many interpretations in film, as well as in soap operas (novelas), is proof enough that her migrating identities have cogently attracted interest both nationally and internationally. It is also remarkable that the leading role of interpreting Xica da Silva in the *telenovela* series of 2005 was the very first time an Afro-Brazilian actress would have such prominence and prestige. One can only speculate about such a corporate decision, layered with political undertones on the prospects of Brazil finally attaining a "racial democracy" in the new millennium. It is debatable whether such a decision would have even materialized if not for the ambivalences and ambiguities that Xica da Silva embodies, thus making it permissible to showcase the nudity of a black female slave who eventually attained freedom from slavery despite the mockery and abuse of her dignity. Somewhere between lowering her standards of dignity under slavery and resetting her boundaries of strategic compromise in the name of survival lies the humanity of Xica da Silva. My reading of Xica da Silva is nuanced and less opinionated in order to bring a balanced perspective to her complexity as a victim and as a villain in pursuit of her astutely defined dreams of freedom.

Who are we to judge Xica da Silva? Her mother was a slave. Her mother may have been sexually violated by a Portuguese man, perhaps also a slave owner. Her migrating identity did not begin with her meeting Oliveira, the Portuguese contractor, but well before she was born, when her mother may have transferred a genealogical trauma to her while still in the womb. A psychoanalytical reading of Xica da Silva thus provides us another dimension of the trajectory of this second-generation female Afro-Brazilian warrior. It takes a warrior-soul to have survived the brutalization of her body through rape; it takes a warrior to survive the nine months of slaving while still carrying the baby of her rapist. We will never know. Yet, in *Post Traumatic Slave Syndrome*, Joy DeGruy offers an insight as to what may have triggered the coping strategy of Xica da Silva when she finally found a strategy to escape slavery and be free. DeGruy explains,

> P.T.S.S. is a theory that explains the etiology of many of the adaptive survival behaviors in African American communities throughout the United States and the Diaspora. It is a condition that exists as a consequence of multigenerational oppression of Africans and their descendants resulting from centuries of chattel slavery. A form of slavery which was predicated on the belief that African Americans were inherently/genetically inferior to whites. This was then followed by institutionalized racism which continues to perpetuate injury.[2]

Without sensitivity and compassion, it is quite convenient to explain away Xica da Silva's actions as reprehensible and self-objectifying, or to use this theory as an exculpatory measure to justify her counterviolent actions, such as her less-than-compassionate treatment of her *mucamas* (bedside maids and maidens) once she became part of the high society. Nonetheless, her shifting identities are directly proportional to the structural inequalities she had to confront. Her anguish is best captured in the classic moment of rejection when, even after receiving her manumission letter that she carries around with pride, she is denied access to the Catholic church, a symbol of purity and power, and told she needed to wait another five generations after being free. She has had to be a different woman to different men in her life. And even the men she bore for Oliveira were taken to Portugal for higher education and administrative occupations for the Portuguese Crown, while the remaining (nine) daughters were left in Brazil—ample evidence of gendered inequality. Regardless of how Xica da Silva is interpreted, that she survived her migrating identities makes her a Brazilian heroine, and not the sexual object she is often myopically portrayed to be.

Beyond the trials and triumphs of Xica da Silva, *Tenda dos Milagres*, in film and print and as discussed in chapter 5, encapsulates one of the *chef-d'oeuvres* of Jorge Amado's literary corpus. What remains an enigma, however, is the subtle semblance of protagonist Pedro Archanjo to Manuel Querino. Although Amado does not openly state the similarity between the fictional character and the real person anywhere in the narrative, the sheer details of descriptions and correlations of historical facts lead to this conclusion. Amado's poetic license allows for a reconfiguration of historical facts into fictionalized experiences that nonetheless leave their social agency, as the protagonist enacts what may well be the life of Manuel Querino in the twentieth century. That some of the cited locations in Amado's *oeuvre* still exist around the "Pelourinho"[3] of life, where debauchery and a living cultural museum preserve for the curious observer a taste of life in the nineteenth century, seems a natural blessing for the curious visitor or researcher. Lover of life and of many women, Archanjo balances rejection by the medical establishment to which he had applied to study medicine, and ironically settles for a petty position as a messenger at the medical school, also finding time to conduct research on Afro-Brazilian culture. It takes the visit of an anthropologist, Dr. Levenson from Columbia University, for the entire

Bahian community to appreciate the value of their very own Pedro Archanjo. Since Pedro Archanjo was deceased, Dr. Levenson hires an assistant, Fausto Pena, a journalist and poet, who, incidentally, is also the lover of Ms. Ana Mercedes, whom Dr. Levenson compensates with a job and ends up with the assistant's lover (Mercedes). The novel adopts a narrative-within-a-narrative style in order to flash back into the life of Pedro Archanjo. The contradiction in the name choice for fictionalizing Manuel Querino raises some questions about the representation of the real and the fictional, in the sense that "Pedro" references Biblical "Rock" while "Archanjo" is often glossed as Lucifer, the fallen angel.

Oscillating between good and evil in his characterization of the protagonist, Amado may be suggesting that Pedro Archanjo is not in any way a perfect man; in fact, he is a mixed-race person, which makes him desirable to white women in the same way that Ana Mercedes is desired by Dr. Levenson. Amado's miscegenation thesis is unmistakable; yet his use of Africa-derived religiosity as practiced by Pedro Archanjo, especially in the scene of apparition of Acotirene, who gave him words to utter in order to protect himself when police return to persecute them, also expresses the vital significance of Africa in Afro-Brazilian culture. Amado assigns Ogum as Pedro Archanjo's orixá, the Yoruba deity that paves the way for others in a configuration that combines African and European value systems, since he seems to prefer white women to Afro-Brazilian women. As a migrating subject, Pedro Archanjo must modify his professional identity and aspiration from that of the Afro-Brazilian desiring a medical education to a nonacknowledged Afro-Brazilian cultural scholar whose validation in Brazil must first come from an American outsider/ professor. In sum, Afro-Brazilians continue to grapple with recognition of whether they are darker skinned or lighter skinned, since whiteness is maintained at the top of the social mobility pyramid.

When compared to the forgoing iconic figures, Orpheus, the Brazilianized Greek musical legend, remains the most representative of all possible Brazilian shifting identities, due to his embodiment of the essentialist characteristics of Brazilian character as embedded in Carnival and the Romeo-and-Juliet story of fatal love, as documented in Vinícius de Moraes's *Orfeu da Conceição* and Marcel Camus's cinematic adaptation, *Orfeu Negro*. My discussion of the different versions and adaptations has something in common in terms of their ultimate humanism: Orpheus is Greek, Brazilian, Yoruba, and universal. In sum, he is potentially everyone. Drawing from Yoruba mythology, I find in the parallel of agency between Orpheus and Obatala—both semi-deity characters with the ability to descend into the land of the dead and return to life—a form of defiance of death. Such a regenerative analysis intersects with the notion of deathlessness and reincarnation in the African worldview. The same inability of Orpheus to live without Eurydice, hence the tragic flaw of looking back, finds echoes in Obatala's weakness, as in the drunkenness that made him make imperfect beings. Both are fallible and gullible, yet regenerative, rebellious, and immortal. Orpheus is not an irrational being; he realizes his limits but cannot help himself, as his tragic decision to be with his loved one in life and death is not about logic, but destiny, suggesting a mythological moral that there are limits to human intelligence and that cosmic forces can provoke order and disorder as they wish—and in so doing, fulfill that which is predestined through what to the human eye reads as a "tragic flaw," or what I prefer to interpret as the metaphysics of the inevitable.

Though Orpheus's dilemma embodies the classical myth of creation—whether of the Judeo-Christian Edenic prohibition transgressed and sanctioned with death, or in the case of Greek mythology, Eurydice's attempt to escape from Aristaeus's rapist advances and the consequent blind stepping on a snake that eventually killed her—Orpheus's metaphoric descent into hell was inevitable. Recovering Eurydice in the realm of death, Orpheus is warned by Hades not to look back, but he does so all the same, and consequently suffers the sanction of death, which is the only way he could remain with Eurydice. Read regeneratively, Orpheus has indeed conquered death; and likewise, he has helped Eurydice to be happy in death by being reunited with him. As the founder of Orphism, Orpheus is endowed with the power of three reincarnations or identities, which makes the descent into hell a mere transition from one identity to another—that is, a reenactment of life in death and death in life. Ever free, ever fearless of life and of death, and at perpetual peace in all his stages of transition, Orpheus exudes the classical migrant identity, for he plays in the crossroads of taunting death and submitting to a permanent quest for life in whatever symbolic guise. In the Brazilian cultural interpretation of the Orpheus myth, the fusion of the atmosphere of Carnival and the life-love-death vicious cycle or triangulation complicates the plot, while also resolving it through the regenerative possibilities that the ending engenders, both in the 1959 version, with the young Orpheus and Eurydice dancing, and the remake of 1999. In the former, the vibrant lives of Orpheus and Eurydice are foregrounded, while in the latter, the whole community mourns the death and "death-lessness" of their national hero. The Brazilian adaptation of the Greek myth, "Black Orpheus," may have been dedicated to the Afro-Brazilian Orpheus, but its essential existential possibilities for human disintegration and reintegration, of love and obstacles resisting that ultimate romantic ideal, embody all the traits of the universal shifting being and identity.

In the final chapter of *Cidade de Deus*, where an entire new gated favela community becomes a character and an allegory for the appreci-ation of collective and individual migrant identities in Rio de Janeiro, a number of characters constitute the face of the Brazilian slum as well as a microcosm of a Brazilian dilemma when it comes to the violence and social death predicated by historical and political conditionings that have kept millions on the margins for many centuries. Whether as a sociological novel or as a riveting cinematic adaptation, *Cidade de Deus* unveils the hidden dramas of a "city" within a city, as the writer or cineaste takes the reader and audience on a different journey that the touristic emblems of the enticing beaches of Copacabana and the alluring Pão de Açúcar (Sugar Loaf) cannot provide. As with the iconic transportation of Orpheus from a Greek legend to a Brazilian and uni-versal symbol, Paulo Lins's *Cidade de Deus* is no longer a marginal text but a work of global impact. While Cidade de Deus as a new slum set-tlement has not yet been a destination of the now-famed "favela tours" organized by the dwellers of the Rocinha favela, its popularity is almost identical to Rocinha's.

The cinematic version by Fernando Meirelles echoes the sociological perspective of the novel, which constitutes an ethnographic study of drug warfare and gangsta violence. The juxtaposition of two key characters, Zé Miúdo (Little Zé) and Busca Pé (Rocket), one who has a certain thirst for violence and ends building his drug-trafficking trade, and the other who realizes his dream of becoming a photographer, betrays a creative tension between the human desire to survive and the social condition-ings that often make violence inevitable. Beyond providing a darker side of Rio de Janeiro often obfuscated to the casual visitor or even to the dweller in Rio de Janeiro whose socioeconomic class protects him from the decadence of poor marginal urban dwellers who must make a living by any means necessary in the squatter settlements, *Cidade de Deus* in film and print vividly captures the lack of emotion in the face of violence, which is the extent to which human life has been reduced: a worthless species worthy of eradication. Marginalization is indeed a social invention when the living conditions of the rich and the poor are compared in Rio de Janeiro. The moral of this major narrative and film lies in its ability to shock its readers and public with realistic images of violence that call for urgent intervention. The shifting identities of the main characters as they negotiate survival between reality and fantasy, between their own desire to escape poverty and the likelihood that they will probably die within it via structural violence at the hands of the police or by their own making, seem condemned to a vicious cycle, as if their destiny is predetermined and cannot be otherwise. The slum of death as represented by Paulo Lins and Fernando Meirelles may be a "problem" indeed, but it will take more than theoretical speculations and police invasions to protect the city of Rio de Janeiro against itself. It is a social dilemma that political expediency coupled with corporate greed and corruption have thus far failed to remedy.

In the forgoing reality of migrating identities dislocated in life and in death, only to be relocated through social mediations that are symbolic, allegorical, and political, the consoling outlet lies in the persistent sense of hope through the primacy of hybridized creative intelligence. At the heart of these dislocated and relocated characters is slavery positioned as an economic excess that opted for the degradation of human life in order to attain capitalist accumulation. Following that experience, each character is indeed playing out the post-traumatic slave syndrome as a stigma that must be confronted, exorcised, mediated, and subverted, even in allegorical terms, in order to make sense of the persistence of oppression in the post-slavery era. The admission that a migrating subject suffers a series of psychological torture as it painstakingly attempts to create new memories and yet is somehow trapped within the aftermath of torturous old memories is not a sign of victimhood but a proactive strategy at engendering therapeutic agencies through which the relics of social captivity are not only reversed but channeled into archetypal creative icons through which the migrating subject self-empowers, as the characters of Manuel Querino, Zumbi dos Palmares, Xica da Silva, Pedro Archanjo, Orpheus, and Zé Miúdo have exemplified. Dislocation need not be a permanent state of mind, nor relocation be perceived as a fixed frame of mind. Rather, the shifting dynamics indeed serve as an empowering agency, as the migrating subject consistently mutates in the quest for relative positive meaning of life, as well as a comforting space for being black and deservingly human.

Notes

Introduction

1. See Toplin, *Freedom and Prejudice*, 91.
2. Ianni, *Esclavitud y Capitalismo*, 33.
3. For a thorough analysis of this slave rebellion, see João José Reis, *Slave Rebellion in Brazil: The Muslim Uprising of 1835 in Bahia* (Baltimore: Johns Hopkins University Press, 1993).
4. Reis, *Slave Rebellion in Brazil*, 5.
5. See A.J.R. Russell-Wood, *The Black Man in Slavery and Freedom in Colonial Brazil* (London: Macmillan, 1982).

Chapter 1

1. Beyond *Casa Grande e Senzala* (The Masters and the Slaves) (1933), see for example, *O Mundo que o Português Criou* (The World the Portuguese Created) (1940); *Um Brasileiro em Terras Portuguesas* (A Brazilian in Portuguese Lands) (1953); *Integração Portuguesa nos Trópicos* (Portuguese Integration in the Tropics) (1958); and *O Luso e o Trópico* (The Portuguese and the Tropics) (1961).
2. For a thorough analysis of the concept as theory, see Burke and Pallares-Burke, *Gilberto Freyre: Social Theory in the Tropics*, 167–201.
3. On the future of Lusophonia in Africa in the twenty-first century, see, for example, Teresa Cruz e Silva et al, *'Lusofonia' em África: História, Democracia e Integração Africana* (Dakar: CODESRIA, 2005), 3–30.
4. A provocative school of historical thought argues that the Portuguese were not only explorers and enslavers but also migrants and settlers. The migrational argument, especially situated in the age of discoveries and mercantilism, is problematic since such a voluntary migration is significantly different from the forced one in the context of transatlantic slavery. As a matter of fact, a comparison is inconceivable except for the purpose of justifying slavery and

exculpating the colonial project. For a more nuanced analysis of this contestation of the colonizer as migrant, see A.J.R. Russell-Wood, *The Portuguese Empire, 1415–1808* (Baltimore: Johns Hopkins University Press, 1992), 58–94.

5. For a detailed analysis of differentiated identities in the lusophone world, the roots of prejudices, racism, and racial discrimination, see Patrícia Ferraz de Mattos, *The Colours of the Empire: Racialized Representations during Portuguese Colonialism* (New York: Begham Books, 2013), 7–36. See also Lívio Sansone et al., eds. *Africa, Brazil and the Construction of Transatlantic Black Identities* (Trenton, NJ: Africa World Press, 2008) and José C. Curto and Paul E. Lovejoy, eds., *Enslaving Connections: Changing Cultures of Africa and Brazil during the Era of Slavery* (New York: Humanity Books, 2004).

6. See Miguel Vale de Almeida, " 'Longing for Oneself': Hybridism and Miscegenation in Colonial and Postcolonial Portugal," *Etnografia* 6.1 (2002): 181–201; see also *An Earth-Colored Sea: 'Race,' Culture and the Politics of Identity in the Post-Colonial Portuguese-Speaking World* (New York: Berghahn Books, 2004), 65–82.

7. A project funded by the Portuguese government, *CIARIS* (Center for Social Inclusion), targets the five Portuguese-speaking African countries, in order to ensure that salaried and nonsalaried workers are included in the government-sponsored social security system. For this project to succeed, a three-pronged approach has been identified: (1) study the impact of the informal economy on poverty and exclusion; (2) develop and maintain a website that will monitor visibility and encourage communication amongst the participants; (3) empower various governments and partners of these five countries to take over the project and implement it over the longer term. While such an initiative is commendable, it neither guarantees any continuity nor does it put in place dependable financial resources to ensure that the implementation goes beyond the experimental and "feasibility studies" stage. Of what use is such a cosmetic agenda if not as mere propaganda for the Portuguese government, as if it were still patriarchally caring for its ex-colonies?

8. See Rebecca Reichmann, ed., *Race in Contemporary Brazil: From Indifference to Inequality* (State College: Penn State University Press, 1999), 173. For a critique of the Brazilian racial project and white domination, see also G. Reginald Daniel, *Race and Multiraciality in Brazil and the United States* (University Park: Penn State University Press, 2006), 53–84.

9. Durban, South Africa, August 31 through September 8, under the auspices of the United Nations.

10. For an incisive critique of Gilberto Freyre's thesis, see for example, Cláudia Castelo, *O Modo Português de Estar no Mundo* (The Portuguese Way of Being in the World) (Lisboa: Afrotamento: 1998) and Edson Nery da Fonseca, *Novas Perspectivas em Casa Grande e Senzala* (New Perspectives in Casa Grande e Senzala) (Recife: Fundação Joaquim Nabuco, 1985).

11. It is estimated that there are at least 1,000 *quilombos* all across Brazil; the most famous, of course, is the *Quilombo de Palmares*, led by Zumbi dos Palmares in the seventeenth century.

12. In the case of South America, much has been written about the rebellions in the "slave quarters" that led to today's *quilombos* as well as actual insurrections by the *quilombolas* against Portuguese colonial enslavement. In the case of lusophone Africa, African resistance took the form of refusal to pay taxes to the Portuguese. For example, in Mozambique, the Massingire Rebellion of 1884 and the 1897 Cambuenda-Sena-Tonga Rebellion were sparked by issues of taxation. For more detailed analysis of these acts of rebellion and resistance to Portuguese slavery and colonialism, see, for example, João Reis, *Rebelião Escrava no Brasil* (Slave Rebellion in Brazil) and Allen F. and Barbara Isaacman, *Mozambique: From Colonialism To Revolution 1900–1982* (Boulder, CO: Westview Press, 1983).

13. For a more comprehensive and comparative study of the white Portuguese colonial attitudes toward their black and brown subjects in Brazil, lusophone Africa, and India, see, for example, Charles Boxer, *Race Relations in the Portuguese Colonial Empire, 1415–1825* (London: Oxford University Press, 1963). See also José Lingna Nafafé, *Colonial Encounters: Issues of Culture, Hybridity and Creolisation: Portuguese Mercantile Settlers in West Africa* (New York: Peter Lang, 2007) and Robert L. Tignor, "Colonial Africa through the Lens of Colonial Latin America," *Colonial Legacies: The Problem of Persistence in Latin American History*, Jeremy Adelman, ed. (New York: Routledge, 1999), 29–49.

14. Octávio Ianni's *Escravidão e Racismo* (Slavery and Racism) (São Paulo: HUCITE, 1978); and for a further understanding of capitalist expansion and the crisis of slavery, see also Ianni's *Esclavitud y Capitalismo* (Slavery and Capitalism) (Mexico: Siglo Veintiuno Editores, 1976).

15. See Walter Hawthorne, *From Africa to Brazil: Culture, Identity, and the Atlantic Slave Trade, 1600–1830* (Cambridge: Cambridge University Press, 2010), 123.

16. For a critique of the claim of racial harmony in lusophone Africa, the reality of oppression, and the fact that the Portuguese did not come to Africa with their wives (hence their need for indigenous African women for sex and company and not for racial harmony), thus debunking the theory of Lusotropicalism as a favorable assimilationist policy to both the indigenes and the Portuguese, see Gerald J. Bender, *Angola under the Portuguese* (Los Angeles: University of California Press, 1980).

17. An important aspect of the transatlantic slave trade and the place of lusophone Africa is yet to be theorized and historicized. As a response to any form of revolt, the culprits were often exiled to one of the islands (such as Cape Verde or São Tomé and Príncipe). However, a number of colonized Africans were also sent to Brazil as slaves. For a detailed analysis of the transatlantic

relations between Angola and Brazil in the context of slavery, see, for example, Roquinaldo Ferreira, *Cross-Cultural Exchange in the Atlantic World* (Cambridge: Cambridge University Press, 2012), 148–165.

18. Studies are gradually emerging on the Brazilian black brotherhoods. See for example, A.J.R. Russell-Wood, "Collective Behavior: The Brotherhoods," *Slavery and Freedom in Colonial Brazil* (Oxford: One World, 1982), 128–160. See also, Elizabeth W. Kiddy, *Blacks of the Rosary: Memory and History in Minas Gerais, Brazil* (University Park: Penn State University Press, 2005).

19. The term used varies from scholar to scholar. Some use "revolt," and others refer to the incident as "insurrection," uprising," "insurgence," or "rebellion."

20. For a succinct analysis of the political significance of the Palmares settlement, see, for example, R. K. Kent, "Palmares: An African State in Brazil," *Maroon Societies: Rebel Slave Communities in the Americas*, Richard Price, ed. (Baltimore: Johns Hopkins University Press, 1979), 170–190.

21. Reis notes his objections to the claim of the rebellion as a *jihad* by such scholars as Etienne Brazil, Arthur Ramos, and Pierre Verger. For a detailed elaboration of Reis's position, see *Slave Rebellion in Brazil*, 122.

22. For a better understanding of how African ethnicity was reconstructed in colonial Bahia, especially with regard to the Yorubas, see Maria Inês Côrtes de Oliveira, "The Reconstruction of Ethnicity in Bahia," *Trans-Atlantic Dimensions of Ethnicity in the African Diaspora*, Paul Lovejoy and David Trotman, eds. (London: Continuum, 2003), 158–180.

23. To see the 1835 insurgents as "plotters" is very problematic because it suggests that the freedom they sought from slavery was not legitimate or that it contravened the law of humanity, especially given that they were the "property" of the state and had no right to initiate a rebellion against the state.

24. Frederic Jameson, "Third-World Literature in the Era of Multinational Capitalism," *Social Text* 15 (1986): 69.

Chapter 2

1. See, for example, John Kloepfer, *Caçadores de Zumbi* (Hunters of Zumbi) (Rio de Janeiro: Novo Século, 2011), and Alexandre Callari, *Apocalipse Zumbi* (Apocalypse Zumbi) (Rio de Janeiro: Editora Évora, 2012). Except where otherwise stated, all translations in this chapter are mine.

2. Contrastively, many works render Zumbi in a positive light in addition to the text under analysis (*Arena Conta Zumbi*): for example, Décio Freitas's *Palmares: A Guerra dos Escravos* (Rio de Janeiro: Graal, 1978), Mário Garcia-Guillén's *Palmares: A Epopéia do Negro no Brasil* (São Paulo: Loyola, 1992), and Joel Rufino dos Santos's *Zumbi* (São Paulo: Global, 2006).

3. Among many other notable institutions set up in his honor across Brazil, the state of São Paulo created an all-black university, named Universidade

Zumbi dos Palmares in 2004, at which 40 percent of declared openings (*vagas*) for student admission are reserved for blacks. This university produced its first graduates in 2008 amidst celebrations and fanfares including a cover-page story in the *Raça* magazine of June 2008.

4. See the Zumbi Archives in the care of Conde Graziela de Cadaval (b. 1938) who inherited part of the inheritance from Rev. Antonio de Melo. The other archives were inherited by Duke Cadaval. The complete archives, containing about 5,000 books and various collected documents acquired in the last six centuries, are kept in Muge, about eighty kilometers from Lisbon, Portugal. One of the prized documents, including personal letters written by Rev. Antonio de Melo himself, says of Zumbi: "At 15, Zumbi had already mastered Latin, the same way that he was gradually improving his Portuguese." See also the Torre do Tombo Archives (Code 9, Sheet F, verse 246) for additional data on the destruction of Palmares as recorded by none other than Jorge Velho, the Portuguese captain who led the decisive assault on Palmares in 1694.

5. Sebastino da Rocha Pitta, *Historia da America Portugueza desde o Anno de Mil a Quinhentos do Seu Descobrimento ate o de Mil a Setecentos e Vinte e Quatro* (New York: Nabu Press, 2010), 49.

6. Robert Anderson, *Theatrical Semiosis and the Theatre of Gianfrancesco Guarnieri*. Dissertation, University of North Carolina, Chapel Hill, 1990.

7. Robert Anderson, "The Muses of Chaos and Destruction in *Arena Conta Zumbi*," *Latin American Theater Review* (1996): 15–28, p. 16.

8. Margo Milleret, "Acting into Action: Teatro Arena's *Zumbi*," *Latin American Theatre Review* (1987): 19–27.

9. Oscar Fernández, "Brazil's New Social Theatre," *Latin American Theatre Review* (1968): 15–30.

10. Margo Milleret, "Acting into Action: Teatro Arena's *Zumbi*," *Latin American Theatre Review* (1987): 19–27.

11. Augusto Boal and Gianfrancesco Guarnieri, *Arena Conta Zumbi*, *Revista de Teatro* 378 (1970): 31.

12. David George, "Theatre of the Oppressed and Teatro de Arena: In and Out of Context," *Latin American Theatre Review* 28.2 (1995): 41.

13. Frances Babbage, *Augusto Boal* (New York: Routledge, 2004), 44.

14. Funso Aiyejina, "Esu Elegbara: A Source of an Alter/Native Theory of African Literature and Criticism." Unpublished Paper.

15. Tiradentes is a pseudonym of Joaquim José da Silva (1746–1796) who led a revolutionary movement in Brazil in the eighteenth century known as "Inconfidência Mineira" (Vote of No-Confidence in Minas Gerais) that sought to declare independence against Portuguese colonial power. Unfortunately, the plot was foiled and led to the arrest, trial, and public hanging of Tiradentes in 1976. He earned the pseudonym during the trial to ridicule him since he once briefly worked as a dentist and the literal meaning of Tiradentes is "tooth puller."

16. See Anderson, "The Muses of Chaos and Destruction, 19–20.

17. See Anderson, "The Muses of Chaos and Destruction," 20.

18. See Bonnie Wasserman, "Breaking the Bonds: Slavery and Rebellion in *Arena Conta Zumbi*," *Metaphors of Oppression in Lusophone Historical Drama* (New York: Peter Lang, 2003), 101.

19. Robert Stam, *Tropical Multiculturalism* (Durham, NC: Duke University Press, 1996), 313–316. Stam further critiques the film as being self-designated "science-fiction," thus betraying a sense of utopianism that may not correlate with the historical correctness of the production. Regardless of this limitation or that of the use of Yoruba that Antônio Risério sees as "Nagôcentrism," since the Yoruba group arrived in Brazil much later and the Palmares group should have been characterized as Bantu and not Yoruba, the assumption that African culture is one in Brazil is not as problematic as it is with African culture in Africa, since different Africa-derived religions have had to be "collapsed" under one predominant rubric of Candomblé (Africa-derived traditional religious worship) in Brazil. Other variations such as Umbanda and Macumba are either Indian-influenced or regionalized.

20. Olakunle George, *Relocating Agency: Modernity and African Letters* (Albany: SUNY Press, 2003), 27. My emphases.

Chapter 3

1. In addition to the novel *Xica da Silva* by João Felício dos Santos, her story was adapted into a movie (*Xica da Silva*) by Carlos Diegues in 1976, starring Zezé Motta. Likewise, Xica da Silva's history was adapted into a *telenovela* (*Xica da Silva*) in 1996, written by Walcyr Carrasco and directed by Walter Avancini. Considered successful in several countries around the world, it starred the actress Taís Araújo as Xica da Silva, the first black Brazilian woman to be given the role of a protagonist of a Brazilian soap opera. Until then, other black women had been given secondary roles such as assistant to the white madam in her bedroom (*mucama*) or as cook (*cozinheira*). Taís Araújo also featured as a protagonist in the Globo television network's *Da Cor do Pecado* (On the Color of Sin).

2. Júnia Ferreira Furtado, *Chica da Silva e o Contratador dos Diamantes: O Outro Lado do Mito* (São Paulo: Companhia das Letras, 2009).

3. Keila Grinberg et al., *Para Conhecer Chica da Silva* (Rio de Janeiro: Zahar, 2007), 2.

4. See Aires da Mata Machado Filho, *Arraial do Tijuco: Cidade Diamantina* (São Paulo: EDUSP, 1980).

5. The thirteen children are identified as follows: Francisca de Paula (1755), João Fernandes (1756), Rita (1757), Joaquim (1759), Antonio Caetano (1761), Ana (1762), Helena (1763), Luiza (1764), Antônia (1765), Maria (1766), Quitéria Rita (1767), Mariana (1769), and José Agostinho Fernandes (1770).

6. These included *São Francisco do Carmo* Brotherhood (exclusive to whites), *Mercês* Brotherhood (exclusive to mulattoes), and *Rosário* Brotherhood (exclusive to Africans).

7. Accounts vary from author to author, but the recurrent number of Xica's children (with Oliveira) was generally known to be thirteen; this differs from Corrêa's account of twelve.

8. Luiz Valente, "The Refiguration of Brazil's Eighteenth Century in *Romanceiro da Inconfidência,*" *Luso-Brazilian Review* 48.2 (2011): 98.

9. Cecília Meireles, *Romanceiro da Inconfidência* (Rio de Janeiro: Civilização Brasileira, 1975).

10. The "Inconfidência Mineira" was one of the most important social and political movements in the Brazilian quest for independence. It probably was not intended to be a national movement, but was restricted to Minas Gerais. It signified the struggle of Brazilian people for freedom against the abuses of the Portuguese colonial government in 1789, a period considered the peak of the cycle of gold in Minas Gerais. At the end of the eighteenth century, Brazil was still under the colonial domination of Portugal, and suffered various political and economic abuses, especially in the form of high taxation. In addition, Portugal prohibited the development of commerce and industry in order to keep the colony dependent on Portugal. Inspired by the ideals of the French Enlightenment and American Revolution of 1776, the conspirators wanted to create a republic in which the leader was elected. Mostly from the white upper class of Minas Gerais, they had studied in Europe and owed large debts to the colonial government. Considering the decline in gold production, the Portuguese colonial government decreed a "derrama" or obligatory payment of debts. Three of the conspirators betrayed the group in exchange for lesser payment of taxes.

11. When not a love story expressed in a narrative form or a narrative about imaginary characters involved in heroic events remote in time or place, a romance in the context used by Cecília Meireles in *Romanceiro* refers to a tale based on the legend of Minas Gerais as a colonial state, medieval romance, adventure, and passionate love. Meireles follows the traditional romance form but sets her stories in colonial Minas Gerais.

12. João Felício dos Santos, *Xica da Silva* (Rio de Janeiro: José Olympio, 2006). Unless otherwise stated, all translations of excerpts from this book are mine. I have chosen to cite English translations to minimize having too many formatting shifts in Portuguese and English while also maximizing readership for the book.

13. Contrary to the suggestion that Oliveira returned to Portugal in 1770 due to allegations of corruption and embezzlement, Antônio Callado insists that he actually returned due to the death of his father, in order to address inheritance matters and not as a reprimand for his scandalous relationship with Xica. See Antônio Callado, *O Tesouro de Chica da Silva* (São Paulo: Códice, 2006), 6.

14. Rubens José Souza Brito, *Dos Peões ao Rei: O Teatro Épico-Dramático e Luís Alberto de Abreu*, doctoral thesis, São Paulo: USP, 1999. While applying the "epic-dramatic" frame to at least six plays by Abreu, Brito, curiously, does not analyze *Xica da Silva*, a play that rightly fits this configuration by virtue of the central character (Xica) and the implication of the narration on national significance.

15. See for example, Randal Johnson's "*Xica da Silva*: Sex, Politics, and Culture" (1980), Deniza Araújo's "The Spheres of Power in *Xica da Silva*" (1992), O. Hugo Benavides's "Seeing *Xica* and the Melodramatic Unveiling of Colonial Desire" (2003), and Richard Gordon's "Allegories of Resistance and Reception in *Xica da Silva*" (2005). While these viewpoints share the commonality of invoking the long-neglected significance of Xica in Brazilian cultural history, they also differ in their ideological and critical foci—from feminist to a general cultural historical intertext.

16. Robert Stam observes that one of the sources for Xica da Silva was the 1962 carnival pageant devoted to Xica da Silva by the Acadêmicos de Salgueiro samba group, in which Xica is claimed to have taken advantage of her sensuality in order to "break the color barrier." For a detailed critique of Xica da Silva as a carnivalesque exuberant performance, see Stam's *Tropical Multiculturalism* (Durham, NC: Duke University Press, 1997), 290–296.

17. Barbara Christian, "The Race for Theory," Angelyn Mitchel, ed., *Within the Circle* (Durham, NC: Duke University Press, 1994), 348–359.

18. Meireles's "Motivo" (Motif) is often referenced as a window into her poetics: "I sing because the instant exists / and my life is fulfilled; / I am neither happy nor sad, / I am a poet." In this laconic piece lies the totality of the ambiguities and contradictions of the poetic world of Meireles. For her, being a poet is everything—not about expressing pain or happiness but just the power of freedom that being a poet entails.

19. Alceu Amoroso Lima, *Fortuna Crítica: Cecília Meireles* (Rio de Janeiro: Nova Fronteira, 1982), 21.

20. Cecília Meireles, *Romanceiro da Inconfidência* (Rio de Janeiro: Civilização Brasileira,1975), 48.

21. Cited in Randal Johnson and Robert Stam, eds., *Brazilian Cinema* (New York: Columbia, 1995), 216.

Chapter 4

1. For a more detailed historical-critical survey, see the works and scholarship of Jorge Amado, Jorge Calmon, Pedro Calmon, E. Bradford Burns, Jaime Nascimento, Jaime Sodré, Maria das Graças Andrade Leal, David Brookshaw, Emanoel Araújo, Luiz Alberto Ribeiro Freire, Eliane Nunes, Kim Butler, Vivaldo da Costa Lima, Antônio Sergio Alfredo Guimarães, and Waldeloir Rego.

2. See *Team of Rivals* (New York: Simon and Schuster, 2005), 351.

3. "Bibliographic Essay: Manuel Querino's Interpretation of the African Contribution to Brazil" *The Journal of Negro History* 59.1 (1974): 78–86. E. Bradford Burns was one of the first North American historians to devote effort to the study of Manuel Querino. In fact, Burns translated one of the seminal essays by Querino, "O Fator Africano na Colonização do Brasil," which appeared as *The African Contribution to Brazilian Civilization* (1979).

4. Maria das Graças de Andrade Leal, *Manuel Querino: Entre Letras e Lutas—Bahia 1851–1923* (São Paulo: Annablume, 2010), 254.

5. Jorge Calmon, *Manuel Querino: O Jornalista e o Político* (Salvador: CEAO, 1984).

6. See Melville Herskovits, *The Myth of the Negro* (Boston: Beacon Press, 1990).

7. See Manoel Querino, *O Colono Preto como Fator da Civilização Brasileira* (Salvador: Imprensa Oficial do Estado, 1918).

8. For a detailed discussion of this controversy, see Ari Lima, "Blacks as Study Objects and Intellectuals in Brazilian Academia," *Latin American Perspectives* 33.4 (2006): 82–105.

9. Cited in Lima, "Blacks as Study Objects," 94. In showcasing many Afro-Brazilians and their denigration by white intellectual elites, the author seeks to expose the contradictions and hypocrisies of the Brazilian Academy as it encourages black participation while creatively excluding same through the accusation of mediocrity and lack of rigor. In essence, the author insists that not much has changed; for in actual fact, blacks even as intellectuals are still treated as "objects" and not subjects, alongside the black groups they study.

10. See Antônio Sérgio Alfredo Guimarães, "Manuel Querino e a Formação do 'Pensamento Negro' no Brasil," Unpublished paper, presented at the 8th Luso-Afro-Brazilian Conference, Coimbra, Portugal, September, 2004.

11. Guimarães (2004) identifies four phases in the formation of Brazilian identity: (1) 1870–1890; (2) 1920–1930; (3) 1940–1950; (4) 1970–1990. These phases coincide with stages of the struggles in the buildup to the 1978 creation of the Unified Black Movement.

12. See Abdias do Nascimento, "African Culture in Brazilian Art," *Journal of Black Studies* 8.4 (1978): 389–402. On page 402 a passing mention is made of Querino, not as an artist or painter himself, but as a "collector of mores, religions, and arts of his brothers." Such a treatment echoes the attitude of the white intelligentsia, making one suspect an underlying bias against Querino even from Abdias do Nascimento, a steady defender of black rights in Brazil.

13. Abdias do Nascimento had been barred from presenting as an official representative of the Brazilian government's group at the third meeting of world black cultures, known as "FESTAC '77" (Festival of Arts and Cultures), at which he had wanted to present on the myth of racial democracy. His controversy with the Brazilian government led Nascimento to write a book on the experience,

Sitiado em Lagos (Barred in Lagos; 1978), and to serialize his "debarred" presentation in the *Daily Punch* newspaper under the title *Racial Democracy: Myth and Reality* (1977). Such a blatant case of racism and discrimination on African soil as perpetrated by the Brazilian government should have rekindled Nascimento's enthusiasm to showcase the efforts of Manuel Querino.

14. Antônio Sérgio Alfredo Guimarães, "After Racial Democracy." Trans. Renato Rezende. *Tempo Social* 18.2 (2006): 269–287.

15. Burns, 81.

16. Cited in Manuel Querino, "O Colono Preto como Fator da Civilização," *Afro-Ásia* 13 (1980): 148.

17. All translations in this study are mine. See Manuel Querino, "O Colono Preto como Fator da Civilização, *Afro-Ásia* 13 (1980): 152.

18. The term *quilombo* translates as "maroon settlement" and refers to those settlements of the colonial era in Brazil during which African descendants decided to run away from enslavement and set up their own free and independent communities that were more inclusive than exclusive in their conceptualization and reality. The phenomenon was not unique to Brazil but also verifiable in the Caribbean and the rest of Latin America under other terms such as *cimarrones* or *palenques*.

19. Manuel Querino, *A Bahia de Outrora* (Salvador: Livraria Progresso Editora, 1946), 14.

20. For a seminal study on the use of photography in the ethnography work of Manuel Querino, see Christianne Silvia Vasconcellos, "O Uso de Fotografias de Africanos no Estudo de Manuel Querino," *Sankofa: Revista da África e da Diaspora Africana* 4 (2009): 88–111.

21. See the blurb of the original edition, Manuel Querino, *A Raça Africana e Seus Costumes na Bahia* (Salvador: P555 Edições, 2006).

22. That Querino included himself in the biographical compilation may not have been a case of arrogance but an effort to be comprehensive. For a detailed entry on himself, see *Artistas Bahianos* (Rio de Janeiro: Imprensa Nacional, 1909), 116–117.

23. *Artistas Bahianos*, 247.

24. *Artistas Bahianos*, 17.

25. Citing Dr. Virgilio Damasio's quote used as an epigraph at the beginning of the book. See *Artistas Bahianos*, ix.

Chapter 5

1. Jorge Amado, *Amor do Soldado* (São Paulo: Companhia das Letras, 2008).

2. E. Bradford Burns, "Manuel Querino's Interpretation of the African Contribution to Brazil," *The Journal of Negro History* 59.1 (1974): 78.

3. Linda Hutcheon, "The Politics of Postmodernism: Parody and History," *Cultural Critique* 5 (1986–1987): 180.

4. Jorge Amado, *Tenda dos Milagres*, 166.

5. João José Reis, "Postface," in Jorge Amado, *Tenda dos Milagres* (São Paulo: Companhia das Letras, 2008), 298–302.

6. See Arthur Ramos, Preface, in *Costumes Africanos no Brasil* (Rio de Janeiro: Civilização Brasileira, 1938), 9. Cited in "From Freedom to Folklore: The Politics of Twentieth Century New World Africanity," http://cgt.columbia.edu/files/papers/Cooper-abstract.pdf. Accessed on August 15, 2018.

7. Jorge Amado, *Morte e a Morte de Quincas Berro d'Água* (São Paulo: Companhia das Letras, 2008). This is one of the carnivalesque narratives by Amado in which vagabondage and hustling form part of the everyday art of survival.

8. See João José Reis, Postface, in Jorge Amado, *Tenda dos Milagres* (São Paulo: Companhia das Letras, 2008), 298–302.

9. Jorge Amado, *Tent of Miracles*, Trans. Barbara Shelby (Madison: University of Wisconsin Press, 2003), 325.

10. Cited in Jaime Sodré, *Manuel Querino: Um Herói da Raça e Classe* (Salvador: Self-publication, 2000), 93.

11. *Tent of Miracles*, 272.

12. See Aimé Césaire, *Discourse on Colonialism* (New York: Monthly Review Press, 2001).

13. *Tent of Miracles*, 272.

14. Autopsy Report as appended to the homicide report on Inocêncio Firmino de Souza, also known as "Sete Portas," in the APEB Judicial Section records, statute 195, box 2, document 5, page 2. See also Josivaldo Pires Oliveira, *Pelas Ruas da Bahia: Criminalidade e Poder no Universo dos Capoeiras na Salvador Republicana (1912–1937)*(Through the Streets of Bahia: Criminality and Power in the Capoeira Universes in Republican Salvador [1912–1937]). Masters dissertation, Federal University of Bahia, 2004.

15. *A Tarde*, May 11, 1922, p. 1.

16. See *A Tarde*, May 11, 1922, p. 1.

17. *Tent of Miracles*, 274.

18. See Richard Brown, "Dialectic and Structure in Jean-Paul Sartre and Claude Levi-Strauss," *Dialectica* 32.2 (1978): 165–184.

19. For a more detailed analysis of the connections between culture and history, see Ana Rosa Ramos, "Historicidade e Cultura Urbana," in *Bahia: A Cidade de Jorge Amado* (Bahia: The City of Jorge Amado) (Salvador: Casa de Palavras, 2000), 29–60.

20. See Arjun Appadurai, *Modernity at Large: Cultural Dimensions of Globalization* (St. Paul: University of Minnesota Press, 1996).

21. Appadurai, *Modernity at Large*, 32.

22. Fábio Lucas, "As Intencionalidades da Narrativa de Jorge Amado," in *Colóquio Jorge Amado: 70 Anos de Jubiabá* (Salvador: Casa das Palavras, 2006), 165.

23. *Tent of Miracles*, 110.

24. *Tent of Miracles*, 167.

25. *Tent of Miracles*, 167–169.

26. *Tent of Miracles*, 169.

27. *Tent of Miracles*, 39.

28. For a detailed discussion of Pereira's *Tent of Miracles*, see Joan R. Dassin, "*Tent of Miracles*: Myth of Racial Democracy," *Jump Cut: A Review of Contemporary Media* 21 (2005): 3.

29. Dassin, 3.

30. Dassin, 4.

31. *Tent of Miracles*, 161–162.

32. Edmar Ferreira Santos, *O Poder dos Candomblé: Perseguição e Resistência no Recôncavo da Bahia* (The Power of *Candomblé*: Persecution and Resistance in the Bahian Basin) (Salvador: Edufba, 2009), 188. The author's conclusion is based on an elaborate study of Candomblé temples in the city of Cachoeira.

33. *Tent of Miracles*, 305.

34. *Tent of Miracles*, 306.

35. For a detailed explication of the life, times, and legacy of Manuel Querino, see Jaime Sodré, *Manuel Querino: Um Herói da Raça e Classe* [Manuel Querino: A Hero of Race and Class] (Salvador: Self-Publication, 2001).

Chapter 6

1. While scholars such as Afolabi Epega and Bolaji Idowu suggest that Obatala or Orisa-Nla (supreme deity) is the highest in ranking among the deities, Wande Abimbola argues that a clear-cut demarcation of seniority among the Orisa is truly unimaginable and difficult to establish. See, for example, Afolabi A. Epega, *Ifa: The Ancient Wisdom* (New York: Imole Oluwa Institute, 1987), 3; Bolaji Idowu, *Olodumare: God in Yoruba Belief* (London: Longmans, 1962), 71; and Wande Abimbola, *Ifa: An Exposition of Ifa Literary Corpus* (Ibadan: Okford University Press, 1976), 3.

2. I use "text" in its multiple meanings of oral, written, visual, and performative productions, including plays and films.

3. Obatala literally translates as the "the white-robed king," who is divinely immune from the soiling of his pristine garb.

4. Wole Soyinka, *Myth, Literature and the African World* (Cambridge: Cambridge University Press, 1976), 26.

5. Femi Abodunrin, *Blackness: Culture, Ideology and Discourse* (Ibadan: Dokun Publishing, 2008), 229.

6. Tejumola Olaniyan, *Scars of Conquest / Masks of Resistance* (Oxford: Oxford University Press, 1995), 48.

7. Richard Seaford, *Dionysos* (New York: Rutledge, 2006), 40.

8. Soyinka, *Myth, Literature and the African World*, 28.

9. For more insights on the plasticity and limited creative agency of Obatala, see also Olaniyan, *Scars of Conquest / Masks of Resistance*, 48; and Omotade Adegbindin, *Ifá in Yorùbá Thought System* (Durham, NC: Carolina Academic Press, 2014), 67.

10. Soyinka, *Myth, Literature and the African World*, 3.

11. See http://oyekuofun.org/who-is-obatala.

12. See http://oyekuofun.org/who-is-obatala.

13. Often referred to as "Adunni Olorisa," Susanne Wenger (1915–2011) was the white priestess of Osun River Grove deity in Nigeria. Born in Graz, Austria, Susanne studied art in Graz and Vienna where she was a member of the Vienna Art-Club. After World War II, she traveled to Italy and also spent time in Switzerland where she had exhibitions at the Des Eaux Vives in Zurich. In 1949, Susanne went to Paris, where she met and married Ulli Beier, a German linguist who subsequently accepted a posting to West Africa. The couple arrived in Ibadan, Nigeria, in 1959 and later moved to the small town of Ede near Oshogo, where Susanne quickly assimilated to the local culture. She later divorced Ulli Beier and married Chief Alarape aka Ayansola Oniru. It was at Ede that Susanne met Ajagemo, a powerful Obatala (native) priest and her guru, who initiated her into the world of the Orisha, the traditional Yoruba religion. She got very much involved in Osun River Grove; her passion and devotion saw her grow through the ranks to become the chief custodian and priestess of the shrine.

14. Obotunde Ijimere, *The Imprisonment of Obatala and other Plays* (London: Heinemann, 1966), viii.

15. Fyodor Dostoevsky, *Crime and Punishment* (New York: Vintage, 1992), 497.

16. Ijimere, *The Imprisonment of Obatala*, vi.

17. "Obotunde Ijimere" is the unfortunate pen name assigned to the anonymous author by the translator. It is so pejorative a Yoruba-derived name that the text might not have even been published in Yoruba culture. "Obo" refers to a monkey, while "tunde" may refer to a returned traveler or an inveterate mischief-maker. And "Ijimere" refers to a baboon. So Beier essentially said the text was penned by one "Trouble-making Monkey Baboon," or a monkey born of baboon parents—which has serious implications, as it may suggest that Beier was either an evolutionist or a masked racist. It must be noted that Nigeria had just attained independence when Ulli Beier, a young PhD from Australia, joined the then university of Ife (Ile-Ife), a Nigerian university. He should have been more sensitive to the implication of a "monkey" writing a play in the African

context! Interestingly, Beier had a pet monkey that also followed him around on campus, or so the story goes.

18. Nelson O. Fashina, "Evolution of Theory and the Problem of Contextual and Cultural Configurations in African Dramatic Literature." *Nawa Journal of Language and Communication* 2.2 (2008): 2.

19. Soyinka, *Myth, Literature and the African World*, 1.

20. Soyinka, *Myth, Literature and the African World*, 13.

21. Soyinka, *Myth, Literature and the African World*, 36.

22. For a better understanding of Soyinka's theory of tragic drama, see Tejumola Olaniyan, *Scars of Conquest / Masks of Resistance* (New York/Oxford: Oxford University Press, 1995), 46–47.

23. Soyinka, *Myth, Literature and the African World*, 38.

24. Soyinka, *Myth, Literature and the African World*, 152–153.

25. Soyinka, *Myth, Literature and the African World*, 144.

26. See, for example, Anthony Appiah, *In My Father's House* (New York: Oxford University Press, 1993).

27. Soyinka, *Myth, Literature and the African World*, 28.

28. Ijimere, *The Imprisonment of Obatala*, 44.

29. For a compelling study of the ritual of sexuality in *The Imprisonment of Obatala*, see for example Amadou Ouedrago, "Myth and the Ritual of Sexuality in Obotunde Ijimere's *The Imprisonment of Obatala*," *Bridges: A Senegalese Journal of English Studies* 6 (1995): 29–42.

30. Ijimere, *The Imprisonment of Obatala*, 9.

31. Ijimere, *The Imprisonment of Obatala*, 36.

32. Ijimere, *The Imprisonment of Obatala*, 40.

33. Ijimere, *The Imprisonment of Obatala*, 40–41.

34. Ijimere, *The Imprisonment of Obatala*, 42–43.

35. Ijimere, *The Imprisonment of Obatala*, 43.

36. Ifayemi Eleburuibon (Chief Priest), *The Adventures of Obatala: Ifá and Santería God of Creativity* (Osogbo: API Production, 1989), 15–17.

37. Ifayemi Eleburuibon, *Adventures of Obatala*, 15.

38. For a more detailed discussion of Orphism, see, for example, W.K.C. Guthrie, *Orpheus and Greek Religion* (Princeton, NJ: Princeton University Press, 1993), Marcel Detienne, *The Writing of Orpheus: Greek Myth in Cultural Context* (Baltimore: Johns Hopkins University Press, 2003), and Salomon Reinach, *Orpheus: A History of Religions* (New York: Horace, 1930).

39. *Eurydice* (2003) is a play by Sarah Ruhl that reimagines the myth of Orpheus from the viewpoint of Eurydice. The play focuses on Eurydice's confusion: to return to earth with Orpheus or to stay in Hades with her father, a new character invented by Ruhl. Of the many structural changes made by Ruhl, Eurydice's calling out to Orpheus and forcing him to look back differs from the version where Orpheus looks back, unable to control his own passionate desires.

In Ruhl's version, Eurydice was split between her fear of returning to the earth and her desire to remain with her father in the underworld. Though yet to be published, *Eurydice* has been performed on Broadway in New York (2007).

40. Virgil, *Georgics* (Chicago: University of Chicago Press, 1966); see Book X (Songs of Orpheus) and Book XI (Death of Orpheus), Ovid, *Metamorphoses* (New York: Norton, 2010), 265–315.

41. Edward Young, *Busiris: King of Egypt, A Tragedy* (London: Gale, 2012).

42. See Charles A. Perrone, "Don't Look Back: Myths, Conceptions, and Receptions of Black Orpheus," *Studies in Latin American Popular Culture* 17 (1998): 157.

43. Quoted in José Eduardo de Mello, *Música Popular Brasileira* (São Paulo: Melhoramentos, 1976), 59.

44. Charles A. Perrone, "Don't Look Back," 159.

45. Jorge de Lima, *Invenção de Orfeu* (Rio de Janeiro: Record, 2005), 7.

46. Jorge de Lima, *Invenção de Orfeu*, 154–155.

47. Jorge de Lima, *Invenção de Orfeu*, 157.

48. Charles A. Perrone, "Don't Look Back," 165.

49. See Glauber Rocha, "Orfeu: Metafísica na Favela," *Jornal do Brasil* (October 24, 1959).

50. See Chris McGowan and Ricardo Pessanha, *The Brazilian Sound: Samba, Bossa Nova, and the Popular Music of Brazil* (Philadelphia: Temple University Press, 1998).

51. See Michael Hanchard, *Orpheus and Power* (Princeton, NJ: Princeton University Press, 1994).

52. Lúcia Nagib, *Brazil on Screen: Cinema Novo, New Cinema, Utopia* (London: L. B. Taurus, 2007), 81–97.

53. Robert Stam, *Tropical Multiculturalism* (Durham, NC: Duke University Press, 1997), 175.

54. Toni Garrido is the lead singer of the "Cidade Negra" musical group of Rio de Janeiro.

55. *Brazil on Screen*, 97.

Chapter 7

1. Bianca Freire-Medeiros, "Selling the Favela: Thoughts and Polemics about a Tourist Destination," *Revista Brasileira de Ciências Sociais* 22.65 (2007): 70.

2. Sommers et al., eds, *Marginality in Space—Past, Present and Future: Theoretical and Methodological Aspects of Cultural, Social and Economical Parameters of Marginal and Critical Regions* (London: Ashgate, 1999), 7.

3. See Frantz Fanon, *The Wretched of the Earth* (New York: Grove Press, 2005).

4. Circe Monteiro, "Enclaves, Condominiums, and Favelas: Where are the *Ghettos* in Brazil?" *City and Community* 7 (2008): 378.

5. L. Wacquant, "Ghetto," in N. J. Smelster et al. eds., *International Encyclopedia of the Social and Behavioral Sciences* (London: Pergamon, 2004), 148.

6. Monteiro, "Enclaves, Condominiums, and Favelas," 380–381.

7. Virginia Maria Trindade Valadares, "O Contratador dos Diamantes e Chica Que Manda" *Caderno de História* 7.8 (2005): 57–66.

8. Monteiro, "Enclaves, Condominiums, and Favelas," 382.

9. Bianca Freire-Medeiros, "Selling the Favela: Thoughts and Polemics about a Tourist Destination," *Revista Brasileira de Ciências Sociais*, 22.65 (2007): 71.

10. Jaime do Amparo-Alves, "Narratives of Violence: The White ImagiNation and the Making of Black Masculinity in *City of God*," *Sociedade e Cultura* 12.2 (2009): 301. For a more nuanced critique of the state for the propagation of violence and marginality in Brazil, see also, Jaime Amparo Alves, *The Anti-Black City: Police Terror and Black Urban Life in Brazil* (Minneapolis: University of Minnesota Press, 2018).

11. Vanessa Fitzgibbon, "O Ressentimento Racial Brasileiro e a Identidade Marginal a Partir da "História de Inferninho," *Cidade de Deus*, de Paulo Lins," *Luso-Brazilian Review* 46.2 (2009): 129.

12. Cited in Claudia Drucker, "Review: *Desde que o Samba é Samba*," *Estação Literária Londrina* 10 (2012): 243.

13. See "O Samba Nasceu Fugindo da Polícia" (Samba was born in the process of running from the police). http://revistacult.uol.com.br/home/2012/05/"Co-samba-nasceu-fugindo-da-policia.

14. Paulo Lins, *Desde que o Samba é Samba* (Rio de Janeiro: Planeta, 2012), 294.

15. Ferréz, *Capão Pecado* (Rio de Janeiro: Objetiva, 2005), 147.

16. Ferréz, *Capão Pecado* (Rio de Janeiro: Objetiva, 2005), 149.

Conclusion

1. See http://lyrics.wikia.com/Chico_Science_%26_Na%C3%A7%C3%A3o_Zumbi:Etnia. Accessed on December 10, 2019.

2. Joy DeGruy, *Post Traumatic Slave Syndrome* (Washington, DC: DeGruy Publications, 2005), 55.

3. Pelourinho has been declared a world heritage center, and the name literally means a place of flagellation, thus echoing the legacy of the violence of slavery. The overall surrounding colonial architecture—including fountains, squares, and churches—serve as colorful relics of the golden age of Brazilian colonial history and culture.

Bibliography

Abodunrin, Femi. *Blackness: Culture, Ideology and Discourse*. Ibadan: Dokun Publishing, 2008. 228–241.

Abreu, Luís Alberto de. *Xica da Silva*. São Paulo: Martins Fontes, 1988.

Adelowo, E. Dada. "Rituals, Symbolism and Symbols in Yoruba Traditional Religious Thought." *African Journal of Thought* 4.1 (1990): 162–173.

Adewuyi, Olayinka. *Obatala: The Greatest and Oldest Divinity*. New York: River Water, 2013.

Adluri, Vishwa, and Joydeep Bagchee. "From Poetic Immortality to Salvation: Ruru and Orpheus in Indic and Greek Myth." *History of Religions* 51.3 (2012): 239–261.

Agnew, Vanessa. *Enlightenment Orpheus: The Power of Music in Other Worlds*. New York: Oxford, 2008.

Agnew, Vijay. *Diaspora, Memory, and Identity: A Search for Home*. Toronto: University of Toronto Press, 2005.

Agualusa, José Eduardo. *Nação Crioula*. Lisboa: TV Editora, 1997.

Aidoo, Lamonte. *Slavery Unseen: Sex, Power, and Violence in Brazilian History*. Durham, NC: Duke University Press, 2018.

Aiyejina, Funso. "Esu Elegbara: A Source of an Alter/Native Theory of African Literature and Criticism." Unpublished Paper.

Almeida, Miguel Vale de. "'Longing for Oneself': Hybridism and Miscegenation in Colonial and Postcolonial Portugal." *Etnográfia* 6.1 (2002): 181–201.

Almeida, Miguel Vale de. *An Earth-Colored Sea: "Race," Culture and the Politics of Identity in the Post-Colonial Portuguese-Speaking World*. New York: Berghahn Books, 2004.

Alves, Jaime Amparo. *The Anti-Black City: Police Terror and Black Urban Life in Brazil*. Minneapolis: University of Minnesota Press, 2018.

Amado, Jorge. *Amor do Soldado*. São Paulo: Companhia das Letras, 2008 [1947].

Amado, Jorge. *Bahia de Todos os Santos*. Rio de Janeiro: Record, 1977.

Amado, Jorge. *A Morte e a Morte de Quincas Berro d'Água*. São Paulo: Companhia das Letras, 2008.

Amado, Jorge. *Tenda dos Milagres*. São Paulo: Companhia das Letras, 2008 [1969].

Amado, Jorge. *Tenda dos Milagres*. São Paulo: Livraria Martins Editora, 1969.

Amado, Jorge. *Tent of Miracles*. Madison: University of Wisconsin Press, 2003.

Amado, Jorge. *Tent of Miracles*. New York: Knopf, 1977.

Amparo-Alves, Jaime do. "Narratives of Violence: the White ImagiNation and the Making of Black Masculinity in *City of God*." *Sociedade e Cultura* 12.2 (2009): 301–318.

Anderson, Robert N. "The Muses of Chaos and Destruction of *Arena Conta Zumbi*." *Latin American Theater Review* (1996): 15–28.

Anderson, Robert N. "The Quilombo of Palmares: A New Overview of a Maroon State in Seventeenth-Century Brazil." *Journal of Latin American Studies* 28 (1996): 545–566.

Anderson, Robert N. *Theatrical Semiosis and the Theatre of Gianfrancesco Guarnieri*. Doctoral dissertation, University of North Carolina, Chapel Hill, 1990.

Antunes, António Lobo. *Os Cus de Judas*. Lisboa: Editora Vega, 1979.

Appadurai, Arjun. *Modernity at Large: Cultural Dimensions of Globalization*. St. Paul: University of Minnesota Press, 1996.

Araujo, Ana Lucia. *Paths of the Atlantic Slave Trade: Interactions, Identities, and Images*. Amherst, NY: Cambria Press, 2011.

Araújo, Deniza Corrêa. "The Spheres of Power in *Xica da Silva*." *Rocky Mountain Review of Language and Literature* 46.1–2 (1992): 37–43.

Araújo, Emanoel. *A Mão Afro-Brasileira*. São Paulo: Tenege, 1988.

Arendt, Hannah. *On Violence*. New York & London: Harcourt Brace Jovanovich, 1970.

Azevedo, Celia Maria Marinho de. *Abolitionism in the United States and Brazil: A Comparative Perspective*. New York: Garland, 1995.

Babbage, Frances. *Augusto Boal*. New York: Routledge, 2004.

Bacelar, Jeferson. *A Hierarquia das Raças Negros e Brancos em Salvador*. Rio de Janeiro: Pallas, 2001.

Bada, Valérie. "Cross-Cultural Dialogues with Greek Classics: Walcott's 'The Odyssey' and Soyinka's 'The Bacchae of Euripides.'" *ARIEL: A Review of International English Literature* 31.3 (2000): 7–28.

Bakhtin, Mikhail. *Problemas da Poética de Dostoievski*. São Paulo: Forense Universitária, 2005.

Balogun, Oladele A. "The Concepts of Ori and Human Destiny in Traditional Yoruba Thought: A Soft-Deterministic Interpretation." *Nordic Journal of African Studies* 16.1 (2007): 116–130.

Baronov, David. *The Abolition of Slavery in Brazil: The "Liberation" of Africans through the Emancipation of Capital*. Westport, CT: Greenwood Press, 2000.

Barreto, Lima. *Recordações do Escrivão Isaías Caminha*. Lisboa: Olympio, 1909.

Bascom, William. *Sixteen Cowries: Yoruba Divination from Africa to the New World.* Bloomington: Indiana University Press, 1980.

Beier, Ulli, ed. and trans. *Yoruba Myths.* Cambridge: Cambridge University Press, 1980.

Beier, Ulli, ed. and trans. *Yoruba Poetry: An Anthology of Traditional Poems.* Cambridge: Cambridge University Press, 1970.

Benavides, O. Hugo. "Seeing *Xica* and the Melodramatic Unveiling of Colonial Desire." *Social Text* 21.3 (2003): 109–133.

Bender, Gerald J. *Angola under the Portuguese.* Los Angeles: University of California Press, 1980.

Benmayor, Rina, and Andor Skotnes, eds. *Migration and Identity.* New Brunswick: Transaction Publishers, 2007.

Berlink, Manoel T. *Marginalidade Social e Relações de Classes em São Paulo.* Rio de Janeiro: Petrópolis, 1975.

Bernd, Zilá. "O Universo Crioulizado de Jorge Amado." Rita Olivieri-Godet and Jaqueline Penjon, eds. *Jorge Amado: Leituras e Diálogos em Torno de Uma Obra.* Salvador: Casa da Palavras, 2004. 131–143.

Bethencourt, Francisco, and Adrian J. Pearce, eds. *Racism and Ethnic Relations in the Portuguese-Speaking World.* Oxford & New York: Oxford University Press, 2012.

Bhabha, Homi. *The Location of Culture.* New York: Routledge, 1994.

Blackburn, Robin. *The Overthrow of Colonial Slavery, 1776–1848.* London: Verso, 1988.

Block, Sharon. *Rape and Slavery in Early America.* Chapel Hill: University of North Carolina Press, 2006.

Boal, Augusto, and Gianfrancesco Guarnieri. *Arena Conta Tiradentes.* São Paulo: Sagarana, 1967.

Boal, Augusto, Gianfrancesco Guarnieri, et al. *Arena Conta Zumbi. Revista de Teatro* 378 (1970): 31–59.

Boal, Augusto. *Teatro do Oprimido e Outras Poéticas Políticas.* 4th ed. Rio de Janeiro: Civilização Brasileira, 1983.

Bond, Edward. *Orpheus: A Story in Six Scenes.* Mainz: Schott, 1978.

Borges, Dain. *The Family in Bahia, Brazil, 1870–1945.* Stanford, CA: Stanford University Press, 1992.

Borges, Heloísa Barretto. "Uma Leitura do Romance *Tenda dos Milagres* de Jorge Amado: A Relação Triádica Real/Fictício/Imaginário no Texto Literário." *Sitientibus* 37 (2007): 113–133.

Boxer, Charles. *The Portuguese Seaborne Empire: 1415–1825.* New York: Pelican Books, 1969.

Boxer, Charles. *Race Relations in the Portuguese Colonial Empire, 1415–1825.* London: Oxford University Press, 1963.

Brito, Rubens José Souza. *Dos Peões ao Rei: O Teatro Épico-Dramático de Luís Alberto de Abreu*. PhD thesis, São Paulo: USP, 1999.

Brown, Kimberly Juanita. "Black Rapture: Sally Hemings, Chica da Silva, and the Slave Body of Sexual Supremacy." *Women's Studies Quarterly* 35.1–2 (2007): 45–66.

Bryant-Jackson, Paul K. "Obatala in Revolutionary (Postmodern) Diaspora." *Theatre Journal* 57.4 (2005): 612–614.

Buller, Jeffrey L. "Looking Backwards: Baroque Opera and the Ending of the Orpheus Myth." *International Journal of the Classical Tradition* 1.3 (1995): 57–79.

Burke, Peter, and Maria Lúcia G. Pallares-Burke. *Gilberto Freyre: Social Theory in the Tropics*. Oxford: Peter Lang, 2008.

Burns, E. Bradford. "Bibliographic Essay: Manuel Querino's Interpretation of the African Contribution of Brazil." *The Journal of Negro History* 59.1 (1974): 78–86.

Burns, E. Bradford. "Manuel Querino's Interpretation of the African Contribution to Brazil." *The Journal of Negro History* 59.1 (1974): 78–86.

Busatto, Luiz. *Montagem em Invenção de Orfeu*. Rio de Janeiro: Âmbito Cultural, 1978.

Butler, Judith. *Gender Trouble: Feminism and the Subversion of Identity*. New York: Routledge, 2006.

Butler, Kim. *Freedoms Given, Freedoms Won*. New Brunswick, NJ: Rutgers University Press, 1998.

Calil, Carlos Augusto, ed. "Orfeu da Conceição." *Vincius de Moraes: Teatro em Versos*. São Paulo: Companhia das Letras, 1995. 51–111.

Callado, Antônio. *O Tesouro de Chica da Silva*. (Coleção Teatro). São Paulo: Códice, 2006.

Calmon, Jorge. *Manuel Querino, O Jornalista e o Político*. Salvador: CEAO/ UFBA, 1984.

Calwell, Kia Lilly. *Negras in Brazil: Re-envisioning Black Women, Citizenship, and the Politics of Identity*. New Brunswick, NJ: Rutgers University Press, 2007.

Camp, Stephanie M. H. *Closer to Freedom: Enslaved Women and Everyday Resistance in the Plantation South*. Chapel Hill: University of North Carolina, 2004.

Campos, Claudia de Arruda. *Zumbi, Tiradentes e Outras Histórias Contadas pelo Teatro de Arena de São Paulo*. São Paulo: Perspectiva, 1988.

Camus, Marcel. dir. *Black Orpheus*. New York: Criterion Collection, 1999 [1959] (DVD).

Castelo, Cláudia. *O Modo Português de Estar no Mundo*. Lisboa: Afrotamento: 1998.

Cavalcanti, Luciano Marcos Dias. "Orfismo e Cristianismo na Lírica Final de Jorge de Lima." *Revista Recorte* 7 (2002): 1–24.

Cavalcanti, Povina. *Vida e Obra de Jorge de Lima*. Rio de Janeiro: Correio da Manhã, 1965.

Césaire, Aimé. *Discourse on Colonialism*. Monthly Review Press, 2000.

Chandra, Sarika. *Dislocalism: The Crisis of Globalization and the Remobilizing of Americanism*. Columbus: The Ohio State University Press, 2011.

Christian, Barbara. "The Race for Theory." Angelyn Mitchel, ed. *Within the Circle*. Durham, NC: Duke University Press, 1994. 348–359.

Cocteau, Jean, dir. *Orpheus*. New York: Janus Films, 2011 [1950] (DVD).

Commander, Michelle D. *Afro-Atlantic Flight: Speculative Returns and the Black Fantastic*. Durham, NC: Duke University Press, 2017.

Corrêa, Viriato. "Chica da Silva." *Chica da Silva e Outras Histórias*. Rio de Janeiro: Civilização Brasileira, 1955. 19–26.

Couto, Mia. *O Outro Pé da Sereia*. São Paulo: Companhia das Letras, 2006.

Cruz e Silva, Teresa, and Manuel G. Mendes Araujo. *"Lusofonia" em África: História, Democracia e Integração Africana*. Dakar: CODESRIA, 2005.

Curto, José C., and Paul E. Lovejoy, eds. *Enslaving Connections: Changing Cultures of Africa and Brazil during the Era of Slavery*. New York: Humanity Books, 2004.

DaMatta, Roberto. *Carnavais, Heróis e Malandros*. Rio de Janeiro: Zahar, 1979.

Daniel, G. Reginald. *Race and Multiraciality in Brazil and the United States*. State College: Pennsylvania State University Press, 2006.

Dassin, Joan R. *"Tent of Miracles*: Myth of Racial Democracy." *Jump Cut: A Review of Contemporary Media* 21 (2005): 2–22.

Dawson, Terence. "The Orpheus Complex." *Journal of Analytical Psychology* 45 (2000): 245–266.

Degler, Carl. *Neither Black Nor White*. Madison: University of Wisconsin Press, 1986.

DeGruy, Joy. *Post Traumatic Slave Syndrome*. Washington, DC: DeGruy Publications, 2005.

DeNeef, A. Leigh. "The Poetics of Orpheus: The Text and a Study of *Orpheus His Journey to Hell (1595)*." *Studies in Philology* (1992): 20–69.

Detienne, Marcel. *The Writing of Orpheus: Greek Myth in Cultural Context*. Baltimore: Johns Hopkins University Press, 2003.

Diegues, Carlos, dir. *Xica da Silva*. Rio de Janeiro: Embrafilme, 1976 (VHS).

Diegues, Carlos. dir. *Orfeu*. New York: New Yorker, 1999 (DVD).

Dixon, Kwame, and Ollie A. Johnson III, eds. *Comparative Racial Politics in Latin America*. New York: Routledge, 2019.

Dostoevsky, Fyodor. *Crime and Punishment*. New York: Vintage, 1992.

Duarte, Cristina. "Carlos Diegues et la Représentation de l'Esclave au Brésil." Étude de Ganga Zumba, Xica da Silva et Quilombo." *Cinémas d'Amérique Latine* 10 (2002): 171–173.

Duarte, Eduardo de Assis. *Jorge Amado: Romance em Tempo de Utopia*. Rio de Janeiro: Record, 1999.

Dunne, John. *The City of the Gods: A Study in Myth and Mortality*. New York: Macmillan, 1965.

Eco, Umberto. *Semiotics and the Philosophy of Language*. Bloomington: Indiana University Press, 1984.

Elebuibon, Ifayemi. *The Adventures of Obatala: Ifa and Santeria God of Creativity.* Osogbo: API Production, 1989.

Espinheira Filho, Ruy. *Nordeste e o Negro na Poesia de Jorge de Lima.* Salvador: EGBA, 1990.

Espinheira, Gey, ed. *Sociabilidade e Violência.* Salvador: Estado da Bahia, 2004.

Fanon, Frantz. *The Wretched of the Earth.* New York: Grove Press, 2004.

Fanon, Frantz. *Black Skin, White Masks.* New York: Grove Press, 2008.

Fashina, Nelson. "Evolution of Theory and the Problem of Contextual and Cultural Configurations in African Dramatic Literature." *Nawa Journal of Language and Communication* 2.2 (2008): 1–14.

Ferreira, Roquinaldo. *Cross-Cultural Exchange in the Atlantic World.* Cambridge: Cambridge University Press, 2012.

Ferréz. *Capão Pecado.* Rio de Janeiro: Objetiva, 2005.

Fischer-Lichte, Erika. "The Theatrical Code: An Approach to the Problem." Ernest Hess-Lüttich, ed. *Theatre Semiotics.* Tubingen: Verlag, 1982. 46–62.

Fitzgibbon, Vanessa. "O Ressentimento Racial Brasileiro e a Identidade Marginal a Partir da 'História de Inferninho' em *Cidade de Deus,* de Paulo Lins." *Luso-Brazilian Review* 46.2 (2009): 129–154.

Fonseca-Downey, Elizabeth Anne. *The Theatre of Gianfrancesco Guarnieri as an Expression of Brazilian National Reality.* Doctoral dissertation, University of Iowa, 1982.

Fonseca, Edson Nery da. *Novas Perspectivas em Casa Grande e Senzala.* Recife: Fundação Joaquim Nabuco, 1985.

Foucault, Michel, and Paul Rabinow. *The Foucault Reader.* New York: Pantheon, 1984.

Foucault, Michel. *The History of Sexuality: An Introduction.* New York: Vintage, 1990.

Foucault, Michel. *The Use of Pleasure.* New York: Vintage Books, 1990.

Fredricksmeyer, Hardy. "Black Orpheus, Myth and Ritual: A Morphological Reading." *International Journal of the Classical Tradition* 14.1–2 (2000): 148–175.

Freire-Medeiros, Blanca. "Selling the Favela: Thoughts and Polemics about a Tourist Destination." *Revista Brasileira de Ciências Sociais,* 22.65 (2007): 61–72.

Freitas, Décio. *Palmares: A Guerra dos Escravos.* 5th ed. Rio de Janeiro: Graal, 1982.

French, Jan Hoffman. *Legalizing Identities: Becoming Black or Indian in Brazil's Northeast.* Chapel Hill, NC: University of North Carolina Press, 2009.

Freyre, Gilberto. *Um Brasileiro em Terras Portuguesas.* Lisboa: Edições Livro do Brasil, 1953.

Freyre, Gilberto. *Casa Grande e Senzala.* Lisboa: Edições Livro do Brasil, 1933.

Freyre, Gilberto. *Integração Portuguesa nos Trópicos.* Lisboa: Col. ECPS, 1958.

Freyre, Gilberto. *O Mundo que o Português Criou.* Lisboa: Edições Livro do Brasil, 1940.

Freyre, Gilberto. *O Luso e o Trópico*. Lisboa: CECC, 1961.

Fry, Peter. "Politics, Nationality, and the Meanings of 'Race' in Brazil." *Daedelus* 129.2 (2000): 83–118.

Furtado, Júnia Ferreira. *Chica da Silva e o Contratador dos Diamantes: O Outro Lado do Mito*. São Paulo: Companhia das Letras, 2009.

Furtado, Júnia Ferreira. *Chica da Silva: A Brazilian Slave of the Eighteenth Century*. Cambridge: Cambridge University Press, 2009.

Garden, Dale Thorston. *From Slavery to Freedom in Brazil*. Albuquerque: University of New Mexico Press, 2001.

Gayley, Charles Mills. *The Classic Myths in English Literature and in Art*. Boston: Ginn and Company, 1911.

George, David, "Theatre of the Oppressed and Teatro de Arena: In and Out of Context," *Latin American Theatre Review* 28.2 (1995): 39–54.

George, Olakunle. *Relocating Agency: Modernity and African Letters*. Albany, NY: SUNY Press, 2003.

Gledhill, Sabrina. "Manuel Querino: Um Pioneiro e Seu Tempo." *Afro-Brazilian Studies Before 1930: Nineteenth-Century Racial Attitudes and the Work of Five Scholars*. (Extracted from Master's thesis in Latin American Studies), UCLA, 1986. 1–75.

Gledhill, Sabrina. "Reflexões Sobre Um Retrato de Manuel Querino." Unpublished Paper, 2002.

Gledhill, Sabrina. "Velhos Respeitáveis: Notas Sobre a Pesquisa de Manuel Querino e as Origens dos Africanos na Bahia." *História Unisinos* 14.3 (2010): 339–343.

Glymph, Thavolia. *Out of the House of Bondage: The Transformation of the Plantation Household*. Cambridge: Cambridge University Press, 2008.

Gohn, Maria da Glória Marcondes. *A Força da Periferia*. Rio de Janeiro: Vozes, 1985.

Goldstein, Norma Seltzer. "Uma Leitura Antropológica de Jorge Amado." *Colóquio Jorge Amado: 70 Anos de Jubiabá*. Salvador: Casa das Palavras, 2006. 77–97.

Goldstein, Norma Seltzer. *A Literatura de Jorge Amado*. São Paulo: Companhia das Letras, 2008.

Gomes, Álvaro. *Jorge Amado: Literatura Comentada*. São Paulo: Abril, 1981.

Goodwin, Doris Kearns. *Team of Rivals*. New York: Simon and Schuster, 2005.

Gordon, Richard A. "Allegories of Resistance and Reception in *Xica da Silva*." *Luso-Brazilian Review* 42.1 (2005): 44–60.

Grinberg, Keila, et al. *Para Conhecer Chica da Silva*. Rio de Janeiro: Zahar, 2007.

Guimarães, Antônio Sérgio Alfredo. "After Racial Democracy." Trans. Renato Rezende. *Tempo Social* 18.2 (2006): 269–287.

Guimarães, Antônio Sérgio Alfredo. "Manoel Querino e Formação do 'Pensamento Negro' no Brasil, entre 1890 e 1920." Paper Presented at the 8th Luso-Afro-Brazilian Congress, Coimbra, 2004.

Guthrie, W.K.C. *Orpheus and Greek Religion*. Princeton, NJ: Princeton University Press, 1993.

Hall, Stuart. "Cultural Identity and Diaspora." *Colonial Discourse and Post-Colonial Theory: A Reader*. Ed. Patrick Williams and Chrisman. London: Harvester Wheatsheaf, 1994. 392–401.

Hall, Stuart. *Critical Dialogues in Cultural Studies*. New York: Routledge, 1996.

Hanchard, Michael G. *Orfeu e o Poder: Movimento Negro no Rio e São Paulo*. Rio de Janeiro: EDUERJ, 2001.

Hanchard, Michael G. *Orpheus and Power: The Movimento Negro of Rio de Janeiro and São Paulo, Brazil, 1945–1988*. Princeton, NJ: Princeton University Press, 1994.

Hawthorne, Walter. *From Africa to Brazil: Culture, Identity, and the Atlantic Slave Trade, 1600–1830*. Cambridge: Cambridge University Press, 2010.

Heise, Tatiana Signorelli. *Remaking Brazil: Contested national Identities in Contemporary Brazilian Cinema*. Cardiff: University of Wales Press, 2012.

Herskovits, Melville. *The Myth of the Negro Past*. Boston: Beacon Press, 1990 [1963].

Hess-Lüttich, Ernest W. B. *Theatre Semiotics*. Tübingen: Verlag, 1982.

Holanda, Heloísa de. "Estética da Periferia: Um Conceito Capcioso." Rio de Janeiro: Programa Avançado de Cultura Contemporânea, 2005.

Hooker, Juliet. "Inclusão Indígena e Exclusão dos Afro-Descendentes na América Latina." *Tempo Social* 18.2 (2006): 89–111.

Hooker, Juliet. *Theorizing Race in the Americas: Douglass, Sarmiento, Du Bois, and Vasconcelos*. Oxford: Oxford University Press, 2019.

Hutcheon, Linda. "The Politics of Postmodernism: Parody and History." *Cultural Critique* 5 (1986–1987): 180–205.

Idowu, E. Bolaji. *Olodumare: God in Yoruba Belief*. London: Longman, 1962.

Ianni, Octávio. *Esclavitud y Capitalismo*. Mexico: Siglo Veintiuno Editores, 1976.

Ianni, Octávio. *Escravidão e Racismo*. São Paulo: HUCITE, 1978.

Ijimere, Obotunde. *The Imprisonment of Obatala and Other Plays*. London: Heinemann, 1966.

Isaacman, Allen F., and Barbara Isaacman. *Mozambique: From Colonialism to Revolution, 1900–1982*. Boulder, CO: Westview Press, 1983.

Isfahani-Hammond, Alexandra, ed. *The Masters and the Slaves: Plantation Relations and Mestizaje in American Imaginaries*. New York: Palgrave, 2005.

Jameson, Fredric. "Third-World Literature in the Era of Multinational Capitalism." *Social Text* 15 (1986): 65–87.

Johnson, Randal. "*Xica da Silva*: Sex, Politics, and Culture." *Jump Cut* 22 (1980): 18–28.

Johnson, Randal, and Robert Stam, eds. *Brazilian Cinema*. New York: Columbia, 1995.

Karade, Baba Ifa. *The Handbook of Yoruba Religious Concepts*. Boston: Weiser Books, 1994.

Kent, R. K. "Palmares: An African State in Brazil." *Maroon Societies: Rebel Slave Communities in the Americas.* Ed. Richard Price. Baltimore: Johns Hopkins University Press, 1979. 170–190.

Kerenyi, Carl. *Dionysus: Archetypal Image of Indestructible Life.* Princeton, NJ: Princeton University Press, 1976.

Kiddy, Elizabeth W. *Blacks of the Rosary: Memory and History in Minas Gerais, Brazil.* State College: Penn State University Press, 2005.

Laurito, Ilka Brunhilde. "Romance da Inconfidência: Uma Releitura." *Ensaios Sobre Cecília Meireles.* São Paulo: Humanitas/FAPESP, 2007. 49–60.

Layiwola, Dele. "The Philosophy of Wole Soyinka's Art." *Journal of Dramatic Theory and Criticism* (Spring 1996): 19–46.

Leal, Maria das Graças de Andrade. "A Dimensão do Trabalho na Vida e Obra de Manuel Querino—Bahia: 1851–1923." Paper Presented at the 26th National Symposium of History, Salvador-Bahia, 2007.

Leal, Maria das Graças de Andrade. *Manuel Querino—Entre Letras e Lutas—Bahia 1851–1923.* São Paulo: Annablume, 2010.

Leite, José Roberto Teixeira. *Pintores Negros do Oitocentos.* São Paulo: Edições K; Motores MWM, 1988.

Lima, Alceu Amoroso. *Fortuna Crítica: Cecília Meireles.* Rio de Janeiro: Nova Fronteira, 1982.

Lima, Ari. "Blacks as Study Objects and Intellectuals in Brazilian Academia." *Latin American Perspectives* 33.4 (2006): 82–105.

Lima, Jorge de. *Invenção de Orfeu.* Rio de Janeiro, 2005.

Linforth, Ivan M. *The Arts of Orpheus.* Berkeley: University of California Press, 1941.

Lins, Paulo, João Luis Vieira, and Vladimir Carvalho. "Cinema: Texto e Contexto." *Intersecções: Revista de Estudos Interdisciplinares* 5.1 (2003): 183–198.

Lins, Paulo. *Cidade de Deus.* São Paulo: Companhia das Letras, 2002.

Lins, Paulo. *Desde que o Samba é Samba.* Rio de Janeiro: Planeta, 2012.

Locke, Liz. "Orpheus and Orphism: Cosmology and Sacrifice at the Boundary." *Folklore Forum* 28.2 (1997): 3–29.

Lorenz, Aaron. "Paulo Lins's *Cidade de Deus*: Mapping Racial and Class Difference in the *Favela*." *Afro-Hispanic Review* 29.2 (2010): 81–96.

Loureço, Cileine I. *Negotiating Africanness in National Identity: Studies in Brazilian and Cuban Cinema.* Doctoral dissertation, The Ohio State University, 1998.

Love, Velma. *Divining the Self: A Study in Yoruba Myth and Human Consciousness.* State College: Penn State University Press, 2013.

Lucas, Fábio. "A Contribuição Amadiana ao Romance Social Brasileiro." *Cadernos de Literatura Brasileira* 3 (1997): 98–119.

Lucas, Fábio. "As Intencionalidades da Narrativa de Jorge Amado." *Colóquio Jorge Amado: 70 Anos de Jubiabá.* Salvador: Casa das Palavras, 2006. 163–171.

Lucas, J. Olumide. *The Religion of the Yorubas.* Brooklyn: Athelia Henrietta Press, 1996.

Machado Filho, Aires da Mata. *Arraial do Tijuco: Cidade Diamantina*. São Paulo: Editora USP, 1980.

Maes-Jelinek, Hena. "'Latent Cross-Culturalities': Wilson Harris's and Wole Soyinka's Creative Alternative to Theory." *European Journal of English Studies* 2.1 (1998): 37–48.

Magaldi, Sábato. *Um Palco Brasileiro: O Teatro de Arena de São Paulo*. São Paulo: Brasiliense, 1984.

Maldonado-Torres, Nelson. "The Decolonial Turn." Ed. Juan Poblete. *New Approaches to Latin American Studies: Culture and Power*. New York: Routledge, 2018. 111–127.

Mar-Molinero, Clare, and Angel Smith. *Nationalism and the Nation in the Iberian Peninsula*. Oxford/Washington, DC: Berg, 1996.

Matos, Patrícia Ferraz de. *The Colours of the Empire: Racialized Representations during Portuguese Colonialism*. New York: Berghahn Books, 2013.

McLeash, Kenneth. *Orpheus*. Dublin: The British Council/Artslab, 1997.

Mead, G.R.S. *Orpheus*. New York: Barnes and Noble, 1965.

Meireles, Cecília. *Romanceiro da Inconfidência*. Rio de Janeiro: Civilização Brasileira, 1975.

Mendes, Miriam Garcia. *O Negro e o Teatro Brasileiro*. São Paulo: Hucitec, 1993.

Mendes, Orlando. *Portagem*. São Paulo: Ática, 1988.

Mignolo, Walter. *Local Histories/Global Designs: Coloniality, Subaltern Knowledges, and Border Thinking*. Princeton, NJ: Princeton University Press, 2000.

Miki, Yuko. *Frontiers of Citizenship: A Black and Indigenous History of Postcolonial Brazil*. Cambridge: Cambridge University Press, 2018.

Milleret, Margo. *Teatro de Arena and the Development of Brazil's National Theatre*. Doctoral dissertation, University of Texas at Austin, 1986.

Millett, Kate. *Sexual Politics*. New York: Doubleday, 1970.

Mitchell, Geoffrey S. "(Lost) Love, Eros and Metaphor: Colonialism, Social Fragmentation and the 'Burden' of Race in *Portagem* by Orlando Mendes." *Portuguese Literary and Cultural Studies* ["Reevaluating Mozambique"] 10 (2003): 69–85.

Mitchell, Geoffrey. "Theorizing the Orpheus Myth: *Orfeu da Conceição* and *Orfeu Negro*." *Marvels of the African World*. Niyi Afolabi, ed. Trenton, NJ: Africa World Press, 2003. 99–123.

Mitchell, Sean T. "Whitening and Racial Ambiguity: Racialization adn Ethnoracial Citizenship in Contemporary Brazil." *African and Black Diaspora: An International Journal* 10.2 (2017): 114–130.

Mitchell-Walthour, Gladys L. *The Politics of Blackness: Racial Identity and Political Behavior in Contemporary Brazil*. Cambridge: Cambridge University Press, 2018.

Moi, Toril. *Sexual/Textual Politics*. New York: Routledge, 1985.

Monteiro, Circe. "Enclaves, Condominiums, and Favelas: Where are the *Ghettos* in Brazil?" *City and Community* 7 (2008): 378–383.

Moraes, Vinicius de. *Orfeu da Conceição*. Rio de Janeiro: Livraria São José, 1960.

Moraes Filho, Mello, et al. *Bailes Pastoris na Bahia*. São Paulo: Cultrix, 1980.

Mostaço, Edélcio. *Teatro e Política: Arena, Oficina e Opinião (Uma Interpretação da Cultura de Esquerda)*. São Paulo: Proposta, 1982.

Nafafé, José Lingna. *Colonial Encounters: Issues of Culture, Hybridity and Creolisation: Portuguese Mercantile Settlers in West Africa*. New York: Peter Lang, 2007.

Nagib, Lúcia, ed. *Brazil on Screen: Cinema Novo, New Cinema, Utopia*. New York/London: L. B. Taurus, 2007.

Nagib, Lúcia, ed. *The New Brazilian Cinema*. New York/London: L. B. Taurus, 2006.

Nagib, Lúcia. "A Língua da Bala." *Novos Estudos* 67 (2003): 181–191.

Nagib, Lúcia. "Talking Bullets: The Language of Violence in *City of God*." In Else Vieira, 32–43.

Nascimento, Abdias. "African Culture in Brazilian Art." *Journal of Black Studies* 8.4 (1978): 389–422.

Nascimento, Jaime, and Hugo Gama. *Manuel Querino: Seus Artigos na Revista do Instituto Geográfico e Histórico da Bahia*. Salvador/BA: IGHB, 2009.

Neto, Aléo, Sharon Brooks, and Rômulo R. N. Alves. "From Eshu to Obatala: Animals Used in Sacrificial Rituals at Candomblé "Terreiros" in Brazil." *Journal of Ethnobiology and Ethnomedicine* 5.23 (2009): 1–10.

Newitt, Malyn. A History of Portuguese Overseas Expansion 1400–1668. New York: Routledge, 2004.

Nicolete, Adélia. *O Teatro de Luís Alberto de Abreu*. São Paulo: Cultura/Fundação Padre Anchieta, 2004.

Nunes, Maria L. "The Preservation of African Culture in Brazilian Literature: The Novels of Jorge Amado." *Luso-Brazilian Review* 10.1 (1973): 86–101.

Oakley, R. J. "The Reader and the Writer in *Recordações do Escrivão Isaías Caminha*." *Portuguese Studies* 3 (1987): 126–148.

Olaniyan, Tejumola. *Scars of Conquest / Masks of Resistance*. New York/Oxford: Oxford University Press, 1995.

Oliveira, Celso de. "*Orfeu da Conceição*: Variation on a Classical Myth." *Hispania* 85.3 (2002): 449–454.

Oliveira, Maria Inês Côrtes de. "The Reconstruction of Ethnicity in Bahia." *Trans-Atlantic Dimension of Ethnicity in the African Diaspora* Paul E. Lovejoy and David V. Trotman, eds. London: Continuum, 2003. 158–180.

Olupona, Jacob K., and Terry Rey, eds. *Orisa Devotion as World Religion: The Globalization of Yoruba Religious Culture*. Madison: University of Wisconsin Press, 2008.

Parente, Moema. *Visitantes Estrangeiros na Bahia Oitocentista*. São Paulo: Cultrix, 1980.

Peçanha, Érica. *Vozes Marginais na Literatura*. Rio de Janeiro: Aeroplano, 2009.

Peixoto, Fernando. *Teatro em Movimento: 1959–1984*. São Paulo: Huchee, 1985.

Pellegrini, Tânia. *Despropósitos: Estudos de Ficção Brasileira Contemporânea*. São Paulo: Annablume/FAPESP, 2008.

Pereira, Armando. *Bandidos e Favelas: Uma Contribuição ao Estudo do Meio Marginal Carioca*. Rio de Janeiro: Livraria Eu e Voce Editora Ltda., 1984.

Pereira, Gonzalo de Athayde. "Professor Manoel Querino." *Boletim da Agricultura, Commercio e Industria* 1–6 (1923): 90–95.

Pereira, Gonzalo de Athayde. "Professor Manuel Querino: Sua Vida e Suas Obras." Salvador: Imprensa Oficial do Estado, 1932.

Perlman, Janice E. *O Mito da Marginalidade*. Rio de Janeiro: Paz e Terra, 1977.

Perrone, Charles A. "Don't Look Back: Myths, Conceptions, and Receptions of Black Orpheus." *Studies in Latin American Popular Culture* 17 (1998): 155–183.

Perrone, Charles. "Don't Look Back: Myths, Conceptions, and Receptions of Black Orpheus." *Studies in Latin American Popular Culture* 17 (1998): 1–19.

Pfister, Friedrich. *Greek Gods and Heroes*. London: Macgibbon & Kee, 1961.

Pierce, Richard, ed. *Maroon Societies: Rebel Slave Communities in the Amercias*. Baltimore: Johns Hopkins University Press, 1992.

Pinho, Patricia de Santana. *Mama Africa: Reinventing Blackness in Bahia*. Durham, NC: Duke University Press, 2010.

Pladott, Dinnah. "The Dynamics of the Sign Systems in the Theatre." Ernest Hess-Lüttich, ed. *Theatre Semiotics*. Vol. 2 of *Multimedial Communication*. Tubingen: Verlag, 1982. 28–45.

Prado, Décio de Almeida. "Arena Conta Zumbi." *Exercício Findo: Crítica Teatral (1964–1968)*. São Paulo: Perspectiva, 1987. 66–67.

Prado, Décio de Almeida. *O Teatro Brasileiro Moderno*. São Paulo: Perspectiva, 2009.

Querino, Manoel. *A Raça Africana e Seus Costumes na Bahia*. Salvador: P555 Edições, 2006. [1918].

Querino, Manoel. "A Raça Africana e os Seus Costumes na Bahia." *Anais do 5 Congresso Brasileiro de Geografia* 7 (1916): 23–24.

Querino, Manoel. "O Colono Preto como Fator da Civilização." *Afro-Ásia* 13 (1980): 143–158.

Querino, Manoel. *A Arte Culinária na Bahia*. Salvador: Livraria Progresso Editora, 1951.

Querino, Manoel. *A Bahia de Outrora*. Salvador: Livraria Progresso Editora, 1946.

Querino, Manoel. *Artistas Bahianos*. Rio de Janeiro: Imprensa Nacional, 1909.

Querino, Manoel. *As Artes na Bahia*. Salvador: Typ. do Lyceu de Artes e Officios, 1909.

Querino, Manoel. *Costumes Africanos no Brasil*. Rio de Janeiro: Civilização Brasileira, 1938.

Querino, Manoel. *O Africano como Colonisador*. Salvador: Livraria Progresso Editora, 1954.

Querino, Manoel. *O Colono Preto como Fator da Civilização Brasileira*. Salvador: Imprensa Oficial do Estado, 1918.

Querino, Manuel. *The African Contribution to Brazilian Civilization*. Trans. E. Bradford Burns. Tempe: Arizona State University-Center for Latin American Studies, 1978.

Quiles, Edgar H. *The Theatre of Augusto Boal*. Doctoral dissertation, Michigan State University, 1982.

Ramos, Ana Rosa. "Historicidade e Cultura Urbana." *Bahia: A Cidade de Jorge Amado*. Salvador: Casa de Palavras, 2000. 29–60.

Ramos, Artur. "Preface." Manuel Querino, *Costumes Africanos no Brasil*. Rio de Janeiro: Civilização Brasileira, 1938.

Ramos, Artur. *The Negro in Brazil*. Washington, DC: The Associated Publishers, 1951.

Reichmann, Rebecca, ed. *Race in Contemporary Brazil: From Indifference to Inequality*. State College: Pennsylvania State University Press, 1999.

Reinach, Salomon. *Orpheus: A History of Religions*. New York: Horace, 1930.

Reis, João José. "Postface" in Jorge Amado, *Tenda dos Milagres*. São Paulo: Companhia das Letras, 2008. 298–302.

Reis, João José. *Slave Rebellion in Brazil: The Muslim Uprising of 1835 in Bahia*. Trans. Arthur Brakel. Baltimore, MD: Johns Hopkins University Press, 1993.

Reis, José João. *Rebelião Escrava no Brasil*. São Paulo: Companhia das Letras, 2004.

Reiter, Bernd. "Portugal: National Pride and Imperial Neurosis." *Race and Class* 47.1 (2005): 79–91.

Ribeiro, Marília Scaff Rocha. "Variations on the Brazilian Orpheus Theme." *Comparative Literature and Culture* 11.3 (2009): 1–9.

Ribeiro, Paulo Jorge. "*Cidade de Deus* na Zona de Contato: Alguns Impasses da Críticacultural Contemporánea." *Revista de Crítica Literaria Latinoamericana* 57 (2003): 125–139.

Ridgeway, Renée, ed. *Migrating Identity: Transmission/Reconstruction*. Amsterdam: SEB Foundation, 2004.

Riedel, Dirce Côrtes. *Leitura de Invenção de Orfeu*. Rio de Janeiro: Brasília, 1975.

Rocha, Elaine Pereira and Nielson Rosa Bezerra, ed. *Another Black Like Me: The Construction of Identities and Solidarity in the African Diaspora*. Cambridge: Cambridge Scholars Publishing, 2015.

Rodney, Walter. *How Europe Underdeveloped Africa*. Washington, DC: Howard University Press, 1981.

Rose, H. J. *A Handbook of Greek Mythology*. London: Methuen, 1928.

Rosenfeld, Anatol. *O Mito e o Herói no Moderno Teatro Brasileiro*. São Paulo: Perspectiva, 1982.

Russell-Wood, A.J.R. *Slavery and Freedom in Colonial Brazil*. Oxford: One World, 1982.

Russell-Wood, A.J.R. *The Black Man in Slavery and Freedom in Colonial Brazil*. London: MacMillan, 1982.

Russell-Wood, A.J.R. *The Portuguese Empire, 1415–1808: A World on the Move*. Baltimore: Johns Hopkins University Press, 1992. 58–94.

Sansone, Lívio, et al., eds. *Africa, Brazil and the Construction of Transatlantic Black Identities*. Trenton, NJ: Africa World Press, 2008.

Santiago, Silviano. "Reading and Discursive Intensities: One Situation of Postmodern Reception in Brazil." *The Postmodernism Debate in Latin America*. Ed. José Oviedo, John Beverly, and Michael Aronna. Durham, NC: Duke University Press, 1995. 241–49.

Santiago, Silviano. *O Cosmopolitanismo do Pobre*. Belo Horizonte: EDUFMG, 2008.

Santos, Edmar Ferreira. *O Poder dos Candomblé: Perseguição e Resistência no Recôncavo da Bahia*. Salvador: Edufba, 2009.

Santos, João Felício dos. *Xica da Silva*. Rio de Janeiro: Olympio, 2006.

Santos, Joaquim Felício dos. *Memórias do Distrito Diamantino*. Rio de Janeiro: Petrópolis, 1978.

Santos, José Eduardo Ferreira. *Cuidado com o Vão: Repercussões do Homicídio entre Jovens de Periferia*. Salvador: EDUFBA, 2010.

Santos, José Felício dos. *Ganga-Zumba*. Coleção Vera Cruz 38. Rio de Janeiro: Civilização Brasileira, 1962.

Santos, Maria José de Oliveira. "Cecília Meireles e o Romanceiro da Inconfidência: O Que a História Oficial Não Contou?" *Cecília Meireles & Murilo Mendes*. Ed. Ana Maria Lisboa de Mello. Porto Alegre: UNIPROM, 2002. 98–105.

Santos, Myriam Sepúlveda dos. "The Brazilian Remake of the Orpheus Legend: Film Theory and the Aesthetic Dimension." *Theory, Culture, and Society* 20.4 (2003): 49–69.

Scheel, Márcio. *Um Olhar Sobre Invenção de Orfeu*. Maceió: EDUFAL, 2005.

Schoenbach, Peter Julian. *Modern Brazilian Social Theatre: Art and Social Document*. Doctoral dissertation, Rutgers University, 1973.

Schwarz, Roberto. "Paulo Lins's Novel *Cidade de Deus*." Trans. John Gledson. In Else Vieira, 8–18.

Schwarz, Roberto. *O Pai de Família e Outros Estudos*. Rio de Janeiro: Paz e Terra, 1978.

Schwarz, Roberto. *Seqüências Brasileiras: Ensaios*. São Paulo: Companhia das Letras, 1999.

Scliar, Moacyr. "Jorge Amado e Pedro Archanjo *versus* Jorge Archanjo e Pedro Amado." *Um Grapiúna no País do Carnaval*. Salvador: EDUFBA, 2000. 227–229.

Segal, Charles. *Orpheus: The Myth of the Poet*. Baltimore: Johns Hopkins University Press, 1989.

Sharpe, Jim. "A História Vista de Baixo." Peter Burke, ed. *A Escrita da História: Novas perspectivas*. São Paulo: UNESP, 1992.

Smelster, N. J., et al. eds., *International Encyclopedia of the Social and Behavioral Sciences* (London: Pergamon, 2004), 148.

Smith, Christen. *Afro-Paradise: Blackness, Violence, and Performance in Brazil.* Urbana: University of Illinois Press, 2016.

Soares, Lúcia Maria Macdowell. "O Teatro Político do Arena e de Guarnieri." *Monografias! 1980.* Rio de Janeiro: INACEN, 1983. 11–103.

Sodré, Jaime. *Manuel Querino: Um Herói da Raça e Classe.* Salvador: Self-Publication, 2000.

Sommer, Doris. *Foundational Fictions: The National Romances of Latin America.* Los Angeles: University of California Press, 1991.

Sommers, Lawrence M., et al., eds. *Marginality in Space—Past, Present and Future: Theoretical and Methodological Aspects of Cultural, Social and Economical Parameters of Marginal and Critical Regions.* London: Ashgate, 1999.

Souza Araújo, Jorge de. *Jorge de Lima e o Idioma Poético Afro-Nordestino.* Maceió: EDUFAL, 1983.

Souza Araújo, Jorge de. *Jorge de Lima.* Salvador: Fundação Pedro Calmon, 2008.

Soyinka, Wole. "Ritual as the Medium: A Modest Proposal." *African Affairs* 96 (1997): 5–23.

Soyinka, Wole. *Myth, Literature and the African World.* New York: Cambridge University Press, 1976.

Stam, Robert. *Tropical Multiculturalism: A Comparative History of Race in Brazilian Cinema and Culture.* Durham, NC: Duke University Press, 1997.

Sterling, Chery. *African Roots, Brazilian Rites: Cutural and national Identity in Brazil.* New York: Palgrave, 2012.

Thomas, Kevin J. A. *Diverse Pathways: Race and the Incorporation of Black, White, and Arab-Origin Africans in the United States.* East Lansing: Michigan State University Press, 2014.

Thornton, John. *Africa and Africans in the Making of the Atlantic World, 1400–1800.* Cambridge: Cambridge University Press, 1998.

Tidjani-Serpos, Noureini. "The Postcolonial Condition: The Archeology of African Knowledge: From the Feat of Ogun and Sango to the Postcolonial Creativity of Obatala." *Research in African Literatures* 27.1 (1996): 3–18.

Tiffany, Joseph D. *Race on the Move: Brazilian Migrants and the Global Reconstruction of Race.* Stanford, CA: Stanford University Press, 2015.

Tignor, Robert L. "Colonial Africa through the Lens of Colonial Latin America." *Colonial Legacies: The Problem of Persistence in Latin American History.* Ed. Jeremy Adelman. New York: Routledge, 1999. 29–49.

Toplin, Robert Brent. *Freedom and Prejudice.* Westport, CT: Greenwood Press, 1981.

Valadares, Virginia Maria Trindade. "O Contratador dos Diamantes e Chica Que Manda." *Caderno de História* 7.8 (2005): 57–66.

Valente, Luiz Fernando. "The Reconfiguration of Brazil's Eighteenth Century in *Romanceiro da Inconfidência*." *Luso-Brazilian Review* 48.2 (2011): 98–111.

Valladares, José. *Estudos de Arte Brasileira*. Salvador: Museu do Estado da Bahia, 1960.

Vasconcellos, Christianne Silvia. "O Uso de Fotografias de Africanos no Estudo Etnográfico de Manuel Querino." *Sankofa: Revista da África e da Diaspora Africana* 4 (2009): 88–111.

Viana, Marcus, comp. *Xica da Silva*. [CD Soundtrack of TV Soap Opera]. Belo Horizonte: Sonhos e Sons, 2007.

Vianna, Antônio, and Manoel Raymundo Querino. *Discurso* (Salvador, 1923).

Vianna, Antônio. "Manoel Querino." *Revista do Instituto Geográfico e Histórico da Bahia* 54.11 (1928): 305–316.

Vieira, Else R. P., ed. *City of God in Several Voices: Brazilian Social Cinema as Action*. Nottingham: CCCP, 2005.

Vieira, Nelson H. "Testimonial Fiction and Historical Allegory: Racial and Political Repression in Jorge Amado's Brazil." *Latin American Literary Review* 17.34 (1989): 6–23.

Wade, Peter. *Race and Ethnicity in Latin America*. London: Pluto Press, 2000.

Wade, Peter. *Race and Sex in Latin America*. London: Pluto Press, 2009.

Walter, Roland. *Narrative Identities: (Inter)Cultural In-Betweenness in the Americas*. New York: Peter Lang, 2003.

Warden, John. *Orpheus: The Metamorphoses of a Myth*. Toronto: University of Toronto Press, 1982.

Wasserman, Bonnie S. *Metaphors of Oppression in Lusophone Historical Drama*. New York: Peter Lang, 2003.

Wasserman, Renata. "The Press in Novels: Credit, Power, and Mobility in William D. Howell's *Modern Instance* and Lima Barreto's *Recordações do Escrivão Isaías Caminha*." *Comparative Literature Studies* 48.1 (2011): 44–63.

Wesseling, Elisabeth. *Writing History as a Prophet*. Amsterdam: John Benjamins, 1991.

White, Deborah Gray. *Ar'n't I a Woman: Female Slaves in the Plantation South*. New York: Norton, 1999.

Whitehead, Anne. "Journeying through Hell: Wole Soyinka, Trauma, and Post-colonial Nigeria." *Studies in the Novel* 40.1–2 (2008): 13–30.

Wroe, Ann. *Orpheus: The Song of Life*. New York: The Overlook Press, 2011.

Wynter, Sylvia. "Unsettling the Coloniality of Being/Power/Truth/Freedom: Towards the Human After Man, Its Overrepresentation—An Argument." *The New centennial Review* 3.3 (2003) 257–337.

Xavier, Ismail. "Corrosão Social, Pragmatismo e Ressentimento." *Novos Estudos* 75 (2006): 139–155.

Xavier, Ismail. *Allegories of Underdevelopment: Aesthetics and Politics in Modern Brazilian Cinema*. Minneapolis: University of Minnesota Press, 1997.

Zaluar, Alba. *A Máquina e a Revolta: As Organizações Populares e o Significado da Pobreza*. São Paulo: Ed. Brasiliense S.A., 1985.

Zaluar, Alba. *Condomínio do Diabo*. Rio de Janeiro: UFRJ Editora, 1994.

Index

www.ingramcontent.com/pod-product-compliance
Lightning Source LLC
Chambersburg PA
CBHW020339270326
41926CB00007B/238